RELIGION
Is God's Way of Showing Us
It's a Lot Earlier in Human Evolution
Than We Thought

The Path of the Doubtful Sojourner:
The Spiritual Quest of Nonbelievers

DOUGLAS FALKNOR

abbott press®
A DIVISION OF WRITER'S DIGEST

Abbott Press books may be ordered through booksellers or by contacting:

Abbott Press
1663 Liberty Drive
Bloomington, IN 47403
www.abbottpress.com
Phone: 1-866-697-5310

ISBN: 978-1-4582-0893-4 (sc)
ISBN: 978-1-4582-0892-7 (e)

Library of Congress Control Number: 2013906754

Printed in the United States of America.

Abbott Press rev. date: 5/13/2013

Dedicated to
all who dare to think
that not believing in a god might not be a sin,
and giving voice to the needs of their most human spirit.

As a First Principle, and to the Question of the
Inerrancy of these Words . . .

ALL THAT FOLLOWS COULD BE WRONG.

Contents

Preface

The heritability of religiosity holds the greatest implications for religion of any science since Darwin published Origin of the Species.

Perhaps one of the most enlightening aspects of modern times will be considered in these pages. That is, how religion evolved with humanity and because of that how a certain "spiritual" nature may have become "hard-wired" within us. In turn, whether from the same or a different source, something gives rise to a spiritual need which feels like an urge that must be satisfied . . . or we suffer the consequences.

Natural selection built some rewards into the makeup of our minds to validate our religious actions, beliefs, and experiences. Why would it do this? Natural selection isn't speculative. It is blind, but it's also cumulative. Minor variations that prove beneficial to an organism are passed on.

The religious drive comes from the same organic source within us all.

Every step of the way, religious activity and religiosity were adaptations that proved beneficial or they wouldn't have been supported by our genes nor would they have made religion the nearly universal aspect that it is across our societies.

Without religion the ultimate questions go unsettled. That unsettledness leaves an unsatisfied or anxious insecurity. Religion is the price we pay to settle the ultimate questions.

Why do people think that through their religions they reach out and communicate with their god? Why do they accept that they have obtained a necessary, if minimal, spiritual level through their religion? We are going to delve deeply into these and greater questions.

If it's not already obvious, in the interest of full disclosure, I am a nonbeliever who's spent a lifetime of study, writing and thought in the field—*Why do we have religion?* Post-modern thought, science, and philosophy have gained significant insights if not breakthroughs in this query.

I certainly do welcome believers as readers as well. A significant portion of this work focuses on them. In the long run I wish to include them in our ongoing dialogue. I have continuously doused the flames of inflammatory rhetoric directed at them. There are, however, points at which I must choose who this writing is to serve, and its issues, my issues, are the issues of nonbelievers in a believer's world and, thus, they necessarily have much more meaning for nonbelievers and that is the master I choose to serve. That is my cause.

There are numerous issues that the religious create unnecessarily for us in our society. As believers continue to demonstrate religiously incorrect behavior it is our duty to point it out. Re-affirming *In God We Trust* as the national motto by the U.S. Congress and similar religious acts are easy to point to as instances of believers behaving badly. The fact that our legislative leaders can vote to disenfranchise us with zeal, trounce our rights, and crush our feelings demonstrates an inexcusable level of disregard (and supports the main thesis of this writing). Until they *get* that and until they choose to care anything about us, our protests will continue and may become more strident still.

Believers are "religiously affected" if not afflicted. (Due to the drive and reward for religio-spiritual activities as explored later.) This seriously affects their judgment to the point of clouding it in at least two ways. One: believers believe they can rationally defend the reasons for their belief while they continue to prove they cannot. Two: their anti-atheist (and anti-other faiths) actions would hardly be tolerated by smaller majorities against other groups. (At the time of this writing, there is a proposal before the Arizona legislature that would bar atheists from graduating from high school in the state and one before the Indiana legislature to teach "creation science" in their high schools.)

Once believers are religiously affected, can they ever be objective, again? Fortunately, we know that new knowledge can soften the stance of, at least, some believers—and there have been deconversions, if rarely, including a number of Christian clergymen.

American Christianity may be less tolerant because it has enjoyed a largely homogeneous Christian culture throughout the continent and even the hemisphere. There were other faiths and nonbelievers, but back in the day, they may have been happy to avoid detection rather than face the repercussions of being outed. In fairness, that's a risk more or less serious in any culture.

This is an ongoing journey of mind and spirit, the path of the Doubtful Sojourner. Wherever the truth may lead . . .

This book may have some aspects of popularizing science and thought as it takes a look at the evolutionary roots of faith. At the same time, that line of inquiry is "liberation theology" for nonbelievers. The New Atheists and others however, don't think religiosity is heritable (they don't think we have "religion in our genes") largely because they aren't open to the idea that religion has ever had significant benefits for believers.

If they could move past that, there's a rich harvest to be had in those fertile fields. It's worthwhile to note that the "hardwired hardware" of religion wasn't recently incorporated into our evolution. What we're saddled with is an ancient mode of religion, that of hunter-gatherers, nomads, scavengers, isolated tribes, and xenophobic clans.

A balanced approach to the hidden aspects of religion can still be made—but, as pointed out above, this field as focused on by this writing has more meaning for nonbelievers yet perhaps, at the same time, more implications for believers. Few writers delve into the rich meaning of religion's place in our evolution—and even fewer religious writers. And so, it falls on us as nonbelievers to determine this meaning for the future of all of us. Ultimately, the implications are significant and extreme.

In light of this new knowledge, the social dynamics will change. Justice can be demanded. A just world can, again, be contemplated. Greater insight into religious bigotry and discrimination can be obtained. For nonbelievers, less of their human spirit will be sapped. Believers can create a world where they have reduced the amount of insult and effrontery they've put on their fellow man. By ending bigotry and prejudice against one more group (us) society becomes healthier, better able to meet everyone's needs and ultimately rewards those who've let go of their bigotry and hatred.

> Above all else, this is for the nurturance of the human spirit of nonbelievers.

Other nonbelievers may be put off by my thesis that we are all spiritual. I ask them to reserve judgment until they see what the reality of this radically different spirituality is all about. Our spirituality—in effect, the feeling of spiritual fulfillment—can be channeled in a good way. It can improve the believer-dominated world that so often has left the nonbeliever unsatisfied.

> Believers and unbelievers alike respond to the instinctual propensity toward spirituality.

This book is multi-thematic. So is life. There is spirituality in this view of life, but an authentic, secular, human spirituality. Too, there is a witnessing of where religion has been, where it came from, and where it will take us—if we let it. And, perhaps, we can consider (for the first time?) where *we* should take *it.*

Yes there's religious criticism. How could there not be in such a worldwide cornucopia of faith? But there's an olive branch to the religious and in fact, more than that—an earnest invitation to a path forward.

Heritable spirituality?

> It is the central proposition of this book that religion requires both the human capacity for it (the genetically transmitted component)—as well as the content of faith and belief (the culturally transmitted aspects).

This writing is intended to bring increased liberation to the nonbeliever. It is hoped that it paves the way toward greater spiritual and psychological fulfillment. Advances in understanding always help or at the very least seem to console. Some of these advances are in the science alluded to in this work.

The scientific study of religion as proposed by Daniel Dennett is a young endeavor that has footnotes as old as the universe. This should be a path to spiritual fulfillment for many nonbelievers much like cosmology or philosophy or anthropology might be. (These "intellectual rituals" fall far short of the authentic spirituality that will be identified shortly.)

Where I have the science wrong, or if I've quoted scientists or others who have the science wrong, I ask your forgiveness. Where I might have it wrong due to my bias or agenda, it would be inexcusable as it would for anyone, be she scientist, philosopher, theologian.

What makes it copasetic for this book, containing a discussion of the evolutionary origins of religion, to also contain thoughts on atheist spirituality as well as religious criticism? It is because of the implications of those evolutionary origins of humanity and religion—the meaning they hold—for all humankind now and in the future.

This is my witnessing. It's what I bring back to the world after what it has given me. There is rich ore in this vein. I hope to share as much of it as I've found.

In the long run, we are all spiritual seekers. It is the way we were made. Many respond to a false positive that makes them think there is a supernatural realm and perhaps beings of pure spirit. We did not respond to that. Do we lack something that believers have—or are we better equipped than they? Either way, we have not lost anything nor failed in some way. We still have the pursuit, the spiritual quest, the authenticity of truth, and the rich meaning that sentient beings can find as well as create in such an incredible universe.

Caveat

Religion has a grip on mankind. Is it waining? Could it have (or has it had) a rejuvenation? Could any new, or for that matter, existing religion get a foothold in this post—enlightenment, postmodern world?

There's a warning here about religion. Read the signs. We must see where it's been in order to see where it could go. Most people today are able to keep their religion in check—but once in a while it becomes an unreasoning monster that looms out of control . . . and when religion is out of control, there is no known way of bringing it under control.

Evolution brought us religion

It sounds disarming to say it is an adaptation for religiosity or spirituality, but it is also something that allows certain memes of a religious nature to lock into our psychology in a way that nothing else can. It takes a certain introduction, and it's most powerful when at a young age, a susceptible person is open to this willing, but unwitting subjugation.

A grave danger lurks where common wisdom would have us believe there is none. We must acknowledge that there are crisis points when society, civilization, and humanity are most stressed—vulnerable points at which the unthinkable can happen. To doubt this is to dispute history (Germany 1933, China early 1950's, Russia early 1900's). It's times like those where mob psychology and other unreasoning fears, if they tie into that susceptible (religion-prone) place deep within us, can loose religion-like memes upon us. Unfortunate combinations of forces and events that can make a people desperate are not so distant that we can no longer hear of them. They have produced some of history's darkest hours and they may have met where our religious and politic urges meet.

Introduction

The Path of the Doubtful Sojourner... A spiritual Quest?

"One quarter of atheists and agnostics said 'deeply spiritual' describes them."

When we sense a spiritual longing within, given the fact that there is no supernatural spiritual realm, is there any authentic spirituality that those of us wishing to ennoble the temporal soul of the human spirit can pursue? Strange bedfellows with believers, but we, too, are seekers of a sort, Doubtful Sojourners on a different path.

Initially, our paths were largely ignored, negated by believers behaving badly because life and culture were all about *their* beliefs. In the mutual denial of the other's position on religion, our spirits weren't nurtured, but rather slighted by both sides—by our knowledge that we had no souls and our assumption that we had no "spiritual" aspects and by believers who were frustrated with our negation of their beliefs.

Our secular human spirits do need nurturance. It's been too long deferred. I cannot start this or any other writing without acknowledging that and attempting to set it right from the beginning. We do have our human, yet, secular spirits. And as you'll see, nature played a little trick on us and gave us a spiritual need even though this is a spirit-free universe. That felt need drives us to seek spiritual satisfaction—and for us that means in ways that are not religious.

We have been intuitively, though perhaps unintentionally, assembling what we need to ennoble the human spirit—we have a history, we have growing traditions and many conclaves. We have fellowship, lore and lessons to share—and we have many causes, issues, and aspirations through which we also nourish our own secular souls.

Every age redefines humankind and in every age we grow. We are, at best, vaguely aware of this progression, this growth, this maturing of humanity. Nothing quite captures that journey like our increasing understanding of our own evolution. It is that great rise, our ascent, which holds the greater promise for tomorrow: there is no upper limit to our rise. Rather than recalcitrant, backsliding sinners, who hope for redemption by grace, we shall forever be humankind becoming.

We are living in intellectually exciting times. The information explosion coupled with the internet has given us the ability to educate ourselves to a degree we wouldn't have thought possible a few years ago. The age is reminiscent of the one symbolized by the printing press. As we stare ahead into uncertain and possibly divisive times perhaps we can come together in an age of cooperative self-education.

If man is the meaning-seeking animal, and I believe he is, our understanding can be the beneficiary of this new access to knowledge. In that respect, we are still in an age of enlightenment. Never before have we been freer to study as we choose. And as Alexander Pope said, for very different reasons, *Presume not God to scan, the proper study of mankind is man.*

Radical understanding of ourselves is now possible to our very core—greater insight into who we *really* are. Where we came from. What our evolution has been, what it has meant and what it means now and for the future. That quest has been an intellectual one, but it also has been a "spiritual" one—and answers with "spiritual" meaning are now possible. Possible for the atheist, doubter, skeptic, humanist, freethinker, or otherwise godless individual that I call a doubtful sojourner. I think that hints at the journey we are on.

From the Barna Group study, 2005 through 2007, its president stated in the June 11, 2007 article, *Atheists and Agnostics take aim at Christianity*, ". . . most of the Americans who overtly reject faith harbor doubts about whether they are correct in doing so." A more skeptical group, in general, they would most likely reserve some doubt about any position. From the same study, "one quarter of atheists and agnostics said 'deeply spiritual' describes them." I think that statement might shock the other three quarters. It does leave a gray area around the "no faith" respondents. Were they atheists, or more likely agnostics? If atheists or agnostics, did they have some belief that informed their status as either? (Based on a telephone survey from January 2005 to January 2007 of adults 18 and over).

When we sense a spiritual quest or longing within, given the fact that there is no supernatural spiritual realm, is there any authentic spirituality that those of us wishing to ennoble the temporal soul of the human spirit can partake in? Can we have the same spiritual experience as a believer? Or is it barred to us by our very knowledge? Can a believer who had spiritual experiences continue to have them if s/he becomes a nonbeliever?

Believers who reject organized religion also say they are "spiritual but not religious." These New Age believers have given us an example. We can wrest our spirituality back from organized religion. New Agers have done it and are continuing to do it. They aren't as noisy about it as we are and their pronouncements, platitudinous as they are, don't sound so threatening to other believers, but then no one's throwing them to the lions. It seems that the lions we nonbelievers face now (as well as in the future) are Christian.

What's exciting about recent insights is that we can see religion, or again more correctly, *religiosity* or *religiousness* as an evolutionary adaptation that along with being aggressive, political, and warlike may have been what carried man through turbulent times in the geologically recent past.

Neurotheology, the science of spirituality, if we stick with the truly scientific portion of it, tells of a stimulating neurochemical soup that "inspires" spiritually religious behavior. Coupling that with how the brain is structured and seeing how these various areas function, we can reach toward a new level of understanding of our spirituality, why we have religion, what its place and purpose was and might be in the future.

In short we will re-explain religion in a way that is intellectually satisfying. Some conjecture is necessary in interpreting the past or even the implications of current thought, but I hope you will come to agree that these insights do answer the nagging questions that have been overlooked or insufficiently dealt with in the popular writings thus far (though I believe *The Faith Instinct, In Gods We Trust,* and *Darwin's Cathedral* have handled them very well). In some instances you'll see how these new insights of others (and perhaps, rarely, my own) extend the implications of some theories while others seem negated by this new understanding.

The intent of this book is not to say, "Here is what I understand, take my word for it," but rather to offer up to you the same path that's brought me to the understanding that I've reached. Perhaps, like me, you will have a couple of "eureka" moments of your own, your secular epiphanies, if you will. (Those are the nano versions of the neurochemically boosted mystical experience that spiritual practitioners relate to us—simply two extremes, poles apart—subliminal in the former, overwhelming to the point of seeming transcendence in the latter.)

I. WHY DO WE HAVE RELIGION?

Why does religion have such a grip on humankind?

Binding at depth

If religion isn't "in the genes" how does it stir humans at such depth? And why, perpetually and ubiquitously, is its omnipresence felt?

In the oft chanted litany, "God & Country," *God* comes before *country* (and for some way before family). All other things being equal, nothing routs the grip of religion.

Plumb some depths? Here we go . . .

DrD4

From Challenging Nature:
Science in a Spiritual World by Lee Silver.

Lee Silver cited a study by David Cummings that found people who had receptors for the neurochemical dopamine which were most active corresponded to people with belief in miracles, those with the least active corresponded to people who were rational materialists. (p. 77 *Challenging Nature: Science in a Spiritual World*.)

Silver also cited Peter Brugger who gave the L-dopa drug to skeptics, who with a dopamine high, showed a new found tendency to accept mystical explanations for unexplained phenomena. (p. 77)

From *Religion in Human Evolution from the Paleolithic to the Axial Age*, Robert Bellah quoted Vaclav Havel describing his mystical-like experience in nonreligious terms such as joy and deep meaning, but also said he was "struck by love" though he didn't know for whom or what.

With dopamine being the "love drug," the one that gives us that loving feeling, this effect seems likely to be within a neurochemical mix that helps some achieve spiritual fulfillment.

"In 2002, the geneticist Robert Morris and his colleagues discussed that the most active form of this gene [the DrD4—dopamine receptor] first appeared as a mutation in human populations 30,000 to 50,000 years ago, and spread rapidly throughout the populations in Europe, Africa, and the Americas." (P. 77 & 78 in *Challenging Nature*.)

"Without a doubt, the new mutation provided a specific advantage. The dopamine system has many functions and we cannot know for sure, today, what that advantage might have been. But it is certainly interesting that the DrD4 mutation coincides with the earliest archeological evidence for a belief in the after life—accouterments buried along with cadavers."

This ties in to page 35 of *Start Your Own Religion*, "[Religion] is a general view of existence which colors everything we say [or] do." This quote doesn't sound as if it would be compatible with the idea of religion as no more than a mere meme. That is, the quote seems to say religion is more "built in" than "bolted on" to us.

OMG, it's in our genes!

People who have a spiritual need to satisfy—and that may be a large percentage of the population—are more likely to turn to religion than those who don't. Religion's benefits, being great and varied, pay off for individuals via a greater reproductive advantage. (There's an argument that this would require natural selection at the level of the group. I don't think it requires group level selection, though that may have occurred, too.)

Individuals who joined the ranks of the religious would have benefitted sufficiently to increase the population. In the early human populations, each with only a single origin myth and no competing ideology, conformance naturally would have been the highest.

Our neurochemicals reward some of our thoughts and behavior. Why? Either we've inherited a system, mostly neurochemical, rewarding us for spiritual thoughts and religious behavior and thus it is ingrained—or it's something we've learned. Our parents and Sunday school teachers inculcate it in us—*yes, Jesus loves us.* That love triggers an early dose of dopamine (the love drug) which may set us up for the later spiritual rewards for considering the divine and a holy host of other thoughts and behaviors.

Mentioned a few pages earlier, the Barna Group study, 2005 through 2007, reports that one quarter of atheists and agnostics said 'deeply spiritual' describes them. Now, either this means they can't help but respond to the spiritual realm and its deities and other supernatural beings or, since none of those exist, something is driving those atheists and agnostics, perhaps independent of their will, in a seemingly "spiritual" way. This is one more piece of evidence that religion is "in our genes." (Keep in mind that everywhere in this writing that religion is said to be "in our genes" is shorthand for the larger thesis that there is genetic support for a predisposition for religiosity/spirituality in the human genome.)

Many of the recent hypotheses about the sources and staying power of religion are compatible and complimentary and may come together to form a greater explanatory whole. There are occasional areas of disagreement, but there is now a feast, and no longer a dearth, of ideas. Hallelujah!

One such hypothesis to splice onto is Richard Dawkins' memes. Though he's dubious about the idea that religion is an evolutionary adaptation, his suggestion that religion performs like a meme—his word for a virus-like idea or belief that can grab a population and spread virulently through it—describes an apparent aspect of religion's nature.

Viewing the meme-like nature of religion as an insidious parasite encapsulates the downside of religion like little else has so far. That thesis will not be diminished here. When the upside of religion is discussed—the prime one (in dispute) being that religion gave us an evolutionary advantage as an adaptation—it's not being done to diminish the negative aspects, but rather to grope for a greater understanding.

Theses explored in this book

Why do we have religion? What's its source?
Why is our sense of spirituality so strong?
Why do we divide against ourselves in such a radical way based on our beliefs about our worldview?

Obviously, we can get along quite well if we overlook each other's beliefs. That's how most of us function in the work-a-day world. Yet we we're urged to go beyond this superficial way of living. We feel that beliefs of the religious kind have a very deep source within us. In that deep core of our human selves, that source may be a bit hidden from us. Along with that or because of it, we need to know the community we are a part of. Perhaps only then can we define who we are as individuals and in the early days this may have been the beginning of knowing oneself. (The body of thought that there is no *self* duly acknowledged, one might consider a more comfortable idea of personal identity like *the individual* or *ones conscious being*.)

Perhaps our need is as simple as this: *We have to know who we are in order to know what to do.* For our ancient ancestors that "knowing" might more rightly have been at level of the clan or tribe. It is at group level where origin, identity, and purpose can be created, agreed upon, and shared. Community was the source of all for the culture, it encapsulated the culture, empowered and validated it.

Maybe the early holy book writers knew that if you confronted other faiths head on, weaknesses in your own might become apparent. Perhaps the very act of noting that other faiths even exist was draining away the strength of belief necessary to sustain the faith. If so, an ever greater level of belief and commitment might be necessary to feel the same neurochemical perks, the tweaks of support, like the energy pellets in a video game.

The rank and file Christians don't seem to expect a spiritual epiphany, but do they scale back their religious enthusiasm, effort, or engagement to fit their expectations? And is there not a more frightening scenario yet? Perhaps, like the hapless witness who's seen a UFO and sadly endured the social fallout, the typical churchgoer wouldn't want a mystical experience that would set them apart as odd and perhaps stigmatize them for life.

It takes, or so it would seem, a certain amount of gall to offer to replace someone's erroneous spiritual beliefs with your own (erroneous spiritual beliefs). Perhaps, they compensate for their minimal religious efforts in other ways. Perhaps, converting another would enliven their taste for their own religion. They might vicariously enjoy seeing someone else's faith come alive. Alternatively, some volunteer work or giving support to a mission might give them some sense of connection to their faith.

More eager Christians volunteer to proselytize out of genuine piety, no doubt, but the zeal with which they offer up the one *true* religion should be tempered with some reserve. Is this the religious version of hubris? Some sort of spiritual Pride?

For the young Christians I know, I would say it comes simply from a charitable spirit with the purest of intentions and an agenda formed around helping others. At the same time, I've heard them tell those they would help, that they *know* Jesus answers prayers. In conversations with international youth ministry volunteers and out of concern for their safety, I've cautioned these evangelists not to get into a situation where only Jesus can save them.

It seems petty in the reality of their missions to quibble about why they're going and what they are going to say there. Their helpful if evangelical missions have more the flavor of, say, Jesus Christ Superstar than of an Elmer Gantry's hellfire and brimstone revivalism.

It seems it is a lot more difficult to say this is wrong—a happy, uplifting, caring message delivered with love, helping, and maybe a few things of lasting good to those of hopeless destitution—than to condemn, say, the early Church missions in the islands off the Carolinas that enslaved native Americans and sorely mistreated them as forced labor.

Still, there is a message. Hopeful, though it is, it isn't literally true. Religious evidence is anecdotal, at best, and apocryphal legend—or agenda-based dogma at worst. What can one hoping to salvage something of benefit for the human spirit come away with?

Believers, we'd turn our backs on that world (that fictional world that you remake each generation while maintaining certain thematic threads) if we could. (From *Confessions of a Christian Atheist.*)

Understanding

It's my thesis, yet probably not original with me, given that we've inherited Nicholas Wade's *Faith Instinct* and given that we have, rather than an immortal soul, a secular, temporal human spirit, that this individual human spirit, perhaps surprisingly, needs nurtured and should be nurtured, as much as those supposedly immortal souls. We are of one cloth. Either we are all immortal souls or none of us are.

The human mind has evolved to respond with certain neurochemical rewards to reinforce what we might term religious behavior (Andrew Newberg, Principles of Neurotheology; andrewnewberg.com), or a certain religiosity, or spirituality. If the reader can't imagine this, think of it like a "Eureka!" moment. We all experience that internal glow—that feeling of validation—at some time or other. Another parallel is falling in love. Do you know or can you remember that swept away feeling? Depending on the strength of that moment, the feeling is usually somewhere on the scale of positive reinforcement. Isn't it apparent that the rapturous love state is similar to the rapturous religious state and that the internal state, and in all probability, the neurochemistry, of one is similar to the other? (That's not to say there is nothing else to a spiritual state. There can be a sense that the self has diffused into great and singular oneness and a number of other profound experiences. In Dr. Newberg's work, he's shown that those experienced in prayer or meditation, when their brains are PET scanned during those activities, have their parietal lobes light up in similar ways.)

It is surprising the number of people who don't see religion as an evolutionary adaptation, especially some of the evolutionary scientists and philosophers. When it became clear to me, I thought this would be "the truth to set men free." This doesn't seem to be the reaction, though, at least not from everyone. I wonder if the beliefs of some of the scientists and thinkers are interfering with their judgment toward the issue? Perhaps, they don't want to consider that religion could ever have had a benefit.

Many science-enthusiast atheists deny the apparent benefits of religion to the modern day believer. Rather than denial, what they need is a scientifically enlightened analysis of the benefits religion delivers to the believer. Delusion or not, the practices would wither away if there was nothing in it for the believer. I believe these scientists who say religion never has had benefits for the follower want to throw baby Jesus out with the holy bathwater.

Consider for a moment the behaviorally modern human roughly equivalent to what was called Cro-Magnon man or more often today, behaviorally modern humans or the hunter-gatherers (though the peoples indicated by this latter designation could pre-date the first two). Given the clan of 150 members or so, with the strengthened unity achieved through identifying their group with a common origin myth, the sense of purpose of a shared destiny, and shared legends and lore to guide their rituals, activities, and morality, and on and on, how could you come to another conclusion? The entire religion complex delivers benefits both in whole or in parts. If it didn't, all the effort it takes wouldn't be invested.

Throughout you'll see how the generic structure of a primate troupe with its alpha male (or sometimes alpha female) pointed humankind in a lofty direction that set us on the religious path. We have had built into us, like an instinct, our own internalized model of that troupe structure. With it subconsciously in mind we apply incessant scrutiny and continual evaluation to our own group/community/society as to how it measures up. Inherent in that quest for ever better leadership and society is the urge to go beyond, to transcend. That may have been the initial spark that led to religion.

Earlier populations, some anthropologists think, went through some sort of population bottleneck 50,000 to 100,000 years ago affecting most or all the human species and maybe a few other regional bottlenecks like the meteor strike on the northwestern coast of the US about 13,000 years ago. Consensus is limited on how few the numbers became in the earlier species-wide bottleneck, but whenever anything like that happens, only the strong survive. Though we may not like it, religion was a community strengthening bond.

For me, that's why we have religion. The winnowing, if not the cataclysmic extinction events of the less resolute clans of men tested by repeated ice age glaciations, Mount Toba's super-eruption, a meteor impact or two, and especially, competition between clans, races, even species of men. Warmed-over, bespeckled flower-children like myself probably couldn't have cut it. It took those fully involved participants in their early form of religion doing their rant, chant, dance, and trance. You can expect, as well, that they were maximally cranked for the clan's missions. Stir into the mix a certain aggressive predisposition toward war-like behavior and there you have him, modern man: Homo religiosus belicosus.

To bring that back to the spiritual need that most of us have, we miss that type of community. We yearn for spiritual nurturance and fulfillment. And if you recite my litany above, you can see that old time religion had survival value and that's how we got it. It's a species-specific behavior—it's a throwback to prehistoric man. Even an atheist can cite that benefit of religion without embarrassment.

Modern holy men

"Why aren't modern holy men transmuting the dross of scientific fact into the spun gold of sacred meaning." Chet Raymo

Understanding is what the meaning-seeking animal covets—as long as it doesn't conflict with his beliefs—and if it does, understanding alone is the paler consolation that we rationalists will have obtained.

I will not leave us there, though. I think we can glimpse the spirituality and secular religion of the future. The question: Can truth without hyperbole generate enough "spark," enough juice, enough buoying of the spirit to matter? Enough to bind us together, enough to fulfill us spiritually?

That brings us to the last two major goals for this writing: To achieve ever more interconnection between nonbelievers and say to those nonbelievers, (though admittedly schmaltzy sounding) *The truth is out there and the truth shall set you free.* Two of those truths—which we can now move from the believer's side of the ledger to the nonbeliever's side—are the innate source of spirituality and the evolutionary origin of religion. Perhaps you've heard others dismiss these hypotheses, some more dismissively than others.

Finally, I whole heartedly accept Chet (blog.sciencemusings.com) Raymo's exhortation from page 167 of his *Skeptics and True Believers*. Raymo gives voice to the authentic question of our actual human spirituality and asks why the modern holy men aren't *"transmuting the dross of scientific fact into the spun gold of sacred meaning."*

In other words, why isn't someone creating fact-based belief for the worldly spirituality of the mortal but unsinkable, collective human spirit?

Let's have a go at that, shall we? I hope you enjoy this product of my spiritual practice. Thank you for the opportunity to share.

Let's begin with the definition of religion.

Religion defined

We all have our own sense of what religion is. You won't see a definition of religion here so different from what you may be familiar with, but some of the foundational concepts for a definition of religion will be revised somewhat radically.

Two concepts are important to an understanding of religion as their definitions interlock with it. *Spirituality*, the most important, has a multiplicity of meanings and shades of meaning, but for our purposes here an operational definition seems best.

SPIRITUALITY is an experience of the internal state created by the brain's neurochemical responses rewarding us (producing a pleasurable state), however infinitesimally (imagine Tom Sawyer in church), when associated with thoughts, beliefs, experiences within what the person may consider the spiritual or religious realm.

At first blush the definition appears circular. It isn't. It is, rather, the *perception* of the experience that determines the experience. Instead of any circularity in the definition, there is a upward spiraling feedback loop between the perception and the felt experience. (I don't want to overburden you at this point. You will see this cleared up later.)

Is it also necessarily such activities as those that buoy up the human spirit whether the person thinks they are of a supernatural origin or not, *if* they elicit the same neurochemical patterns that produce the same feelings or excited experiences that happen within a spiritual or religious dimension? This too will become clearer as it is discussed.

RELIGIOSITY, the second concept, has definitions with both negative and neutral connotations. In its simplest neutral connotation it is the quality of being religious.

Wikipedia defines it this way:

> Religiosity, in its broadest sense, is a comprehensive sociological term used to refer to the numerous aspects of religious activity, dedication, and <u>belief</u> (religious doctrine). Another term that would work equally well, though is less often used, is *religiousness*. In its narrowest sense, religiosity deals more with how religious a person is, and less with how a person is religious (in practicing certain <u>rituals</u>, retelling certain myths, revering certain symbols, or accepting certain <u>doctrines</u> about deities and <u>afterlife</u>).

Scientific scales, usually in psychology, have been devised over time to measure religiosity and religiousness. In those instances the terms seem to be interchangeable. Some tests measure as few as three or four factors or dimensions of religiosity, others as many as twelve.

Religiosity, spirituality, and religion—the internet is awash with definitions and shades of meaning. One definition worthy of note states that spirituality is how we address the divine. Another indicates it is how we relate to the supernatural. I would say that those were defined from the point of view of a believer or at least in high deference to it.

Consider how different the meaning of all these terms and definitions are in light of religiosity as a species specific behavior of Homo sapiens. Let me cast it in these words: The believer has an experience. Consider the believer and her spiritual sense, her spirituality, and the underlying reality of it. If there is no spiritual realm, no divine beings, why does her experience feel like she's experiencing the divine?

It is because the right neural pathways fire; the right neurochemicals flow into the right brain regions such that the believer has a believable experience. The believer senses she's had a brush with the spiritual realm, perhaps her god or her savior. She senses it physically, emotionally, and *infers* that she's experienced it spiritually. That is, it feels to her like she would expect a spiritual experience to feel. (Again, the believer experiences a release of neurochemicals that rewards her by producing a pleasurable state when associated with the stimuli of spiritual thoughts, beliefs, activities or experiences. This is not to say that we didn't have to learn to make this association before rewards would come. It is almost certain that we did.)

The nonbeliever has a somewhat different experience as he doesn't attribute his buoyant mood or intellectual epiphany to the supernatural.

Admittedly, a peak intellectual insight may not reach the ecstatic peak of someone who thinks she's receiving a message from God. That expectancy is obviously a little more open ended.

That may have something to do with the *value* of belief in the supernatural: if there was a creator of the universe that took an interest in humanity and our welfare, what could be greater than that? (It might be that there are things we could imagine now that could rival this, but in the dearth of our earlier days, probably not.) So our psyches, our cultures, and our evolution opened us up to the value of belief.

Now, let's say, I have an experience as a nonbeliever while considering and writing aspirational thoughts on the ennoblement of the human spirit. Consequently, I have the same neural complex fire in the same way and the same neurochemicals reward my brain the same as the believer. I have an ebullient feeling of wellbeing and my own sense of "spiritual" fulfillment.

Is the believer's experience spiritual while mine is not? Arguably not. I'm willing to admit that the believer may be able to have a greater peak experience than I am. Not every believer has them, of course, but I'll give them the benefit of the doubt; some seem to have mystical experiences or religious epiphanies as well as experiences lower on the scale. Ann Taves said in *Religious Experiences Revisited* we should refer to these experiences and others as *experiences deemed religious*. Her obvious distinction is very much in alignment with the theses expressed here; religious experiences are experiences in the absence of any spiritual realm or supernatural beings.

Polls have indicated something like thirty percent of believers have had some kind of experience which they deem religious (See Ann Taves, above), but this could have ranged from the mildest neurochemical tweak rewarding a simple religious thought to the full-blown born-again experience. There was no information if there were a few mystical level (the pinnacle?) experiences among them.

Such experiences, though, are described in the book *Quantum Change*—a reasonably objective account of individual first person descriptions by ordinary people who had a one time experience of the spiritual kind. (Nonreligious people described *moments of insight* in that book in place of religious experience.) It may be a question of magnitude.

The religious epiphany may be greater than the intellectual epiphany, all other things being equal. Natural selection programmed us to experience a tweak with a little something extra from the religious experience—a little bump to make believers out of us. Some satisfying level of intellectual pleasure may have piggybacked onto the religious equipment though we don't seem to be programmed to have our insights reach as high as the religious peaks—maximally rapturous joy—the crème filling, the cherry inside, the hidden prize in religion's box of Cracker Jacks.

My question, then, would be this. Can a disillusioned believer have an experience after his disillusionment of an equal magnitude to the experience he could have before his disillusionment? I'm willing to accept that s/he may not. Then does it take a brain structured over time (molded via some sort of self-training or teased out by some process of neuroplasticity?) to be rewarded by belief? Is it, the achievement of that greater peak, conditioned upon such a "prepared mind" and an appropriately enabling belief? It may take science a while before it can answer that question.

The pinnacle religious experience is somehow different from that of the trained mind of religious practitioners that Andrew Newberg shows us in his neurotheology work scanning the religious brain. Neither the Carmelite nuns Newburg scanned nor the Buddhist meditators used their trained minds to reach an overwhelming rapturous state. Though theirs seemed to be a fulfilling or satisfying state it seems more of the type accessible to one who follows a discipline, a religious practice. (Both religious and secular epiphanies are discussed in *Quantum Change*.)

That swept away experience, the state of rapturous joy, seems serendipitous as to who has it or when. It may only come to a mind with certain predispositions or a certain state of anticipation or readiness. Such minds have a certain religious longing, but not the aspects of religious practice that the practicing devotees have above.

It seems that both these (secular) *insights* and the rewarding state reached by the accomplished religious practitioner may be on the scale of, but not the magnitude of, religious epiphanies, mystical experiences, or rapturously joyful states.

Consider the "little brother" to the rapturous religious state, the intellectual or secular epiphany. It seems closer to the religious practitioner's state as far as the magnitude of emotion. Do they have something in common? How would you capture the unexpected secular epiphany in a brain scan or the rapturous religious state for that matter?

What is most interesting is the question of the true cause. What triggers any of these experiences? Is it all learned? The religious or meditative practices are learned and practiced and the brain develops and grows toward a capacity for a greater experience. It is extremely telling, however, that as a rule meditators and spiritual practitioners are not commonly having religious epiphanies or other pinnacle experiences anything like those that are having them.

But what of the somewhat more "wild and free" nature of the pinnacle experiences? Only sheer conjecture, but it seems that there might be a mind both predisposed genetically to have rewarding spiritual experiences (and that could include the secular person and their *Eureka!* moment by virtue of our expanded definition that, in short, what feels spiritual is spiritual) and a mind that, if it hasn't explored, has at least flirted with thoughts and feelings in the same general area of the epiphany.

God gene? Not so simple

As you may have gathered, always suspected, or already known, religion or at least the wellspring of religiosity/spirituality has an organic source within us. It grew up with humanity. It is in our DNA, probably not a God gene, possibly an accretion of scattered genes or mélange of genes and epi-genes as suggested above, a part of which contributes to a phenotypic expression akin to the religiosity or spirituality which people obviously demonstrate. Or at least that is the hypothesis that seems to have the most explanatory power and best fits the reality we are experiencing. It may remain for genomic research to sort out.

Nicholas Wade in *The Faith Instinct* has given examples of a similar nature to this vision of inherited religiosity/religiousness/spirituality (rather than any neatly inherited religion). He reports it is somewhat analogous to our inherited propensity for language and syntax. We could no more genetically inherit Christianity than we could English, but we could inherit a predisposition for language as well as another for religion.

Another way to think of it is this. Genes (inheritance of capacity) determine our hardware; Culture (specific content) supplies our software.

Religious behavior, to state the thesis another way, is the typical response that people make to their spiritual need, a need that is genetically instilled and ever after instinctually motivated. The participants may mistakenly infer their having intuitively grasped it (a gut sense of the rightness of their pursuit of their faith practice or aspects of it or for Providence providing it, or God inspiring it), and through which they may achieve or fail to achieve some level of psychological satisfaction.

We as well as others may choose to make a nonreligious response to our instinctual spiritual need. For a major portion of the people in the U.S., it is through the institutions that grew in response to that spiritual need, the organized religions, that they meet that need—or fail to.

Millions of Sunday-only Christians have no doubt fallen below even a subliminal satisfaction level. A few have no doubt turned away from church attendance because of this. They, however, still poll as Christians (See the Pew Forum on Religion and Public Life: pewforum.org). There are myriad reasons why people continue to stay perfunctorily involved with religion. It would be interesting to know from a clinical point of view whether they are having any neurochemically supported reward, i. e., do they feel any internal perk at all on the spiritual scale?

It also seems likely that to feel rewarded for religious practice may be a choice. Perhaps to a similar extent that love is a choice. A person may have learned as a child to feel rewarded for church attendance and church activities. The person may continue to choose to feel rewarded for those activities throughout her life. In fact, wouldn't the very feeling of the reward tend to support the person's continuing to seek it?

At the same time, a person who decides there is nothing there for him, may cease to feel any reward. The wild card to this experience, though, as described in *Quantum Change*, is that a person at low ebb, can have a transformative experience of the religious kind. It may have a lot to do with the person being at a point of crisis or unconsciously seeking a sea change in their lives.

This "satisfaction" may vary from a certain intellectual satisfaction (below or above the "aha" or Eureka! threshold) through a range of psychochemical rewards in various brain centers (possibly even experientially formed synaptic pathways developed and strengthened through habitual use or spiritual practice) from serotonin, dopamine, oxytocin, epinephrine and possibly others.

These neurochemicals support a gradient of possible emotional or mental states ranging from a spiritual feeling through peaks or epiphanies such as an (eventful) enlightenment, God-struck-me-dead, born-again, or other unnamed experiences even though the everyday layman may not reach above an occasional, almost subliminal, low—little more than a warm and fuzzy feeling. As with a number of human activities, religious behavior is strengthened if not magnified by group or communal activities. In fact, the thrust of the social aspects may be considerably underrated. The religiosity/spirituality drive may come from a greater underlying need for the social unit to be of a single homogenous religious orientation. Consider how marriage partners, families, groups and villages, if not nations, seem desirous of conformity to a single belief.

Today that might include social pressure from outside the religious practice to conform to the society's religious doctrines and beliefs and to join and perform the necessary rites and rituals, no matter if perfunctorily performed. In fact, perfunctory performance may be the socially acceptable mode at present. (Consider taking a communion wafer and a sip of the sacramental wine and having a religious epiphany on the spot—the priest or reverend will call the men in the white coats to take you away rather than share in your joy, awe, and reverence of the spiritual event.)

If religion is universal, the most likely explanation is that something in our genes supports the activity. We couldn't very well inherit communion or baptism. Religion of any specific variety wasn't passed on. It would have been some mix of religiosity and a felt spiritual need. It appears that both of these are universal or nearly so and probably passed down for tens of thousands of years.

Some so-called primitive cultures within modern times, and these may give some insight into early human cultures, had long communal dance rituals where the participants joined in trans-inducing activities—repetitive dancing to rhythmic music or drums and perhaps chanting and/or using sacred ritual drugs.

Hold on, you might say. What about God, supernatural beings, the soul or being saved? All that and more was left out of this definition of religion.

They were left out for good reason. It seems with every definition of religion there is an example that has an important exception and that seems to make a definition elusive. Buddhism doesn't have a god. Some religions don't have immortal souls. Most or perhaps all have supernatural realms, beings, or events. Most or all have myths.

What are the important aspects without which something would not be said to be a religion? Must there be a spiritual practice, prayer or devotion? Or some aspect of transcendence, something beyond the mundane world? Obviously, there is a set of elements of which every religion partakes to a large degree—a complex of things that each religion draws from—a matrix of religious aspects.

Most or all religions address a few ultimate questions that seem to lie beyond our reach: Being, of one and all; identity of the group and by extension, the individual; destiny of the group and individual. Further, there's usually a narrative myth, a set of beliefs, some inspired or revealed knowledge.

Critics of nonbelievers say that atheism and humanism are religions. Can that be? Is there a minimal number religious elements below which a thing is not a religion? If we want atheism or humanism to be a religion, does that change anything?

In the simplest definitions of the word "religion" it means to bind people together. It's a little surprising that it is such an insightful definition. You would think believers would have defined it as *How we communicate with God,* or something more spiritual than religious.

Of course that all depends on whose religion we're talking about. And that is where the complexity comes in. Most, but not all religions have a god. Some have an afterlife, others have reincarnation.

To say that religion is how we deal with the divine or supernatural may come close, but many philosophies deal with them academically or intellectually and they aren't religions. There are many definitions of religion arrived at by many learned people. Each one who brings a special insight tells us something more. Some of the definitions are complex if not convoluted, nebulous and generally without specifics. Many don't mention that religion binds people together in a special way, into purposeful social units that can garner great levels of moral force if not political power and may use this power to achieve good—or ill—of the highest order. It is on the internal strength of these religious groups that members find the motivation and inspiration to under take rescue projects, emergency aid, and all sorts of humanitarian projects.

We join with others to be religious, to practice whatever is religion to us—but that doesn't rule out being fans of professional football with all its lore, legends, rituals, and superstitions.

Emile Durkheim, father of sociology, defined religion as a unified set of beliefs and practices relative to sacred things set apart and forbidden where by such sets of beliefs and practices the participants form a moral community. This and other's definitions are discussed in Principles of Neurotheology by Andrew Newberg. Definitions cited there are by Carl Jung, Clifford Geertz, and others.

The social nature of religion is the tip of an iceberg signaling much greater complexity. Can a person be religious who makes no contact with like believers? Perhaps a single church attendance as a child is the only social contact with other believers the person had. Then, throughout the rest of the person's life she sees herself as part of a nebulous community of believers, she prays and sends money to televangelists. Can you say she doesn't practice her religion? (Granted, she may be an errant satellite of a social force that was forged eons earlier.)

It seems there are many iterations of this beast called religion. We've hardly touched on other aspects of it. How it can dominate people's lives and wield the power it can have over them. In eighteenth, nineteenth and early twentieth century America the Christian culture became the American culture and zeitgeist. It was a moral force for good, a model for morality and civility. It became the de facto religion if not the civil or state religion of the U.S.

Throughout the world there may be a billion people not affiliated with a particular religion (though I suspect many of those have an affinity or leaning toward one or another), but that leaves six billion believers. They're not going anywhere soon—except to worship. Rick Warren, Saddleback Church, likes to beat humanists over the head with the fact that a major shift of Christians to secular humanism isn't in the immediate offing at least in the U.S. People here are tenacious about their religion. Or is it that religion is tenacious about its people?

Perhaps it will take evolutionary time for us to drift away from religion. At any rate, it is inevitable if we survive long enough. As each religion inevitably suffers from entropy, ennui, and eventually extinction, the singular truth of humanity's climb toward worthiness will become ever clearer.

Religion defined in chart form

A functional definition:

The software	(the cultural, the human, the living contribution)
RELIGION is a communal practice	(immersion in lore & legend with fellow believers—living it, as it were, makes it real)
using group rituals in observance,	(rant, chant, dance, & trance)
invoke or commune with the divine	(prayer, ritual, singing, affirmations)
with respect to ultimate questions	(ranges from origin myths to afterlife)
surrounding beliefs or thoughts	(Why are we here? What does God want?)
meant to go radically deep,	(as deep or deeper than personal identity)
to the core or origin of our being	(God created the world, Earth is center of universe)
represented by legends or myths	(Genesis, crucifixion, Buddha's enlightenment)
to fill our unknown nature.	(We are clan of Cave Bear; 5th street Baptist Church)

This is not nearly all there is to it. This "software of religion" module consists, further, of anything the culture can add, anything that individuals can come up with. For example, a compelling charismatic leader can be a substantial catalyst in religious practice. On the other hand, primitive cultures may seemingly have little more than lore.

The hardware of religion	(the innate religion complex)
The human being and its community	(tribe, congregation, commune, cult)
The imprinted primate troupe structure	(social or pecking order)
Human imagination, wish, desire, projection	(visualize deity or object of prayer)
Extensive instinctual programming	(innate, inborn, "hardwired")
includes many predispositions ranging from:	(predisposed to a certain behavior)
control a function: new born suckling response	(produces a response as if learned)
to species-specific psychological modules:	(music & dance joined for trance)
for example, Xenophobia or from	(fear/hatred of strangers)
reverence to spiritually-inspired rapturous joy	(Self-escalating feedback spiral)
ties to neurochemical reinforcement like	(the brain's self-administered drugs)
Dopamine ("love drug"), runner's high	(our neurochemistry reinforces our spirituality as we reflect on it)
Esprit-de-corps, loyalty, attachment bond	(ultimate, mutual group commitment)
High cost, high support community	(must conform, but mutual aid offered)

This isn't an exhaustive description. You can be sure many archaic and modern cultures blindly developed endless iterations modifying the basic theme. How extreme can a variation be and still be a religion? Everyone who defines religion will probably usurp the power to make that call. Possibly most significant of the above factors are reinforcement of community or communal aspects of religion (See Nicholas Wade's *The Faith Instinct*), any religiosity instinct which may include a felt need for spiritual behavior, and the generic primate troupe (alpha male) structure as an influencing structural form.

With some punctuation and clarification, the two outlines above form a rough definition of religion. There are many things to quibble about. If there is no divine or supernatural component most people think it's not a religion. A deity seems integral to religion, but this isn't essential. Buddhism has no god, but does have reincarnation and a sort of supernatural exchange for recycling a soul to its next incarnation.

At any rate, religions, in the broadest brushstrokes, seem to celebrate the being of the believer and show it to be meaningful over and against the totality of all being or existence in the abstract and that "abstractedness" is above the mundane nature of the everyday world. It is the universe and more, the transcendent aspect of being. The religion celebrates how our being and destiny are meaningful in relation to the transcendent nature of all being.

Is humanism a religion, a graceful life philosophy, a philosophy, or an ideal? It depends on how it is used; how it is intended; how it was motivated. It could be any of those. Can't a person use Christianity the same way? If a practice falls below some minimal level of ritual and community, does it, perhaps, become a graceful life philosophy?

Is the belief in an afterlife necessary to a religion? According to historians, that wasn't a part of any religion until the Axial Age (Karen Armstrong, *The Great Transformation*), the formative period of most modern religions. The belief in an afterlife, a soul, even a deity may be woven throughout ancient folk lore or legend in our past. Today, they are just some of the lines of code in our religious software.

Granted that most religions incorporate these things, but don't confuse a shopping trip down the grocery isle with the contents of your shopping cart. The first is the pursuit: "It's all about the journey" as the slogan of an EUM (Evangelical United Methodist) Church says. Most grocery trips include putting milk in the cart, but is it not a grocery trip even without the milk?

Most definitions are about the "software" of religion, the cultural content. This is understandable as that is what's visible. It's demonstrated. It's what the participants practice. It's the variable from one religion to the next. The believers might prefer that's all there was to it: The faith, the seeming blank slate (See Steven Pinker, *The Blank Slate*) of the human brain, the person as a philosophical or spiritual unit of being, and the object of worship, God.

What is essential? Enough of the hardware above to perpetuate the need and desire and capacity for a religion; enough of the software to function as a religion. The typical vociferous objection to one thing or another being criticized as *not* a religion may come from a critic in a competing religion. I've heard a Methodist say about a Unitarian Universalist church, *That's no church!* She wasn't talking about the structure. It was obviously a church. She was talking about the spiritual practice performed there or more precisely the failure of the congregation to conform to her minimal expectations of religious practice or belief content.

What of the underlying "hardware?" When you reflect on what you know about religion in general, you may at first find the following at odds with that if not counterintuitive. First a relatively concise definition:

An operational definition of religion is that behavior which arises in response to the "hardware of religion," i.e., the innate, hardwired, instinctual behavior manifested by the individual, possibly in group context, and augmented by the culture, its religious cultural content, and the social forces through which the participants enjoy social bonding and through which the individuals may collectively achieve a sense of spiritual fulfillment.

Then a more expanded definition with an eye to incorporating more of the "software" and "hardware" outlined earlier above:

Religion is that cultural complex (the software) that the individual's innate religiosity-spirituality matrix (the hardware) supports and interacts with. At the same time, that cultural complex facilitates the inborn religiosity-spirituality matrix's interaction with itself (catalyst, e.g. neurochemical release). The specific religion is that part a person or group manifests of the content of their religious cultural complex. The activity is motivated by their genetic predisposition to spirituality buried within this religiosity-spirituality hardware and generated by interaction with the cultural complex, perhaps with fellow actors within a communal setting. Mutual interaction of all factors can help the participants experience a mutually heightened sense of spirituality.

That's only a glimpse of the beast. We will continue to appraise its nature. A significant portion of this book is devoted to that purpose.

Almost as challenging as defining religion is fully defining what it means to be *Christian*. Though Christianity is but one of the world's religions, there are about two billion followers of that religion and it is the major religion of western civilization, and therefore, of prime interest as a religion. Over two thousand years, many denominations, and with a worldwide reach, there have been quite a few iterations of that theme.

Though postmodern Christians have to some extent incorporated dealing with their own doubts into their faith practice, the politically salient and ascendant religious Right seems more monolithic. Critical introspection on their religion is rare—they hold it above and beyond scrutiny, they see it as sacrosanct. Or they don't see it at all; their worldview incorporates it to the extent that it becomes invisible, an integral portion of their reality. Yet it is the source of all they know of ultimate reality, the foundation of their being.

Religion more broadly, when at its nadir, is a "cultural reality" adaptation—a complex whole that unifies or fleshes out the identity, perhaps, the origin, but at least the myth, of the people and culture. It's somewhat like a tribal mission statement or the "about" page on a blog, but that so grossly underestimates the power religion can have and the all encompassing domination of a culture and society that religion can achieve.

Though religion is considered only an aspect or subset of the culture, that misinterprets the true relationship. The culture and society are reframed by religion to the extent that the culture can appear to become a tool of the religion. (Note this bit of evidence that religion is an evolutionary adaptation: religion couldn't reach this radical depth in a person if it was only a combination of "a la carte" traits or other psychological devices [see Dr. Andy Thomson for his explanation of many of these devices on his youtube video (www.youtube.com/watch?v=9T2umUoY00A) or his book, *Why We Believe in God(s)*]).

It's implied, though perhaps it should be more openly restated, we are not all affected to the extreme degree by our religions that radicalized believers are. These radical, literalist fundamentalists are at one extreme, nonbelievers at the opposite end, and a spectrum of believers, who range through a gradient of all possible beliefs, lies in between.

Will we eventually find that the range of believers and beliefs corresponds to some precise genetic mix? Or since it may be a relatively smooth continuum—our affectation by religion—will it correspond to the degree to which our individual brains are able to produce serotonin or some of the other neurochemicals that reward religious behavior?

The religious urge and humankind's myriad responses to it may be tied to our genetics, certainly to our cultures, in many ways, and to more psychological devices and mechanisms than we may know.

And we frame it in myth and narrative so that we may understand it to some extent. Perhaps, we frame something in a narrative so that we may elevate it for focused concentration, to get a handle on it. When we float this paradigm aloft we have a person, maybe a hero, at least a nominee who represents everyman, a stand in for each of us as our single selves. This could be us up there in this narrative myth. He is an actor, he takes action. He may be caught up in the actions of others or even cataclysmic events that act on him.

We consider him, we study him . . . and everything he does and all that happens to him. This myth seems like his vehicle, but it is really our vehicle for going from where we were before his action to where we are after his action and his story play out.

The Holy Roman Empire

Conquering empires such as classical Rome used religion to gain the submission and eventual allegiance of the vanquished. But religion has that power by virtue of its all-encompassing coping mechanism. It locks into a society and culture and an individual in such a way as to remake them in its own image. Religions may fall short of this power, but when a strong one gets a hold of a people, it doesn't let go. A piecemeal explanation of religion's strengths by various brain/ psychological modules, as most scientists and thinkers like to use, just doesn't add up to the tenacity that religion often demonstrates itself to have.

How religions found their strengths

The argument: In the competition of religions over the millennia, they evolved to incorporate any elements that would serve to strengthen the religion—to strengthen its grip on people. Christianity had a redeemer, a savior, a first person deity—he was a god, yet he was human, he could feel their frailties. He spoke to them directly things they were desperate to hear. He sacrificed himself for them—a god who died for you.

What about psychological mechanisms that others (Thomson, Boyer, Dennett, and more) say gave rise to religion? Attachment, HADD, and others. The alpha male thesis discussed elsewhere— that's where psychological attachment meets higher primate sociology. When you add this third dimension of religious functions, this resulting power makes the son of God an heir who's very much apparent.

Perhaps, too, when this country was peopled in part with religious refugees, that immigration brought with it a strong religious gene variant (the innate need and capacity for religion). When coupled with a strong religion (a meme or virus-like cultural content), they make for a tenacious faith. (This is a hypothesis that considers the "why" of the fact that some of the most energetic denominations of Christianity seem on the rise (or holding their own) in the US, and yet waning in Europe where much of America's ancestral immigrant stock originated. That migration may have drained off some of the strong genetic variant from the European population. Alternatively, the immigration to America may have reset the "clock" on the Christian culture here and renewed it sufficiently to outlast the European version that may have continued to decline according to some sort of life cycle of religion in line with its earlier timeline. It's, of course, sheer conjecture at this point.)

When a religion eventually wears out its welcome it either dies out, evolves into another religion, or is replaced. Is there some new danger facing a society if, in fact, it's more difficult for a religion to be replaced in this relatively enlightened age?

In our postmodern cultural reality, new myths may be difficult to come by. The New Age religion might be an example of a sort of evolution in this new environment. I can't verify the factuality of this statement, but someone said that new religions don't spring from nothing; they always arise from an existing one (Cargo cults come up as a question in my mind—it may have originated within a people who had a religion that it rejected and replaced with their cargo beliefs, but did it technically come from their religion before? Or is it that no culture without a religion could create one?

Perhaps, the would-be axiom is rigged. What culture doesn't have a religion associated with it? [See Pascal Boyer's argument that many modern day primitives don't have true religions.] So perhaps, it is trivially true that every religion "starts" from a previous one.) It does seem likely that most religions would have sprung from a previous one. Perhaps, then, everyone's religion comes from a religion which has fallen away. It seems surprising that believers are OK with that progression, but I suspect it is yet another tracing of the beast.

Remember, though, that religions are abandoned—the Greek and Roman gods—and they are imposed—Christianity by the Roman Empire.

When religions fail . . .

It's one of the few times people are freed, but is it also a dangerous social crisis? (For example, when the Greek & Roman gods no longer held any interest for their laity.) Yes, it would be a critical time in a nation or a civilization. Even if large numbers are freed, they won't think of it as being freed unless they see themselves as having been subjugated by the religion. It's not the nature of religion to let its believer think that.

Antithesis: the case against religion as an evolutionary adaptation

There are at least two cases that, while they seem to support the thesis that religion is an evolutionary adaptation, might be fooling us (me).

First, some of the evidence. Rather than being the instinctual religious behavior that it seems, it may be learned. (Some of it probably is learned anyway.) It seems highly likely that we do have to learn or even be taught, at least in part, to reward ourselves with neurochemical releases which amount to producing neurochemical "highs" for our religious, or more likely, our spiritual thoughts and behavior.

As a perhaps familiar example, consider an uninitiated child at his first day of summer Bible school. He was given a box of crayons. He has just colored the picture of the flowing robe on a man with equally flowing hair. *Good, Jimmy,* the teacher says. *You know, Jimmy, Jesus loves us,* she says and points to the man in the picture.

Jimmy feels something when she says that—a little inner glow. As the teacher tells Jimmy of Jesus's nobility, divinity, and even a certain bravery and heroism, Jimmy feels more and more of that inner warmth.

The next day, Jimmy wants to hear more about Jesus and his love for Jimmy. The teacher passes out more pictures to color and tells more of the myth in narrative. It shows on Jimmy's beaming face how he is responding.

Of course, the foregoing is just a hypothetical, but something like it has played out over and over for millions of children in the Christian culture in the U. S. As mentioned before, let's grant that some part of this stimulus and response behavior is learned. How much? Does any of it tie into an instinct-like behavior (religion in our genes)? How much of it is a response by other psychological systems, those that Andy Thomson says account for what we might erroneously be attributing to an inborn religiosity?

Let's consider how something might become an evolutionary adaptation. It seems likely that before a behavior becomes an adaptation it might have become a learned behavior. And might not a learned behavior be a candidate for becoming an adaptation (it's a requisite that the behavior actually bestow an advantage), evolutionary time frames permitting?

Might we in our iteration as hunter-gatherers have been coached into how to trigger our neurochemicals via a dance-til-you-trance marathon—part of this could still be inherited if only the capacity to reward our minds for spiritual thoughts and behavior. Even then, a learned aspect or component seems essential, at least originally. The telling question is, is there a component of this capacity that is not only heritable, but part of a heritable array of genetic material that (someday) can be identified as the religious suite of genes and epigenes?

In the second case, still counter to the primary theses offered in this book, it might be that a group of existent psychological functions like the Hyperactive Agency Detection Device, attachment (bonding to another person), inferential thinking, deference to authority, conformance to groupthink, decoupled thinking, fidelity to troupe and alpha male, as well as all the others may make the contributions described and coincidentally give rise and support to each and every religion WITHOUT anything else heritable being passed on.

Going even further, it might be that no extra coordinating element arose as an adaptation to pull these and other adaptations together to function as if they were a seamless whole, just as there would be if religiosity is the adaptation that it appears to be.

And, finally, it might be that there is no religious or spiritual drive, need, or capacity that's heritable—nothing that all the religious who came to America for religious freedom brought with them, genetically speaking—no propensity, no inclination, no predisposition.

The two following objections present about as strong of a case as can be made for the thesis that religion is *not* an evolutionary adaptation.

1. Adaptation to do what? This argument looks, perhaps, myopically at Europe's effete religions of today. Those religions seem to promote a little social interaction, some social criticism and other minor benefits. Supporters of this thesis deny the ubiquitous nature of religion by saying today's primitive cultures have some religious thoughts and behavior but don't have true religions—and by extension the ancestral human population didn't have true religion either. I believe a number of oversights exist in this argument. These will be explored at greater depth.

2. Natural selection doesn't take place at the level of the group. Groups don't have genes, only individuals do. On the face of it, both of these statements seem to be textbook and true. Still, individuals have traits like altruism that seem to benefit the group at the expense of the individual. Genes like this should disappear if nothing else is going on. These arguments will be picked up later on.

Given whichever religion is, adaptation or not, why don't nonbelievers have these spiritual experiences? Granted, it's possible some do and these form the basis of a conversion experience. Still it's unlikely to go from true nonbeliever to born-again Christian. It seems more likely that such folks come from the range of errant or tepid believers perhaps bearing more feeling of guilt than an avowed atheist.

Are we nonbelievers just the statistical few, the outliers at the negative end of a normal distribution? Or do we have the petit version when, for instance, we extol the rise of humankind? What does Europe's wholesale defection from the faith tell us about their statistical distribution or ours?

This issue will be picked up more fully in the section on Pascal Boyer. In his book *Religion Explained* he challenges the notion that any aspect of religion or religiosity are heritable.

We behave as if we are spiritual

People want the spiritual experience. To transcend the world, to be above and outside the mundanity. Life seems unvalidated without it. They want to have faith, to believe, so badly that they simply do it. That's the reality they want so they accept it, adopt it, and live it.

Given humanity at its present stage—we are quite special beings in a fantastic world to some extent of our own creation (through our technologically advanced cultures), but truly on the shoulders of all who've gone before. This world seems so great and miraculous that it suggests some great purpose—and some auspicious origin. So much so that even now many people can't imagine our source to be anything less than some deity. Although, I wonder if we'd infer a deity if we hadn't raised the question until we'd obtained our current level of knowledge and intelligence.

We have been on a journey: the ascent of humankind, a noble enough enterprise. If an observer from our day had been there at the dawn of man, it surely would have seemed that our ancient ancestors couldn't accomplish much . . . but it's there, proof, in our rapid improvement, our journey of becoming humankind. It means something different today than it did a thousand centuries ago. And it will mean something different a thousand centuries from now.

On some level we know the spiritual nature of every human is temporal, mortal—that's the experience of the everyday world we live in. On the other hand it seems as if we have souls. Everything we've felt, hoped, dreamed under God, every inspired work of art, every musical note performed, achieved as if there were souls, spirits, gods. But as far as anyone knows, all art, all inspired works, were also achieved, in reality, in the absence of the same. It belittles humankind none to say we did it all on our own without any supernatural help . . . except for the inspiration a few of us felt when we contemplated the idea of something greater than ourselves.

This has been our rising, organically as believers. To those early minds, even scant knowledge came hardscrabble. The great chasms of understanding were filled with belief. For eons we crossed ignorance with our speculative religions and envisioned ourselves spiritually as darlings of the gods. In legends perennial we've seen ourselves out of favor and striving to regain it.

It was scarcely yesterday when our knowledge turned a corner. We flirted with logic and courted science. We accumulated a body of knowledge. Still, we very much had our faith, or belief. At the same time we rejected it intellectually. We found ourselves adrift, doubtful sojourners on a spiritual quest facing the impossible task of spiritual fulfillment—in a secular universe. We worried ourselves seeking spiritual salvation or a higher reincarnation, but by everbecoming humankind, a truer greatness was accomplished. And the more becoming, the less remembrance of the great unrest and the tenuous faith in the divine, the more evolved a maturing faith in humankind, until such time as it will be said, *What was the fuss?*

We'll consider our authentic, organic spirituality further along the road.

The appeal of Christianity

The desire for spiritual fulfillment or the discomfort of nonfulfillment may have led to a shift from people making figurative statements or aspirational wishes to (near-) literal statements. For example, when someone died it was common for the person consoling those who had experienced the loss to say the deceased had *gone to a better place* or *that they had gone to live with God.*

This statement about the essence or spirit of a person surely predated the modern religions. Certain common or folk ideas sort of bump around in a culture and may have later been assimilated into the emerging belief systems to become one of Richard Dawkin's memes.

The idea of ghosts is a long-lived myth. The lore, if not the fear, associated with them is rich in our culture as it must have been in ancient times. Now as then, ghosts thrive in folk culture even in very Christian America where very little quarter is given for such thoughts.

As incomprehensible as existence is, non-existence of our own self, our own being is even more incomprehensible. If we don't dig too deeply, existence seems to be pretty much a given. Although death certainly seems like a concrete example of nonexistence, it is less comprehensible than the actuality of being—a person right in front of us. It is the proof of the incontrovertible counterpoint to life that is the sticking point: existence can end abruptly.

In the face of the loss of a life, the discontinuity with being seems ludicrously incongruous. The "flow" of a person, the seeming spiritual essence, that modulation of self upon being, how can that just end? Mortality seems such a frivolous, wasteful end to the complexities of a human life. How can the dreams, aspirations, goals, wishes, objectives, intelligence, and caring of a person just end so abruptly?

It's as if a person's growth and progress were charted on a graph. It seems more satisfying to think that that graph doesn't end at death,

43

but, rather, that you could extrapolate a few points further into the beyond . . .

This is just one more reason that Christianity or perhaps any religion espousing life after death would be such an easy sell.

How religions found their strength

In the competition of religions over the millennia, they evolved to incorporate any elements that would serve to strengthen the religion—to strengthen its grip on people. Christianity had a redeemer, a savior, a relatable deity/person—he was a god, yet he was human, not only could he feel their frailties, he could feel his own. He spoke to them directly things they were desperate to hear. He sacrificed himself for them—a god who died for you.

What about psychological mechanisms that others (Thomson, Boyer, Dennett, and more) say gave rise to religion? Attachment, HADD, and others, how do they fit in? The alpha male thesis discussed elsewhere—that's where psychological attachment meets higher primate sociology. When you add this third dimension of Jesus as the maximally appealing religious icon, the power of synergy makes the son of God an heir who's very much apparent.

Religions that tied into various reservoirs of strength such as those above, whether hit or miss or by design, would tend to survive. Winners in the competition that is the marketplace of religions.

Given man, will religion arise?

All the different deities of the world and their quirky personalities— logic even sparingly applied to those sorts of gods—make them highly unlikely. It seems as if each religion had to make their myth more fanciful than the last. However deeply religion is ingrained within us, myth and narrative seem every bit as basic.

Humankind seemingly has to structure a story around anything significant to understand it. The problem is: you can't be prepared to cope or be equal to a challenge if your story doesn't incorporate enough perceived (spiritual "truth") truth, or moral, or maybe it's gravitas, to allow it to bind your religious community around it. Our possibly innate drive for myths which we can revere may be problematic if it renews our perpetual conflicts, and, therefore seems to hold the seeds of discord and perhaps of our destruction (e.g., Holy books of the Abrahamic religions or the *Left Behind* series). Somewhat contemplative, peaceful myths such as parts of Buddhism have flourished by comparison and brought serenity to many.

Joseph Campbell said in the *Power of Myth* that [western] religion is an inoculation against the divine. For early humankind, I think, religion was an inoculation against the individual becoming bogged down in analyzing the philosophical implications of anything and everything new that comes along which is perceived as significant or meaningful enough—in today's parlance, a game changer.

If our clan knows how touchy the Big Kahuna can be, then we will be better prepared, when he metes out some natural disaster, to continue on, to carry on our routine and survive. The hapless tribe across the river who doesn't know the Big Kahuna is a trickster god, however, may be so stymied by the Mount Toba eruption that they sit around fiddling with their toes as the ash cloud catches them.

A Little Bit of Soul

From *Confessions of a Christian Atheist*

We say there is a soul because we conclude there is. Our individual existence seems to suggest de facto a unit of being, a soul. We are ignorant when we come into this world and when we become self-aware conscious beings we recognize we have been totally dependent on others. Obviously, we have not been self-created.

Our being suggests, in the introspection of the self, that our spirit seems like it should have a source outside us, beyond us. From that vantage point of mind, it seems as if we, our souls, are just occupying a body and could be transportable. We fool ourselves into thinking, *I could have existed at another time and place. Why was I born as me? Why wasn't I born as_____?*

We seem spiritual. Our consciousness experiences itself, but can't explain itself to its own satisfaction. Religion is a software program for that. Did our holy men invent our beliefs? Or did those who invented our beliefs become our holy men? Looking back to simpler times, it seems that individuals may have reached for the divine on their own in their folk religions (See Daniel Dennett, *Breaking the Spell*). Being a shaman, holy man, medicine man or woman appears to have been a cottage industry that attempted to co-opt that power of the divine (actually the *power* came from our unknown instinctual, hidden spiritual drive).

Wouldn't it be interesting to know what people thought the philosophical meaning of things were at each age in our ascent? We have a little of that in our philosophies and religions.

It also seems to us that it would be impossible for us not to exist. How could the universe go on for eternity without my consciousness? So some sort of continuity of being, the essence of being, the animus, probably did crop up in religions often. We're prone to metaphor, then the metaphor becomes real. *She's gone to live with god. He lives on in our hearts.* The battle cry, *Send them to their gods!*

II. Evolving Religion

God Seeking Ape

Back in the day of early man, a good religion was one that resolved the unknown and allowed the believer to move on. Those who were in awe of the unknown may have stood still in rapt contemplation of causes and meanings. In spite of what religion tells us, contemplation doesn't have survival value, moving on does.

If you were a hunter-gatherer on the African savannah 100K ybp (one hundred thousand years before present) immobilized in awe of the universe, some believer from another clan would come by and knock you in the head.

Man becoming human was faced with the hard questions of reality. So too it would have been with the rising hominoid apes. Reality was in their face bringing with it danger, disaster and death. Who . . . ? Why . . . ? Maybe we became human answering those questions.

If apes have those questions so far they haven't told us so, but the more their minds and its linguistic and symbol-handling abilities are studied, the closer it seems they are. Perhaps apes don't share those questions because early man bludgeoned every creature out of existence who stumbled into his niche. There's a distance between us and the other apes—a no man's land for no man . . . but man.

With greater minds, we had greater questions—and a greater need for answers. Only those with religion survived in the niche of man. Coincidence or natural selection?

II. EVOLVING RELIGION

God Seeking Ape

Intuiting the resonance of instinct

The divine right of kings is simply a (human) alpha male's attempt to link his primate level authority to the level of cosmic reality. With that comes a metaphysical link to the source of all legitimacy and thereby a certain transcendence is achieved.

In our prehistory as well as our history, we have apotheosized the seeming mystery of being. The nonbeliever can see that that is a non-answer. The intractable question is, "Why is there being; why is there existence?" While it has often been thought of as a philosophical or religious question, those answers seem less reliable—and less relevant—as time goes on. And we more commonly look to astronomy, cosmology and astrophysics and now we reach into quantum theory, string theory, and particle physics when we ponder these imponderables. (I believe that awe we feel, when we let our thoughts progress in these deep directions, is that same "spiritual" reward that believers feel. [And I suggest that those spiritual feelings of believers and non—are one threshold of reward above those believers of perfunctory piety—those who feel nothing. {Related aspects are considered throughout.}])

Earlier, it was said that most archaic people within their social or communal groups made up, (or more kindly) cultivated over time an origin myth or (less kindly) had one foisted upon them by outsiders. However they got it, they then shared it. In some societies, not all, these myths align with the thesis of legitimate authority of the alpha male (or female, in matriarchal groups). It is easy to imagine how this alignment could serve to strengthen the unity of the whole group by fortifying each of the elements: the origin myth tells the story of group and, thereby implies the authority of the alpha. (For the grand spectrum of myths see Joseph Campbell, though I don't find in his work direct implications for the theses expressed here, mine or others.)

What I propose here is how our instincts are wired and how we can *intuit* them by being alert for the resonances of our beliefs and

51

"truths" that are bumping around in our collective unconscious (This is somewhat more figurative than scientific). In other words, we live the corollaries and metaphors of our primate and early human past. Over time, through tens of thousands of generations, life experimented with our ancestors. Life placed its genetic bets then brought them to life. What would be, would be. Through macro changes in climate, ice ages, super-eruptions, meteors and comets, war and competition, some died, some survived, some thrived. With only those surviving genes on the roulette table, Life again made its bets. On occasion, it was allowed to apply a mutational fudge factor to the genes in question just to make life interesting . . . and interesting it is.

Why is there religion, again?

Many possible sources or explanations of why we have religion have been proposed. We should remain open to all of them—except maybe a divine source—each of them may describe a facet of this megalith. If not a megalith, a thousand-headed hydra? Each factor may have had some influence. Maybe the following is one reason among many, maybe not.

We have a need that so far appears peculiar to humankind, perhaps with roots in our ape ancestry. Consider an ape society. There's leadership most often by an alpha male. Even within the apes, they seem to have more esteem for, or accord more status to, the respectable leader and less for the lesser ape. Even this society has rules and values.

So it seems that even among the apes there is a precursor; they consider their leader's merits. They are capable of considering their own identity (self-recognition in a mirror after a period of familiarization). But can they ponder, *Who are we?*

With language, symbolism, and refined thought, we continually check our identity to see if we are still who we thought we were. Something drives us to do this. But something steadies us not to find a reason to change at the same time. Our more human psychology perhaps? Goals of self preservation, if they do not function at a group level, and I think they do, must function at the individual level, so change, even if necessary for survival, is resisted. This, too, is a survival strategy.

Perhaps the human mind's great breakthrough was the sharpened ability to discern simple cause and effect. The apes have some of it and it appears that some animals pretty far down the scale do, too. Some suggest they can look beyond . . . to the future. Is it imagination? Apes have the ability to fashion the occasional crude, simple tool, solve problems, and maybe dabble with creating primitive art (I'll concede that maybe they don't).

Off on the tangent of mental ability, something seemed to put humanity 'over the top' about 35,000 years ago. Perhaps, it was as simple as the fact that evolution, in bringing a primate on line who had the superior mind among all hominids, and some say there were a number of hominid species present, had so very much on the ball in that arena, that when it had the chance to bring any innovation in its culture, language, or rudimentary technology to fruition those things enhanced its power and prowess even more. And this greatness was implicit in that best of early minds.

(It seems most likely that that 35K ybp manifestation of a superior Homo sapiens was the fruition of ascending abilities pulled together by multilevel selection in a cross-percolating mix of human, humanity, and culture. Look for this to be revisited later.)

Perhaps early man who lived within nature could see that his separation from the other animals was due to his superior abilities rather than a supernatural component merged with an animal being. Perhaps, at some earlier time the connection of man to the other animals and the world must have been so obvious as to be *almost* unnoteworthy. The question is often posed rhetorically, *When did we become human?* It may have been when humans started noticing the difference.

Now after multi-millennia of denial we have members who not only cannot see the animal connection of the human race, they can't even imagine it. No doubt, quite an ironic reversal. Believers of Christianity believe we have souls. Many of those that might be dissuaded by our earthly animal origins don't seem too put out by evolution and accept it as valid science. For them, this natural way, then, is the way God put us here and, therefore, their beliefs are intact.

This accommodation to reality may have sprouted the seeds of entropy for the middle of the roaders, religiosity-wise. The less energy or emotion they put into their religious practice, the less return they get out of it, as a matter of normal course. Added to that, there's nothing priming the pump of the epiphany-challenged believers' neurochemical releases so there's (generally) the loss of opportunity of any greater rewards. Little wonder that the evangelicals and born-agains are putting enthusiasm and emotion into their religion. They must certainly be reaping positive rewards that reinforce their behavior. (These may be observable by brain scan, neural activity, or neurochemical release in the brain.)

Evolution Created Religion, God did not

Do we *feel* the positive experience, via its underlying neurochemical tweak, of our various brain centers as belief's verification?

Evolution couldn't generate knowledge, only raw intellectual capacity. Since wisdom lagged behind, religion came to the fore as a cohesive, purposeful, aligning social force, evolution's substitution for wisdom.

Somewhere between the early great apes and modern man, I think evolution gifted us with something of a tabula rasa, a blank slate, at least with respect to our higher consciousness (with agreement and acknowledgement of Steven Pinker's position that human nature is not a blank slate). I think the evidence of the semi-blank slate that I'm referring to is that great surplus of neurons that a baby is born with, but loses as the child matures. I think that is our tabula rasa and our uses and focuses reserve the portions of those neurons we keep. This may be one of the factors that has given mankind its over-lording preeminence in nature—more neural capacity than we use.

Early humans attained a surprising level of intelligence. We applied that raw brain power to our world. It gave us prowess over our competition in our culture and technology. But the ultimate questions, the fabric of our reality was too complex for our undisciplined minds. We did what we could with what we had, nascent thought and rudimentary language, and what we could invent, myth and narrative which sometimes became ritualized. Inspired by our fears and weaknesses and directed by our animal instincts, superstition, magic, and religion were the result. We would have to await philosophy, logic, and science before much improvement could be made.

The following thoughts are inspired by Barbara King's Evolving God (although she says our religious nature is *not* an evolved trait).

Humans once responded to their world with mutuality. The world puts this out to us and we wish it would do this instead, e.g., feed us a mammoth feast rather feed us to a pack of hungry wolves. The target of that mutuality has been raised and refined over time. Humankind began to seek to interact with the sacred. Over time, perhaps God became "perfected" in our religious imaginations and raised above the mundane.

Now a sky god, a high god. He didn't lose any power. He could still rain down destruction whenever he chose. He was, though, more the architect and executive and less the machinery operator of the world. In relatively recent times, God has been seen as a wish—as hope personified—an expression of love for all humankind.

For some religionists, it is anathema for God to be seen as the personification of society or the world, especially when the thing personified is far from perfect, even somewhat schitzoid, and, therefore, on the seamy, mundane-being-side of unworthiness, the dirty, worldly side of things. The fundamentalist sees the world as corrupt beyond redemption and that there is only a brief window of opportunity before the End Times in which some may be saved.

Humankind deserves much more than that. Perhaps, we deserve the greatest god we can imagine. Some do imagine that god and within the limits of typical god/worshiper parameters, more or less, they have him or her. An echo of Voltaire's "If God didn't exist, it would be necessary to invent Him" pronouncement can be heard in this thesis.

"Human ancestors began to experience mutuality in ever deeper ways," Barbara King says, p. 188 in *Evolving God*, "Hominids began to express themselves through self decoration, rituals for the dead, (. . .) Some of these (. . .) brought hominids into a different plane of relating, an imaginative plane that brought them at least to the verge of relating with God, gods and spirits."

"(. . .) [E]motional transformation was present from the first stirrings of the human religious imagination. The expansion of belongingness to a spiritual realm emerged from mutuality and from hominids' talent for constructing their lives around emotional engagement with others."

In keeping with the perspective of this book, a question forms. Is it possible that imagination is at a place in the human mind where faith and belief can feed directly into it and it into them? And while the person can sense the exchange within the imaginings, does s/he *feel* the energy of positive validation via its underlying neurochemical tweak, as belief's verification?

Give me that hardwired religion

Dean Hamer's thesis in the *God Gene*, more than suggests that our brains are hardwired for religion—Barbara King doubts that. It's the thesis of this book that there is probably neither a single gene nor a specific god spot in the brain that will be identified, but more likely a nuanced spectrum of genes and epi-genes that contribute something piecemeal to give humans an innate propensity toward religiousness. This may be a newer arrangement of neural circuits used for something else that proved out to be capable of dual duty, say, the neural pathways of love, ecstatic happiness, and loyalty.

This is a very imperfect example meant to hint at brain functions that perhaps give form to some of the emotional states or instinctual behavior that could underlie or support higher thought processes that might make up a person's spiritual practice or religious beliefs. (See the earlier citing of Robert Morris' work by Lee Silver, "the DrD4 mutation coincides with the earliest archeological evidence for a belief in the after life . . ."

Pascal Boyer in *Religion Explained* suggests the concept of *belongingness*: a term for the undeniable reality in which humans thrive in relation to others. Humans crave emotional connection, he says. He further points out about this vital need that, as he sees it, relating emotionally to others shapes the quality of our lives.

This can be seen in the other great apes as well. Apes co-create meaning by responding to each other contingently when they interact. In seeking this, primates may be revealing an instinctual urge to be social. This point might be the birthplace of Barbara King's *mutuality*.

"Because apes represent the jumping off point of our evolutionary platform, our legacy is to be transported moment by moment through the process of being social and emotional with others," Boyer continues.

"There is a need for belongingness, not just a want.

"The test of conformance to the [wrong] opinions of planted actors [this appears to have been a study] wasn't due to going along knowing it was wrong, rather their perceptions changed to thinking it was right."

It seems that Boyer, and in fairness, many others believe religion is best explained by already familiar psychological and emotional aspects of human social interactions. He apparently believes the example of conformance, above, would be an example of a sort of belief realignment mechanism that might be a force supporting uniform, coherent beliefs. Perhaps even dogma?

III. Religion's Alpha Male

Why do beliefs engender such tenacious adherence?

It is that tenacity to faith that other theories of religion's source don't seem to equal. The only explanation that seems to approach the roll religion has had in the lives of men is that there are genes which support some or most components of it.

Some aspects of religion may extend from the organically legitimate authority of the alpha male. Consider the generic primate group and its social structure. There are definitely variations on this theme throughout the primates, but there are similarities which may indicate a shared and heritable trait.

A primate naturally owes allegiance to his alpha male, though chimps show us they can be less than enthusiastic about a particular individual holding the position. Like a wide range of species, the alpha in a chimp troupe may be challenged by another male. In the chimpanzee troupe, an alpha may reign for years, even beyond a decade.

The alpha chimp may be an object of general contempt, barely tolerated in his troupe with seething enmity characterizing the general mood. His authority over the troupe seems a mockery of legitimacy. It is only a matter of time, then, when a challenger with an entourage of his own, starts a scuffle which can be incredibly violent and topple the alpha in order to replace him.

Underlying that real world relationship is, in all probability, a genetically imposed pattern, an instinct, to encourage an individual to be loyal to the alpha male or female. Think of it as being similar to the imprinting of a mother on her young. That, too, is instinctual.

Both chimps and humans seem to sense that there's an underlying legitimacy to the ideal alpha's "divine right," but do they ever scrutinize the current alpha for telling signs of weakness in that legitimacy! Consider the full range of political behaviors—continually testing the alphas, attempting to form contrary coalitions, perpetrating deceptions, springing ambushes. If you want to see the seamy underbelly of politics in action, get to know a chimp troupe intimately—you'll see it all. (Jane Goodall has seen chimp society from the inside and writes lively accounts of the lives and exploits she's observed. [Greater depth on the implications of the generic primate troupe will be explored later.])

Certain beliefs that we hold seem stronger, perhaps more valid, than others, though that may have to do with the evidence for their probability. There is another sort of belief that we hold more tenaciously to—beliefs that go to our core. Beliefs imbued with nationalistic pride or loyalty to the local sports franchise, or membership in the church.

When humanity's genes of instinct were being hammered out, there were purer plays of belief and allegiance. This is when group identity and adherence as an evolutionary adaptation were being refined. *We were Clan of the Cave Bear* with the myths and beliefs appropriate to that identity.

These sorts of beliefs—ideas that underpin our world—maybe beliefs such as these, beliefs of our identity and community, are given a greater than typical status, a higher order, something that we owe more than passing fidelity to. They go to the greatest depths. They tie deeply, radically, to our core—like the dynamically revered duo, God and Country.

For that to be true, people, it seems, would have to attach supreme importance to such beliefs—like they do with religious beliefs. These beliefs would have to rise to the level of specially revered, ultimate beliefs that seem to be attached in a most basic way, part of the foundation of the primary social organization of the people. Perhaps these beliefs devolve in some way that assures the most legitimacy for the society. And somehow, as a result, there's this invisible structure connecting the individuals who sense the similitude or resonance of the belief with their social organization.

The statement that religious beliefs alter our worldview is telling. That is the level at which religion can attach to our belief structure. It colors everything about us to such a radical extent because that's how and where religion interacts with mind and belief. It's basic, essential. It reorders and reorganizes our reality. This beast isn't just a meme. It is a meme that has an underlying vehicle and that vehicle is a complex of genes, genotypic, and phenotypic behaviors that make up our predisposition to religion.

That's not to say that some, even many, don't let it rule their lives. Is that a newer phenomenon? Maybe it is the secularizing aspect of modern culture. Or maybe we are just now at that point in the life cycle of the current religion. Maybe some have always had a modicum of neutrality toward religion, a certain disinterested detachment from it. At any rate, the disaffected numbers are greater than just we nonbelievers. There is a certain pragmatic point of view out there that says, *Let's don't get carried away with this.*

It isn't this most polite, most civil, most humanistic religion that is of concern. And it isn't just any belief to which people attach importance of the religious magnitude. I think the people are aware of an alignment of certain basic beliefs with their particular troupe; they go together. I'm making this stretch because I think it would go a long way toward explaining why the ideas don't have to be logical or true. That is, the beliefs have the support of the members simply because they <u>are</u> the beliefs of the group and not for any special intrinsic value of the beliefs in and of themselves. Still, the group will say these do have intrinsic value and call these beliefs their 'sacred truths.'

What chance would a contrary idea have when it butts up against such entrenched beliefs?

Not much. We see that all the time, though, don't we? These beliefs are of such a prime order, so basic to the social order, that to threaten or challenge them is to do likewise to society. In other words, to challenge the religious beliefs is to attack the right of the society to exist. And conversely, due to the beliefs of other societies, beliefs that we don't accept, it suggests to us that they are not legitimate societies and should not exist. We yearn to attack them, destroy them . . . out of our allegiance and piety (c.f., God & Country).

That might have been your caveman, you might say, *but modern man is fully rational.*

Well, we may be striving to be, but we haven't fully made it yet. Early man had no significant body of reasoned thought. All they had was superstition and myth—of course, for that to become a religion it had to have the protection of being pronounced "sacred" in order for it to be *hands off*—not to be subject to ridicule or belittlement. Otherwise the normal advancement of human culture and thought would continually invalidate the religious proclamation of the day before. (This points up how much easier it would be to sustain a religion than to start one.)

Just as we primates are predisposed to groom those bugs right out of each other's hair we similarly apply 'What's wrong with this picture?' thinking to the other's religious dogma and soon it's picked apart. For proof of this we need not look any further than a thought experiment in which Believer *A* is asked to examine the truth value of the differing religious statements of Believer *B's* religion. Only a most enlightened or liberal Believer *A* will refrain from rejecting Believer *B's* beliefs.

Of course, we won't allow the tables to be turned and for the others to criticize the logic of our sacred truths. We insulate our beliefs from that scrutiny by the special way that we treat that revered and revealed knowledge. Knowledge that is only handed on by special invitation or at the end of a ritual initiation—you have to achieve manhood or womanhood in the tribe to have such a privilege as receiving this wisdom. As a result, you are now one of the vessels that will carry forward the sacred knowledge of the culture. It's a solemn responsibility entrusted to those who have earned it.

Globalization is certainly testing today's religions. Archaic man's religions weren't meant to come face to face—but here they are becoming more face to face all the time. The result for some is more tolerance, but for others it means more friction, anger, and trying times.

The Fourteenth Dalai Lama has called for a move *Toward a True Kinship of Faiths* (his book title). If humanity's spirituality is the common source among religions, let it be the uniting force. In our global village a marketplace of eclectic spirituality frees humankind to select the best from every religion, every discipline, every philosophy, everything . . .

Can you remember when some wanted to force others to believe their beliefs? What was all the fuss? We have risen above that. We will continue to rise, it's what we do.

Humanity is our best hope. It's who we are and it's all we have. When the world wants to badly enough, we can all come together, then slowly we will be healed and become whole. The highest aspirations of humanity will be realized, the oneness of humanity in the treatment of all, and even the spread of the best of religion without the dogma, the erroneous cosmology, or the flawed morality. We'll be aware of our oneness because it will be made real.

We are waiting for Neo

We have always been waiting for Neo.

In the void that the world can be, man is continually seeking the Chosen One. This is an anthropologically hard-wired imprint of higher primate behavior, at least of the social primates, though, admittedly not uniformly among them. But it is something of a pattern, an imprint that comes with the stock human mind as one among other simian minds.

Search for the Ultimate Cosmic Alpha Male: Our need for legitimate authority

A couple of millennia ago many thirsted for a prophet of God to bring that soul-quenching *something*—some word or deed that would make everything all right. We're warned about the rabble-rouser who could whip his listeners to a frenetic act through mob psychology or the charismatic cult leader that could make his followers believe anything— even that a prophesied messiah would bring God's Kingdom to Earth.

Meanwhile, on that Earth, an alpha male, sometimes female, is the local nominee for the people's group leader, possibly a chief or tribal strongman. Typical of the overarching primate pattern, the allegiance of the group to this title-holder legitimizes their authority.

In the human troupe the alpha male may have gotten to this position by politics, charisma, or divine right, rather than fighting. Though fighting occurs among numerous primates and closer to home, chimps can be murderously violent while all degrees of conflict have occurred among men.

Indeed, *the recognition of legitimate authority may be an adaptation that allows the higher primate troupe to avoid the need for a struggle.* This cuts down on wasted time and people in fighting. It seems to work inside human groups, but not very well across groups. Consider leaders of other teams or groups and the lack of recognition of legitimate authority in that instance, for example, the waning recognition of the legitimate authority of King George by the residents of the thirteen American colonies.

In spite of routine in-fighting, humanity yearns for an orderly hierarchy in its groups, teams, societies, workplaces, governments, and so on. Tension is lessened where a hierarchy and leader are considered legitimate. Tension is greater where something in the hierarchy seems amiss.

(A very real concern, I think, is the extreme political polarization in this country, as yet not leading to widespread violence, but to the worst political gridlock in recent times and that portends more of the same. Rather than acknowledge differences in political philosophies, one side indicts the other with high crimes and illegitimate leadership. Politics ties into the God & Country identity factor discussed elsewhere and could lead to the most deeply based conflicts.)

Rank hath its games

Games of order can demonstrate the ever-present desire for unity and allow for the achievement of stress reduction in a playful, yet symbolic way. Especially popular are card games with the royal faces, Jack, Queen, King. Fun as they are, those games are the social equivalent of chewing gum and have a similar calming effect.

Gossip is a more serious "game" of social ordering. It can be exhaustive in its scope as well as its detail and is equally seductive to the dilettante and aficionado alike. Previous to a recent study, it was thought that about one third of human conversations were of gossip content, more recently an anthropologist has reported that the proportion is more like two thirds of the time.

Gossip, like the card games, is social ordering or hierarchical ranking. In other words, the rank and file as it falls in line under the alpha male, the king, or the popular kids. Gossip as a social function has at least one added *critical* element: The ever-present critical judgment of social propriety or infraction of social norms by anyone and everyone. As a natural by-product of gossip, social justice can be meted out as necessary. The offender's reputation and status can be immediately affected. As a result, she or he may even be shunned by the community.

In society, gossip can take the alpha male down—read the headlines, watch the news. The newest scandal of a political leader or a wannabe—that's the pinnacle of social gossip. Gossiping over the water cooler or online is the daily work in refining the social rankings of everyone we know or can somehow identify. These results are shared, catalogued in the minds of the recipients, and disseminated into the culture. If it's starting to sound insidious, it can be. For some of the participants it is a compulsion of sorts.

More correctly, though, it falls into the category of species-specific behavior. We're hard wired for it; it's instinctive. Those games of order, cards or chess, are a placebo, again, the chewing gum of the social order. They allow us to obey the Imperative to Rank, to categorize, and to be somewhat relieved of the seriousness that can attend the "official" efforts when we are not playing at it.

The continual analysis of social status and the ranking of the hierarchy one finds oneself in helps solidify the entire social structure. As the members of the society compare notes on who out ranks who and what scandal wrecked whose career, they are in effect acceding to the architecture, they may not like it, but they've acknowledged it. Although if something goes too far awry, the "rumor mill" may kick into disaster mode and exchanges between participant/observers (potentially everyone) will increase and swell to action, say, to overthrow or defeat a leader who failed in morals or is widely felt to no longer be legitimate, cf., Arab Spring.

IV. THE SOCIAL ORDER

Culture, the vehicle of human life

Life is precious, but so precarious. We're all way out there—everyone, believers, nonbelievers. Exposed. Vulnerable. Not just a little. Everything about us, it's all at risk, every moment on the line. It's a world of uncertainties.

Our risks seem to have escalated before our eyes. In part, blame the News at 11:00 or in reality, the News 24/7. It's a more complex world, a fully interconnected world. It seems from our perspective that the world of, say, a hundred years ago had few worries. By contrast, now it seems our doom could come from anywhere at anytime with little or no notice that it's coming.

Discussed earlier, there are a half dozen forms of destruction that could come out of deep space or originate within our solar system and a couple of nearly planet wide catastrophes from within the earth that could wipe out much of the biosphere and the life on earth. The super volcano at Yellowstone and the reversal of the magnetic poles are both overdue.

What else could get us? Global warming—costal cities flooded by rising sea levels—or another ice age, other major environmental disasters—nationwide drought, pandemic, nuclear terrorism (not to mention the U.S. and its national debt seem to be careening threateningly between a fiscal cliff and economic collapse—though this would relate only to social upheaval). So many paths to destruction, which one's it going to be? Will it be only one? We can only hope juggling the lot of them doesn't overwhelm us.

In that cold, sometimes impossible environment out there (picture your ancestors living on the beach because the inland was covered with those mile thick ice age glaciers), our cultures do their part. That's why our ancestors slowly evolved them (or should we say our ancestors survived to become our ancestors *because* they evolved them?)

Our cultures give us figurative sources for ourselves in our creation myths. That gives us a oneness, a connection with all. It says we are not alone. There's strength in that. If a religious sentiment is inspired by an urge to express camaraderie to a fellow human being, it is well motivated. Most people have an urge to be communal and that, too, arguably rises to the level of an instinct.

Today, the internet has made the entire world accessible to us in wholly new ways. It's not about the internet, though, any more than the connections that the telephone made for us were about the telephone. Television, still a favored companion, in its early days showed us an unrealistically high moral image of the world. Computers and the internet are urbanely amoral. Too much so? Well, at least it is openly admitted.

One of the internet's greatest offerings is the chance for those rejected by their local, if provincial, society to reconnect to the larger society. The rebel child or marcher to a different drum can find a place in a more richly diverse social fabric—even if they run the risk of falling in with a more radical crowd.

The internet hints at the possibility of the much maligned (in fiction and political theory on the right) universal network that might approximate the super-consciousness of humanity (a little over-blown from our present perspective, but so would be launching, then repairing the Hubble telescope if we tried to explain to Homo habilis that that's what his stone tools would one day lead to).

On some bright, but distant day we may dream that some over-arching collective mind will reach out to the individual who is cut off by the limits of her own imperfect nature or remote provincial place or family shortcomings—and perhaps give her what she needed from a god.

As hinted at before, there is some danger, too, that a closeted radical will find emboldening support from others of his bent that will lead to violent action. It can be hoped that many more are able to reconnect in cyberspace in ways that tell them they are not alone. That shoring up and support tells them that society isn't a totally uncaring wasteland.

If we all can see the future social fabric as a rich tapestry strengthened by its diversity then it will be that much stronger for its open-mindedness and tolerance. Certainly all religions and all nonbelief will be represented there as they already are on the web. The larger society's plurality pales in comparison to the democracy on the internet. That holds forth promise for us all, made real by the tremendous connection it has already given us.

Even the least connected of those who tend to be social outcasts, the outliers of political, philosophical, or social thought (usually those put upon by insensitive local forces), could be encourage to dialogue and release building pressure. Pressure that the local society *should* wish was more constructively vented, but too often local society frustrates the minority opinions and silences them or, at least, supports no public expression of their view.

The public good is much better served by allowing, if not encouraging, the 'stump' speech. It allows an all important venting, rather than stifling dissent and keeping it bottled up until it explodes. The internet, social media, and the blogosphere allow that venting at the risk of occasionally putting a couple of sociopaths together or would-be patriots who pull off a groundswell revolution.

Along this line, or rather at the extreme of it, is the school shooter. Certainly he is so disaffected by his culture, his society that he sees it not only as failed, but a vile, repugnant lampoon of what it should be: that thing which would nurture him, give him what he needs, and, in fact, celebrate him rather than reject him as he believes it has done, leaving him in the position of a pariah.

The Pariah Factor

Ingrained within man, from his hominid past, is the capacity to act out against authority, to challenge it. There was survival value in this for the early human troupe as well as today's social or political unit. By the testing of authority, the strength of it can be determined with a view to judging, *How legitimate is the authority?*

How loyal are the members of the troupe? This is another gauge of the alpha's right to rule. The alpha may hold power by brute force, but there still is a question of legitimacy and if that is missing it takes a lot more brute force to maintain power.

An election can be the ratification of legitimate authority—or the proof that the authority is not legitimate from the only source that matters . . . the governed—and, as developed elsewhere, there is also a necessary alignment, loose though it may be, with the genetically programmed and hardwired template (within our brains) of the human/ primate social structure (the underlying model of sociopolitical reality for us)—and on up through the individuals to the alpha.

Hidden, maybe not so well, within a challenge to authority is the offering of the challenger's leadership in place of the current leader's. Within a healthy sociopolitical unit testing will still take place. In fact, it is probably not a well functioning unit if testing does not take place (where one is risking his life to test, though, a quiet calculus may be all that's performed). Thus the procedure of free elections institutionalizes this testing as a foundation of legitimate authority and, in that way, protects the unit against the most radical challenges to its authority and legitimacy.

The thesis, here, is that each person looks within himself/herself for a sort of sympathetic resonance of the existing social or political order with the model "hard-wired" within him (his instinct, if you will) and every other human being. In other words, man checks to see if his sociopolitical order is aligned with his ideal (internalized) image for it.

Is Jesus Christ the ultimate alpha male?

As the rank and file human or chimpanzee surveys his place in his primate troupe and looks forward in his pack to his "A. dog," he senses this political structure is right. He'll quibble about it always; it is the nature of the beast to forever examine the reality of his social order. Is it legitimate? Is his ruler deserving of allegiance?

For the individual person to be able to look up from his position in the ranks to his alpha male, then, more figuratively, on up to his Chosen One—perhaps his savior, as he ascends to and becomes the skygod—can this legitimacy be anything but beyond question? Perhaps this is what earthly authorities lack and strive to obtain; they are so temporal, so tentative, so short-lived and fleeting. Many a leader has tried to lockstep with powerful religions thus legitimizing their authority.

The thesis here is that "alphamalism" is a hardwired imprint of higher primate behavior. In the human troupe, the alpha male may have gotten to this position by politics, charisma, strong-handed tactics or other means short of physical fighting or intimidation (Certainly, physical force and intimidation have been all too typical as well.). [See Anthropology of Belief for a deeper discussion.]

This instinct makes humankind yearn for an orderly hierarchy in groups, teams, societies, workplaces, governments and so on. In fact, tensions are lessened where a hierarchy and leader are considered legitimate. Tension is greatest where something in the hierarchy seems amiss.

Perhaps this hints at some important improvements in human groupings over the great ape model of the alpha male. Where chimps can only grumble about their leader who holds the reigns of power like a strongman, until the next stronger man comes along, we can elect or at least respond to the charisma and natural leadership skills of our leaders.

We can also have a "world-perfecting" religion, one that shows us a utopia of justice, of karma by which we can judge our world and perhaps this religion equips us to tolerate a difficult world. Our religion can give us an otherworldly, transcendent leader (or in religions lacking supernatural beings or deities, at least a just order of things.)

The immense value of language and thought as an improvement over the chimpanzee model is too lengthy of a digression to make here, but it serves to bring us closer together in ways the chimpanzee can't imagine.

Particularly adept at this, the feudal system of the Middle Ages was also one that tied into an overt alpha male pattern. Where that structure led to a feudal lord it could eventually lead to a king at the top; they pointed to their 'divine right' to rule. They happily associated with the legitimacy that proceeded from a god. Once obtained, how, then, could that authority possibly be challenged? The perfected ideal of God pretty much bestows a high degree of legitimacy. Power and authority don't get much more just than to proceed from the Source of All. It's a thing of cosmic proportions, anchored in their metaphysical reality.

It makes one wonder, how often in human prehistory have the religious leaders become the political leaders? Even in written history, the lesson of the legitimizing influence of being in a seamless relationship with the agents of the gods (religious leaders) was not lost on the powers that be. They courted and co-opted that influence at every chance or paid the price for not doing so.

Social Hierarchy of Feudal Systems

Divine right of kings

—

God/divine

King/Queen

Prince/princess

Earl/other royalty

Lord/Landlord

Vassel/Sheriff/tax assessor

Business

tradesman

Tenant/farmer

peasants

———

Admittedly, this chart slips into socioeconomic classes as well, but it is only an approximation, a suggestion of the social order. Those classes, though, may still have some relevance in how we see authority or power distributed. The chart is more for comparison with the primate alpha male hierarchy chart, aka, the orthomorphic primate chart below.

Generic structure of Human/Chimp troupes
(The Orthomorphic Primate Hierarchy)

Alpha male

Primary supporters/lieutenants/dauphins/sycophants

Potential aids / Potential rivals

High ranking females

Young potential rivals

Other special rankings

Rank & File Members

Juveniles/ Charges-in-care

Hangers on/Near outcasts

—

The crude outline above is only a suggestion of how a primate socio-political structure might be envisioned. Some aspects of it may be more chimpanzee than human or vice versa. No interlocking religious components have clamped onto this social structure at this point.

If you're skeptical, as you should always be, you might ask, *How would a religious model become ingrained in a human troupe to such a great effect?* You're looking at it backwards. This is, rather, how the generic primate group structure led to human socio-political structure and may have served as a template that natural selection might have used for a religious model. The former, the primate social structure, led to a model for what other social structure arrangements could be.

Those that are reminiscent of every person's innate, internalized model certainly would have the most natural appeal—they are what might seem to come spontaneously, intuitively to mind.

Are there weaknesses or criticisms of this hypothesis? Oh, yeah. First, how could this schematic outline have been any different? That is, doesn't it simply decline from the most (physically) powerful at the top, the alpha male, down to the least powerful at the bottom? If so, then how could it be different?

Perhaps it can't be much different when considered across primate species. Even other mammals demonstrate alphamalism in mating opportunities and often feeding privileges. Birds have their pecking orders. The physically strongest can impose their will on the less strong and achieve the same ends. What would be the need to internalize, in effect, the idea that a bully will come along and take your lunch away from you?

A few things to consider. A number of species have been able to ritualize the challenge between the top two males so that a duel to the death isn't necessary.

Chest-pounding gorillas demonstrate that their posturing and intimidation is usually all that's necessary rather than actual combat. Still, that doesn't invalidate the alpha male model.

One case that's pretty close to home is the bonobo, the so-called pigmy chimp, but actually a separate species with very different behavior. They generally use a brief, even momentary, sex act in lieu of a handshake, greeting, or salute. It seems to work; they have much less violence in their lives than chimps. In fact, rather than an alpha male at the top, this is a female hierarchy. Males only have social rank and political capital through the females and their relationships with them.

Does the bonobo model invalidate the orthomorphic (alpha male) primate model? Not really. At the same time, the alpha male model isn't something to defend, but only a tool for gaining possible insight.

Chimpanzees are the most violent of the great apes including man (those cute little tykes you love to watch are just that—infants and toddlers. By the way, for those of you concerned about the great apes, please don't support exploitive TV commercials and movies—any use is abuse. You've heard the horror stories—mothers have to be killed to capture the young, they're yanked from the world they know, they're traumatized and depressed, then, if they live through it, they are a problem in their adult years—and they are abused like one. Backyard cages, road side zoos—an isolated hell for a gregarious social being.)

Chimp troupes have true hit squads. The alpha male and his lieutenants (supportive underlings) form a unit that will go on raids against threats from other opposing troupes to defend territory, females, and food sources. It is a defense from the point of view of the alpha and his cronies, though perhaps not human observers of such attacks (the alpha's genes are the primary beneficiary of the action).

Perhaps, a more serious charge against the alpha male model is the currently accepted hypothesis that hunter-gatherers lived an egalitarian (presuming no leader, no alpha male) lifestyle with everyone being of equal rank. This is, it is said, what the primitive tribes of today demonstrate. The assumption is made that the hunter-gatherers lived as these primitives do today.

That may be a valid inference. If so, those who argue for it say it means there were no alpha males among the hunter-gatherers. Would it mean no alphas for the 200,000 years of anatomically modern humans? Perhaps. Did this egalitarian state of equanimity become an ingrained, innate model?

There were millions of years of primate evolution and many more millions of years of mammalian evolution that must have placed alphamalism in our genes. Two hundred thousand years, though, is sufficient time for selection to change us. Probably we've changed for the better. If *hunter-gatherer* was the economy that placed us living communally within a tribe, and social equality was the norm, then evermore human exchanges and refined social behaviors surely took hold.

Still there are alphas on this end of that 200,000 years in both primitive cultures and modern. Not all of the Native Americans were agriculturalists and yet they had chiefs. Polynesian and Hawaiian Islanders had chieftains. And almost all modern cultures had leaders. So was the alpha male model suppressed for 200,000 years only to spring up anew when settled farmers and villagers accumulated property? It seems questionable at best.

Still, it should be remembered that we almost certainly had alphamalism hardwired in our genes as well as our minds for *millions* of years. Whether that seemed to leave us with an unmet need, who can say? Our earthly tribal fathers may have met that need or may have proved inadequate to the task. Surely, they must have felt inadequate next to the hostile world they brought their children into, a world that dealt cruelly harsh realities to young and old alike.

Perhaps, it helped these fathers deal with their inadequacy to at least put that world in some sort of context for themselves and their children, perhaps with a narrative of how the nature god and the tribe came together. (Bear in mind, though, that present thinking places our capacity for language no farther back than fifty to seventy-five thousand years and some would place it under fifty thousand years. [With less agreement, some place it over a hundred thousand years ago.])

Still, the more we understood, the greater the gulf might have seemed between our earthy existence and the overwhelming natural world—an adequacy gap. If our fathers weren't equal to the task of taming that dangerous world, perhaps an elder or wise man was? The need to seek wisdom or expertise in a tribal band must have certainly created a well worn path to those with experience. (At some point, the elder who could offer some understanding, even if no greater handling of the world was possible, caused the "skill" to be added to the future holy man's job description.)

Looking up the supernatural chart for answers, short though the chart might have been in our ancestors' early days, would have gone something like this (in ascending order): self, mother, father—huge void—then the unfathomable natural world. It seems likely that this short list would have run through the minds of the members at least once in a while.

Even if the egalitarian model (the leading hypothesis) of the hunter-gatherer life totally dominated their existence, it seems possible that there might have been the odd shaman or moonlighting tribal holy man in some instances. And if so, where these existed, they could be plugged into the chart like this: self, mother, father, holy man, nature—supernatural.

Admittedly the tribal holy men have come to the chart last. (The cynics among us might say that the holy men came into the picture as the result of doing a sales job on their public—convincing them that they were necessary for their expertise in placating and cajoling the gods into listening to them.)

If no such specialization of the god-appeasing arts were possible because the hunter-gatherers were (believed to be) egalitarian (all equal, all worked, no alphas, no holy men {there may have been part-time holy men/women or medicine wo/men]), and "alpha male" rule didn't re-appear until settled agriculturalists would support them, that chart might have looked like this:

The (apparent) Natural Order of Being
Ancestral humans

—

Supernatural Realm

Natural World

Holy Man

(or void)

father

mother

self

*

The case can be made that there was a demand for knowledge of and communication with the supernatural. We can certainly sympathize with the typical member of the village who felt inadequate to the task of petitioning the supernatural realm for favors, perhaps to halt a disaster in progress, or to spare the life of a sick child.

Perhaps tribes, their members, and holy men drew their own charts as they saw them. Initially, this chart may not have interested the individual like the alpha male chart did. That's where they lived, after all, in the alpha male's world.

As Homo sapiens matured as a species, these two charts tumbled over each other—disciplined models in otherwise undisciplined minds. Some behaviorally modern human minds must occasionally, even if dimly, have noticed the potential overlap of the two charts. Perhaps, that allowed an opening for the holy men. Perhaps, it was the future holy men who superimposed one chart on the other and liked where that placed them on the resultant chart.

Was that the beginning of the end of "direct spirituality?" Did the holy men, those spiritual middlemen, usurp the power of the spiritual? Or did humanity need their expertise in making contact—religious professionals—and this gave rise to the priestly class. (Folk religions probably bumped along imbedded within the cultures keeping the people in touch with the spiritual realm—and being the bane of the major religion—c.f., Christianity vis-à-vis pagan religions. There were no modern western holy men in favor of folk religions—no direct spirituality. {Direct spirituality equals just you and your god, no intervening holy man.} [New Age seems to encourage direct spirituality—does that make it a folk religion?])

[Where no dates and no species are mentioned, I am typically talking about the ancestral human population (*Homo sapiens*) over the last 200,000 years and generally of the most formative periods of fifty to one hundred thousand years ago. The term behaviorally modern humans is applied to our ancestors from ~100,000 years ago forward.

I do occasionally refer to earlier species, sometimes naming them, sometimes leaving them unnamed depending on the purpose of the passage. The context will clear up for you as to whether knowing the dates and species is relevant. It's left open, in part, because the intent isn't especially to date the acquisition of a specific human (or primate) function as it is to discuss what the function means to us—the meaning it holds for us now and in the future. It may also be the case that no one knows as yet when a trait was acquired.]

Religion formed true to the alpha male hierarchy

One aspect of the alpha male hierarchies of apes and men that could lead to a religious hierarchy is that, from our place within the hierarchy of men, we look *beyond*. We can and do decouple our thought from the task at hand, we look ahead and behind. As we look toward our alpha leaders, we do project ahead and wonder what lies beyond. Our ultimate questions could come out of that as much as from any other source.

As mentioned earlier, if you observe chimpanzee society in the wild (anywhere there's more than one chimp, actually), you'll see alpha males ruling as a strongman might. Some may be liked, but many are cruel. Typically, all have coalitions with one or a few loyal supporters necessary to maintain power. The alpha chimp is always just one skirmish away from losing control over the troupe.

In the ultimate troupe—some idealized, perfected hierarchy—the alpha's legitimacy elevates everyone in the troupe. It's utopia. There is no reason to look beyond this troupe and alpha; there's nothing better, or so it seems.

As hunter-gatherers, though, we looked beyond our alphas—our fathers and patriarchs (duly acknowledging the current theory cited elsewhere that hunter-gatherer's had no alphas). We've visualized the power behind nature, the Great Spirit, as something of a personality. We know the Great Spirit truly has power, this legitimizes his reign and thus, his rule is just. The alignment of our troupe hierarchy—our mothers and fathers, our alpha male, his lieutenants—under our scrutiny, are all found wanting in the leadership role; their failings are great when we contemplate the perfect candidate in the idealized role.

Is it any wonder that religion does us the service of setting up a realm of supreme justice and righteousness and of legitimate authority, in some cases a loving, benevolent deity, one that watches over us, that sees all and knows all?

Fast forward to the classical period in Rome, Greece, and the Middle East

By this time the Abrahamic holy men had rolled out a new iteration of themselves, the prophet, largely a messenger from God, still a man, but one who has a more or less direct link to the deity. The Hebrew Bible had prophesied a messiah would come. Each new prophet was considered as this messiah, then rejected. Eventually, a messiah appeared, one that was half god, half human.

Jesus of the Bible brings together numerous appealing qualities both human and divine. Son of God, half human by a miraculous virgin birth and half God by a holy gene splice, portended by a star in the east. Son of the one and only creator of the universe. A healer, political and religious activist, spiritual teacher, and inspiring, charismatic leader of a ministry and movement of love. He appears to have had unbounded compassion and as hidden talents go, performing miracles is always a crowd pleaser.

Jesus may have been given some of these qualities by writers of the New Testament. That doesn't really matter now, at least with respect to the reaction the Biblical Jesus engenders in his believers. Every act of Jesus and every event he brought forth served to endear believers to him. In fact, he was probably given some of these traits specifically because they would engender spiritual effects in people and thereby enable their conversion.

Reason, Augustine's rebuked harlot, will not forever be denied

Perhaps, one should not condemn, but rather, admire the search for God. One should, perhaps, condemn the leap of faith by which so many before have *found* Him. There is a flaw in how one *comes* to their knowledge of God. We understand now that we, or perhaps only *they*, were hearing a call, not from the heavens, but coded within our every cell. That inner voice, that *still small voice*, it's from deep within, but it's not God. It calls us to a god, but was programmed by a different designer. Evidently, the godwish is strong in us. The wiser course might be to yet stand vigil, waiting, ever waiting . . .

It is a ludicrously clichéd analogy, the eight blind men and the elephant, but it's too functional in this instance not to use it to describe the different possible sources for the origin of religion. In case you were just rescued from a religious home school environment and having your first brush with secular civilization, the aforementioned parable tells of each blind man's experience of a different aspect of an elephant. One feels a rope-like tail, another the trunk, yet another the foot and so on.

Let me be the first blind man so as not to more greatly offend any other than I necessarily must (that's not the purpose here at all). The aspect of the "elephant" that I experience is that the garden variety Sunday morning religious experiences are neurochemical experiences and may give us enough juice to feel reinforcement for our spiritual pursuits and findings. Because of that and the myriad benefits religion can bestow on its followers, and all the other evidence throughout this writing, it will become apparent that religion is an evolutionary adaptation.

Another blind man sees a god gene or a god spot in the brain. A third credits us with a hyperactive agent detection device with which we often project the likelihood of hidden agency (*Who's there?* Rather than, *What was that?*). A fourth detects a minimally counterintuitive hidden agent (the least implausible *Who's there?*) to whom we ascribe supernatural aspects and given our psychological attachment adaptation, we project our attachment to our father who art in the supernatural realm.

Another blind man hears a repeating meme that makes the believers seem deluded, as if they are infected by another's metaphorical God virus. A seventh envisions our mental template for "person" which we apply to our concept of God and process it with our vital inference systems by which we give religion its strength. The eighth blind man thinks religion is a spandrel, a by-product of other factors, not something formed for its own use or value.

Who's right? Like the eighth blind man, the first seven may be right about their specific contribution to our understanding. None of the theses above, even in detail, (and these are representative, there are more and some are considered in more detail elsewhere) are mutually exclusive and the entire lot of them might be coordinated into an enlarged hypothesis much as Pascal Boyer or Andy Thomson have done.

The only area of significant conflict is the question as to whether religion is a spandrel or an evolutionary adaptation, in other words, heritable, i.e., in the genes (Redundant, I know, but it isn't exactly religion that's heritable. That's just short hand for religiosity, religiousness, or spirituality, and even those terms are only an approximation. That instinct, like all others, is written in DNA code to produce certain neural paths and synaptic connections, to activate and quiet certain brain regions, to produce and release at specific times certain neurochemicals of pleasure and reward. Ultimately, we respond as our genetic preprogramming trains us to do. In the broadest of terms, Religio-spiritual behaviors are rewarded.).

Those who say, *No, No predisposition to religion or spirituality is heritable,* say it in a way that seems to dismiss, if not to miss altogether, the grip religion has or has had on humankind. In part, that's what makes those of us on the pro religion-as-an-evolutionary-adaptation side think they've underestimated religion, its strength, ubiquity, universality, etc. They counter with, *It isn't universal.* They say that primitive peoples, even though they are immersed in the lore of their deity in their daily lives, don't have true religions.

Can't Get No Satisfaction

Most people would settle for a low level religious experience. Most aren't reaching even that level of spiritual satisfaction. I would combine this thought with Joseph Cambell's statement cited elsewhere and sum them up together: The typical person's experience is that modern religion doesn't provide a spiritual experience, but is, rather, just an inoculation against the divine—to plug a hole where a spiritual experience belongs—a place holder.

A person who wishes desperately to have a religious experience, especially a transformative experience, can't achieve it without choosing to believe some religious claims. I suppose (sadly?) that all but a few statistical outliers won't achieve anything spiritually significant at any time in their lives. They'll have the wish, the longing, the knowing that there should have been something more. In sum, they'll have experienced the spiritual drive, but not have fulfilled it.

Yet, there is no expectancy of having a religious experience among the rank and file Christians. Outside the Born-agains, Pentecostals, and evangelicals, the typical Christian looks askance at religious experiences. In the muddle of the middle, when someone overhears another talking about a true (relative term) mystical experience they have had, the typical listener either rolls their eyes or slides a little further down the pew. At best, they assume the speaker is mistaken. For the typical Christian, then, divine beings and the supernatural realm are neither accessible nor at hand.

And what of us nonbelievers? Are there transformative experiences for the secular person? Or are they forever barred from it? Even if it could be achieved while denying all religions, what would its content be? What would one consist of? How would it be significant? What would it mean?

In *Quantum Change*, William Miller and Janet C'de Baca describe the transformative, but nonreligious experience as an *insight*. "They have a quality of growing out of life experiences." "They tend to follow from the person's development rather than being an intrusion into it." "Suddenly the person comes to a new way of thinking . . ." Several of their interviewees "likened the instantaneous force to a lightening bolt." Pages 18, 19 *Quantum Change.*

The religious or mystical experience no doubt serves a purpose besides a consult with a god. It would release the believer from the burden of reality, the oppressive nature of it, of the real world. So, too, religion attempts to perform this function to a lesser but much needed degree. Mystical experiences seem to be well above some minimal level or, let's say, the garden variety experience of everyday religion. Perhaps their intensity matches the felt need, the religious ardor, or the piety of the believer?

It would be only temporary relief as are most other escapes except for death and purportedly, wealth or power. Other would-be reliefs: celebrity, sex, meditation, sedation, transcendental *medication* (i.e., drugs). Being a monarch? (*"It's good to be king,"* Mel Brooks, History of the World, Part I.)

The more a person or a community could pitch themselves a maximally rewarding hypothetical world, albeit of their own creation, and remain immersed in it, the more release from the mundane world there would be. There's an often overlooked, even unknown strength to communal beliefs. Perhaps through the communal mind believers can float aloft of a "sight for sore eyes," a vision, a blend of the best of all possible worlds with enough of the real world in the mix to say of this spiritual quest that it's grounded. The religious worldview can be like that and for those that choose to color it as an idyllic, pastoral life of loving gratitude, the good life is theirs for the making.

Others—those that choose a negative worldview base their lives on the vision that their world could have been great if it weren't for someone messing it up—they may blame the blacks, the LGBT community, the Jews, the liberals, the atheists. In other words, God made their world good until someone came along and mucked it up. These folks then like to point out the dogma that the rest of us ignored and how, by ignoring it, we're forcing God to bringing retribution down on all of us. It hasn't happened yet, but we surely will feel His wrath sometime soon. And those affronts to God that we bring into the community are as offensive to those righteous few as they are to God.

And that's how the rest of us mucked it up for them and how our abominations foul their world and God's.

It's not until society at large "gets it" all over again as it has for each denigrated minority who's been the object of hatred and bigotry—and steps away from the hate community and sees it for what it is. The hate community enjoys hiding within society at large playing on its prejudices to keep it riled up and angered to the effect that the minority is oppressed by the majority. The haters can lash out with relative impunity under the cover of the as-yet-unenlightened culture.

As hate radio panders to the lowest common denominator among its listeners it legitimizes hate speech and hate speech legitimizes street violence or at least continued demonizing, dehumanizing and denying of rights of the minority and keeps the core group on *high alert* with zero tolerance for more imagined offenses by the denigrated minority.

Do we want the polarization we've achieved in this country? We've made it happen one sound bite at a time. We've demonized each other. We've accused each other of greater offenses than we've actually committed. We accuse the other of intending the worst we can imagine. We demand total victory and if unable to have that we'll settle only for total defeat of the other even if we have to go down, too, in order to make it happen. I don't think we're going to like this world that we're making.

V. Is There a God?

Whether early humankind had to answer the god question from the beginning or whether we evolved both the need and the spiritual pursuits to deal with the question, the resultant existential imperative was deeply felt: *Seek the creator . . . and find Him.*

Fortunately for humankind, early man picked up a confirmation bias. Most pursuits and questions came back positive—a false positive, but a positive that one could act on, a positive that put the person into motion. Evidently, that, too, had survival value. Here we are.

It's a world worthy of a god. Humanity deserves a god. They say you can't get to an *ought* from an *is* (I don't know that they're right about this. You do the symbolic logic.). This, though, is getting to an *is* from an *ought*.

The believers' reality is this: In the best of all possible worlds, there would be a god. In short, there ought to be a god, therefore there is one in the believers world.

Still and all, here was a being thrust into the world on several levels at once, becoming man, if not human. As he grew from an unknowing infant, he became conscious as an individual—and found himself, within his own self—that particular state of affairs remaining unexplained to him and to all.

And his family? They were here before him. Where'd they come from, and his tribe? And his world? No one knew. Nobody he knew created any of it or even claimed to see it created. Maybe wherever lightening bolts and leopards came from . . . ? Yeah, better get on *their* good side quickly. Whoever *they* were.

And so, perhaps many millennia before civilizations formed, humanity had been on a god quest. In rudimentary form it may have originated with the ultimate question, *Why?* Or was it because out of the animal kingdom came one who *could* ask why? That was a totally amazing ability, but it far outstripped that animal's or any animal's ability to answer.

Did we become human when
we could ask the question *Why?*

Agriculture is given credit for enabling civilization to rise, but religion may have been an omnibus force for social cohesion. Man accepted its authority to answer those questions he had, but couldn't answer. For their day the answers were wise.

Religion is what the deepest thinking australopithecines of two million years earlier lacked when an alpha male's legitimacy seemed inauthentic or insufficient. When sickened of their Hobbesian world, generation upon generation, perhaps even species after hominid species, they longed for deliverance, for transcendence from the grinding daily want and suffering. Did some proto-ritual, rhythmic and numbing, developed by trial and error over millenia, become their existential—though temporary—relief?

Their questions demanded answers: Who were they? Where did they come from? The human brain reached the capacity to ask the big questions. But man, even primitive as he was, couldn't stand immobilized waiting for the answers. Yet without the answers, immobilized he would stand.

Or did we become humankind when we created religion around the quest for an answer? Perhaps, if human communities have greater strength, if they are bound together by a higher purpose—religion can create that purpose, that radical depth of meaning—and arguably no higher purpose is possible (though, in reality, humanity is its own higher purpose).

We began the search with the question *Why?* Humankind didn't have a means or a channel to pursue that question, yet it seemed to be in its face everyday. Death rates were high in early cultures. Even minor diseases without medical treatment can kill. Some of today's surviving primitives go to war or on raids regularly and, so it is surmised, did their counterparts a hundred millennia before.

I suspect, though, that the pursuit of *Why* didn't become *religion* until we had an answer—or at least a belief—until some name was put to nature or the supernatural power behind nature's veil. Its apotheosis, if you will. Lip service is occasionally paid to the nebulous unknown, but few get excited about it until it has a name, an identity, a persona.

Society was God, some said. Well, it ought to be, but I believe we defaulted to the shiny object instead—the supernatural was more exciting when it came to a head—God. Reality made more sense when you think of the forces in the world as directed by an overarching actor for his own purposes. It was after all, early man's psyche that unwittingly designed our early religions and even more unwittingly, it was under the influence of selection.

If you remember the hierarchical chart of the primate/human troupe, it can be considered a simplistic model of a small society—a tribal band or a clan, say. Based on the model of a just society as an ideal, one might project a just supernatural realm. Or perhaps more poignantly, in the absence of a just society one might project a just heaven with a rectifying deity, intent on making things right. Perhaps that heaven, too, would conform to the hierarchical chart—could the deity be other than an alpha male? We're still primates, after all.

(In many a description of the generic chimp troupe, an uneasy tension underlies the reality of an alpha who rules by force with political allies who add to his strength over and against the apparently unhappy lot of his subjects. Could it be that those subject apes long for justice? If the unspoken source of our morals is heritable, and if, as it seems, there's some rudimentary thing like it within chimps, perhaps they forever will ache for a justice that can never come.)

The troupes of the hunter-gatherers supposedly were egalitarian and had no head, no chief—no alpha male—so perhaps that society without one, wished all the more *for* one? Perhaps they came to idolize a perfected vision of the legitimate alpha male by virtue of the great ape-primate social structure in the back of their minds. Perhaps where you as hunter—gatherer would envision that ideal leader at the head of your pack, and as there was none, you might look up, above and beyond into the great unknown and project a leader up and out there so that you could rejoice in finding that leader.

Our frugivore ancestors had to be generalists in their food seeking. These generalist were rewarded with a reproductive advantage as they developed a brain that had the capacity to let our late ape-early man ancestors specialize to a depth when it was beneficial. The great apes have the ability to mentally catalogue all the fruit and nut trees and all the edible plant products in their environment and to know which ones would be ripe and when (this will be picked up again later).

The modern human brain was overkill—evolution trumped ecosystem, big time. Here was a human mind capable of language—even a high degree of culture in a world where there was none (or little, say. We probably couldn't posit any being we'd call man without some culture, at least, more than chimps seem to have). And in that absence, humankind seemed to arrive inexplicably (from its own perspective) on the scene.

With no real trace of their own origin, origin myths were all there was to fill the void—and so they stood unopposed. Don't you feel on some deep level that creation myths aren't supposed to be questioned? But it's more than mere reverence, creation myths are to be accorded more than just a suspension of our disbelief—they are held as a greater truth.

When the clan's myths of the tribal Great Spirit yielded to the village totems, the way for civilization may have been cleared. Settled communities supposedly began with agriculture about 15,000 years ago. Those mile thick glaciers covering much of the land may have forced settled life and subsistence agriculture on most human cultures as all life may have been isolated to the margins of the continents.

As the glaciers receded the new way of life spread settlement and agriculture far and wide. Skills were honed, surpluses allowed trade. Ingenuity spawned tools and the trades, labor and ownership of land and wealth . . . and conquest. And somehow the conquerors' sacred narrative could be imposed on the vanquished as if they acknowledged that there very conquering was due to the stronger myth of the conqueror.

The vanquished became subject to the conqueror's reality. It was their quill and papyrus, after all, with which history was written. Chiefs, feudal lords, and kings extended their myths over newly acquired territories. Consider the symbiosis of state and religion at work in the Holy Roman Empire.

Nations employed religion, but that was only made possible by how it served—or ruled—humanity. Religion was incredibly intertwined within the community, the culture, and the individual and for good reason. Who were they without their myths? They'd have no identity then—but it was so much more than mere identity. It was their essence and their essential connection to All Being. Surrounding their myths is their religion. It elevates them to ultra relevance, to mythic relevance to the world of all being. It is the answer to the meaning they seek. Why *would* they give that up? It would mean cultural or social suicide, in some instances death.

Why would we give it up? Is it the price of the "examined life" of Socrates or of intellectual honesty? Or does keeping the culture alive stave that off? Maybe those of a common myth band together and raise their voices as well as all the noise they can. In the competition of myths and cultures, only the strong survive.

To offer science or other knowledge is of little consolation as an enticement to quit one's faith. Religion claims an unfair advantage. What can compete with communing with the divine or supernatural and the spiritual feelings that such experiences engender? The bare, unvarnished truth holds no appeal to rival that. If the truth will cause you to be ostracized from your world, what appeal would be sufficient?

I'm wondering if humankind doesn't so commonly adopt religion because the benefits are too great to do without. There is the use of myth to explain the inexplicable, but much of humanity derives greater psychological benefits from religion than that, a sense of harmony with the universe, oneness with nature, inner peace, a spiritual endurance and strength, benevolence toward all mankind, and eternal hope.

This is a believer at his best, of course. So very many fall short. And with all their short comings—religious wars, persecution, prosecution, inquisitions, terrorism, and more—should we ask the believer to trade off all her benefits in exchange for the naked, unpopular, even ugly truth? Again, are the benefits of religion too great to do without? Or perhaps, is the human animal predisposed to adopt, adapt, or develop a set of beliefs that meets his need to have the very same?

Save me! The Garden Varieties of Religious Experience

Perhaps the interior sensations of being 'saved' constitute a certain type of peak experience. Maybe the human mind when fully convinced that it's part of a peak experience, or maybe a transcendent one, releases a psychological payoff not unlike, say for example, winning a contest or wager but only amped up to a higher level yet. Perhaps along with this there's a small release of serotonin, dopamine, or another neurochemical reward stimulating the person to this series of thoughts: *Could I be saved?* (This triggers rising thoughts and moods and another round of neurochemical positive reinforcement—a reinforcement that's so pleasing it encourages us toward more and more of it); *I think I'm saved!* (more neurochemical reinforcement—this could be an upward spiraling loop [self-feeding], with evermore neurochemical validation) *I feel it! I am saved!*

Other forms of religious experiences may have similar *Eureka!* moments with neurochemical underpinnings. Each form of mystical experience could be different. Do "secular moments" share some of the same elements?

This understanding brings us back to the question that was touched on earlier, whether secular people can have as much of a "spiritual experience" as a religious person—even if it is defined as an upward spiral of positive feelings and reinforcing neurochemicals feeding each other. Or do the "reality-based" face an obstacle here?

Does the knowledge that it's not true—that the spiritual experience is not and cannot be supernaturally influenced—eliminate the secular person's chance to have a spiritual experience? Or an experience of that magnitude?

That is, one would think the secular mind is not fooled or tricked into such a state, with the possible exception of a drug induced high or hallucination. The believer, on the other hand, is necessarily somewhat taken by surprise by the experience as it sweeps them away. Similarly, a number of years back, Richard Dawkins donned Persinger's God Helmet in hopes it would stimulate a religious experience in him. It didn't. If that is possible (and I'm not convinced that it is in the sense of creating a spiritual experience of the religious kind in a person who knows there's no legitimate source for such experiences), would it be a tricking of the mind? And could it reach a joyous, ecstatic level of emotion?

Throughout, we've been discussing religious/spiritual experiences that might be calibrated on some scale of the neurochemicals released or certain brain activity that may escalate to a peak of overwhelming feelings at the extreme high end. Granted, there could be visionary experiences, as another type of religious experience where, say, you and Jesus just stand there looking at each other and nothing else happens— this hypothetical event being a more sedate, serene experience like something that might come out of meditation.

The believer [barring temporal lobe epilepsy] that has a vision of an iconic religious person she admires from the past could be experiencing spiritual-visual synesthesia. Just as the synesthete who might experience the number 28 as being, say, the color chartreuse, this special believer who's experiencing some spiritual stimulation my have a brief flash, a vision of sorts, of a historically significant religious person.

One the other hand, the phenomenon of inducing religious visions by extreme focus on the sainted person appears to be a historically accurate one. Such scripted visions were "facilitated" by the person focusing intently on the object of said vision and related prayer while cloistered in their monasteries.)

Is it possible that a believer (barring temporal lobe epilepsy) that has a vision of an iconic religious person she admires from the past could be experiencing spiritual-visual synesthesia where "spiritual" might be a feeling or a sense. Just as the synesthete who might experience the number 28 as being the color chartreuse, this special believer who's experiencing some spiritual stimulation may have a brief flash, a vision of sorts, of a historically significant religious person (or other spiritual feelings and resultant sense experiences. The, perhaps, "normal" side of experiences of these kinds, to place the above experiences in context, might be when a person hears violin music that brings them to tears.)

Consider one's internal state when completing a work of art that one is ecstatic about or a superlative performance that receives well deserved accolades, which the artist is overjoyed with. For more, there's the sexual orgasm, winning a Nobel prize, the McArthur "genius" award or another important academic/intellectual discovery. Despite any external validation from these events, don't we experience something *real* internally?

Maybe a similar internal psychological reward comes from putting one's beliefs out there, vocalizing them to your community of like minded believers, reinforcing other believer's beliefs—acting on them in ritual or song or putting them to practice in public. On the flipside, there's the diminishing aspect of being within a community of differing beliefs, some invalidating your own. (Some say we all worship the same god. If there is one god, why isn't there just one religion? Why can't they identify one god? "Many paths to God." We've heard that one before. Few believers are willing to point to the other guy's god and say, "Yeah, that's my god, too. They must necessarily be all the same.")

I can testify to the negative reaction of hearing beliefs espoused as if the speaker is speaking for all of us. The more that espousal takes place, the more we react as if society has authorized that set of beliefs and disenfranchised anyone who holds beliefs to the contrary. The more that those types of public displays by one religion are tolerated, the less appropriate other, especially secular views, seem by contrast. There is the risk of shame or derision or worse to identify one's self as being of a true minority belief. But most secular people feel a certain urge to yell out, "Hey! That's not me. Here I am. This is who I am."

It's funny that believers say they are such a minority in a secular world. If they believe that, then they surely must realize how much they are imposing their beliefs on what they see as the 'secular majority.' But in a society where over seventy percent claim belief, it's difficult to understand what majority they're talking about.

Might they be saying, *We Born-Again Christians aren't in the majority?* Maybe that is it. Different denominations see each other as other-than-themselves rather than seeing them as being alike.

Maybe that calling to the religious experience, like a pastor's calling, was in the sense of those who, for whatever reason, felt the spiritual reward of something . . . perhaps it was just belief? And for that person, the reaching of the spiritual 'dimension,' and by that I don't mean another realm, I mean that felt psychological reward in the brain, that oxytocin surge rewarding our thoughts while dopamine (the "love drug") rewards us for loving our god and our fellow man. (Does religion structure our thoughts, maybe even our minds, for those rewards?)

Meanwhile, serotonin boosts our mood. And if this happens to be a grand event, a pinnacle—a full blown mystical experience—our mood continues to climb ever upward. Various brain centers that participate in the religious epiphany will light up or quiet down depending on whether they contribute to that sense of diffusing into the universe and becoming one with it or heightening their mental state to one of hyper-awareness. Epinephrine (adrenalin) helps power the internal event. We'll leave it there so as not to overly define all experiences as one.

Is the event itself "in charge" or is the mind of the person in control? In other words, what shapes the event? What determines whether it stays *petit* or whether it reaches grand proportions?

Neonate religions in the Newer Age

Is the world ripe for a religion to sweep through it? Broad appeal would be necessary but may not be sufficient. Would it still be necessary for something in that religion to ignite the spark in prospective believers? (It certainly seems it would have to have some advantage.) Or are those days gone with the advent of the postmodern world? Are modern seekers looking for a more nuanced, more graceful-life, more humanistic belief? Something urbane and sophisticated? Is there an unwitting acknowledgement that the "spark" is gone? (The spark being that in a religion which causes the psycho-spiritual responses in a person to activate and perhaps shape that person's actions in that direction.)

And yet you can be certain that existing religions will evolve. There's no certainty any religion will evolve enough to survive, but it is certain that any that do survive will have evolved to do so. If you look back a generation or so in the history of most faith traditions you'll find significant change—maybe not in the sacred writings—but with accommodation to the present culture. Those religions that don't change will be showing the strain of their anachronism. Considering where the established religions seem to be heading (religious orthodoxy, institutionalization, rigid conventionality) and the esoteric direction of New Age and graceful-life philosophies, it seems unlikely that any new socially binding beliefs are going to be forth coming that will gain a significant portion of any population. (It seems to me that New Age may be the default forming of a queue waiting for the next bus. {It should be noted, though, that incipient religions are being identified.})

Should we be concerned that as societies have less and less formal religious affiliations there might not be a sufficiently energizing level of common beliefs to bind us together and then social vitality will wane? (Oh, wait—that's already happened.) With social indifference comes danger. Divisiveness, rancor, and ennui can expose the social fabric to the risks of failure or destruction.

Both Russian and Chinese communism sought to set religion aside during the course of their "experiments." They saw a conflict and wanted their populaces to have the greater allegiance to the state, or more charitably, to the people. It may not be impossible for a political philosophy to generate the internal drives and rewards that a religion can engender in us, but it wouldn't be easy—and it would be difficult to maintain for a long duration. This would seem to be especially true in a large state. (The forming of smaller collectives may have been an unconscious groping for the prehistoric ancestral clan of one hundred fifty members.)

There is some aspect of the believer or his religious group that wants all the members of the society (parent group) to be of the same faith. There's something ancient that drives this. No doubt the same thing that drives religious xenophobia.

(Alternative perspectives may be just as valid. Case in point: It may be no more meaningful or correct to say "Religious xenophobia" originates in a broader base of human xenophobia than it is to say it is an aspect of our proto-religions that survives to this day.

(The many and varied thoughts and behaviors we may attribute to religion may have been part of other psychological modules that came earlier for other reasons. These thoughts/behaviors may function in response to religion in people whether they are locked into some suite of genes we may someday label "religiosity or spirituality genes" or not.

(Totally unconnected genes may contribute to religiosity. The psychological mechanism of attachment like that of child to parent may be coopted by an association or suite of genes that we may collectively refer to when we say religiosity is heritable. Certainly, if a piecemeal association of genes functioned to give the individual the religiosity advantage, so be it. It doesn't make the complex of religiosity/spirituality any less of an evolutionary adaptation, no matter how it is selected, transmitted, or expressed.)

Eternal Truths

It seems that a person today only has to put two thoughts together in order to reach a mistaken conclusion. This flaw is obvious in everyone but ourselves. Is man the meaning seeking animal that at once finds it too easily and yet finds too little of it?

When meaning is explained in terms of ultimate questions or answers, meaning is most often misunderstood—or little common agreement about it can be found. The most rigorous applications of the scientific method do offer some hope of knowledge. Dogma, at best, can only be considered useful for its aspirations and ethical suggestions.

You would think someone who is adamant that they will not change their beliefs no matter what new and contradictory facts come along might realize the contradiction they are incorporating into their views (These aren't all Christians, just the ones who get in our faces). Because every word of the Bible must be held to be literally true, they are forced to deny or restructure all new information that comes along to fit their particular interpretation of dogma. (This is not to condemn all Christians by any means; many, if not most, are rational.)

I think this discussion points up Daniel Dennett's thesis and the title of his book, *Breaking the Spell.* By breaking the spell, he meant ending the taboo against a true scientific scrutiny or study of religion (though there have long been objective university courses and departments of religion, the study has not been approached as a full-blown science).

Aside from it not being thought good etiquette to "talk religion," I think there is something in us that causes us to give our own religion a pass. A certain self-acceptance for the individual and society is essential to function. It might have been an essential adaptation for believers not to question their faith. Perhaps that's why *not* questioning it appears as if it is a successful testing of the strength and quality of our faith. How steadfast are we? How pious?

Religious Truth

Some religious or cultural ideas that may not be strictly or literally true may hold a teaching or offer an idea which resonates or rings true with the beliefs of the culture. A somewhat crude example, perhaps, but there was at least one primitive culture where it was an absolute commandment that the first child must be a male and, as abhorrent as it may be to us, first born females were killed or allowed to die. This was in keeping with what was right and wrong according to their culture.

We can say it was wrong that the precious lives of these infant girls were not preserved, but this is ethnocentrism on our part. Of course, for many people this just opens the argument about moral relativism, but we can't say these primitives were wrong without applying another culture's standards (our own) to the situation. So 'truth' for a culture may be a logical conclusion based on the culture's values or even statements of fact that are consistent with their belief (or knowledge).

Take special creation as an example. For the literal interpreters of Genesis there are many scientific statements that are "wrong" from their point of view. Some of the proponents of this, young earth creationists, have accepted Reverend Usher's calculation that the world is 6000 years old. For scientists to say it is over four billion years old seems wrong to those believers. Though we've now slipped from moral right and wrong into the area of factual right and wrong, if you're factually wrong about something literal in the Bible you're pretty close to morally wrong for these literalists.

Of course, you might say everybody thinks the other guy's opinion is lousy. And with respect to matters of fact that can be proven, it is readily apparent to reasonable people who's right and who's wrong. But it's more than that. These believers participate in a culture that has a seamless body of knowledge and beliefs. They are so fully invested in the culture that contrary thoughts are ridiculous to them (even if they are objectively and demonstratively true).

If we are not receiving the brunt of their approbation, we may even appreciate these champions of metaphoric truth. Consider aspirational thoughts that cheer us on or champion our cause. Consider, especially, the stirring of our hearts by the hero of a fable. Being rallied to persevere by the lessons of a fictional tale—aren't our emotions then being fired by a metaphor?

What's the story?

Is spiritual truth a metaphor that ought to be true? Or that would be true in a just or perfect world? In the believer's world as perfected by the existence of the believer's god?

We find that some of the "usual suspects" from fiction have a few things in common with religion. Certainly religion asks us to suspend our disbelief albeit surreptitiously. Don't some of the clandestine proselytizers' hushed tones set us up for special knowledge—to accept received wisdom? The sort of thing that to the uninitiated sounds crazy or stupid, but to us who have been chosen to see the truth revealed, we shall know.

It's a supernatural tale of supernatural beings as contrasted with us weak and sorely tested humans who shall be shown the *light* and given the opportunity to do the right thing.

Touched on earlier was the concept in fiction, especially Sci Fi and fantasy, called world-building. The writer must construct her fictional world to be self consistent and logical even though it may have magic and supernatural powers in play.

Probably for the benefit of religion, and in turn its benefit for us, we developed this skill of world-building. That is in a microcosm what we do as we take religion into our culture, although it could be what we do when we remake our culture to fit our religion as well.

I think this is about where the concept of *story* comes into how we world-build when we coordinate, or less charitably, make our culture subservient to our religion. With our origin myths we tell ourselves our spiritual stories. Elsewhere, you'll see how we have this need for identity. Early humans had to grapple with this, I think, as they became thinking beings. For nascent humanity, I think they had to know where they came from in order to say who they were.

Our origin myths tell our stories. Who we are, where we came from, what our destiny will be. It tells us of our relationship with Being. We share a special knowledge about All Being. We have been chosen and initiated as a rite of passage in order to share that knowledge. These things give us meaning as we give them meaning. These myths and events become aspects of who we are. Through them we become relevant in the nature of things. Naturally, we band together over these extensive commonalities.

The tribal story tellers would also have individual stories to tell. The hero's tale is always a favorite action story. The story of another man's disgrace, ousting, and shunning can demonstrate an important moral. Each youngster who listened to these stories around the central fire was anxious to see what his or her story would be. As they grew toward their rites of passage, they knew their hearts would be revealed as their stories began.

Meaning: How story relates

If religion has the evolutionary advantage that it seems, it may have been one of the three greatest culture borne adaptations along with language and industry/technology (if you don't count war making arts and skills as a separate cultural adaptation).

Part of what gives our religiosity its power depends on the creation within our culture, suspended by our mutual minds, of an ultra-relevant, immediately responsive world, seamlessly mythologized and superimposed on the larger, colder reality of the outside world.

The creation of the world, or sometimes more humbly, just our people, as described in our origin myths, elicits a story that all chose to be represented by and therefore banded and bound together by.

We are the meaning-seeking animal. How often does an event take place in our lives that makes us wonder what it means? For somewhere between one and two hundred thousand years we've had a mind built for knowledge and yet so very little to fill it with. So we inferred meaning, sometimes where there was none.

. . . And man saw belief and said it was good—and, thus, he was seduced into the strange realm of faith.

A more likely narrative

For a boy quite a few eons ago, his curiosity was immense. His crackling neurons strained pulling for anything he could know, from his senses, from his memory, from his mind, itself. His inadequate language hobbled his knowing. It was frustrating.

Why did cub wolf play with him when old wolf would kill him? Were the shapes he saw beyond the fire light real? He thought he saw Old Pa. Maybe Old Pa lived in the shadows since he was dead to the daylight world.

The ancestral lines brought with them an alertness of mind, tuned to listen and watch. Made to figure out things. *Where did we come from?* "Not know, Son." *How can we not know?* "Not know." *Who are we then?*

Why does the wind bite my ears now? "Old Pa say wind-spirit fight water-spirit." *What makes the sun stay low in the sky?* "Not like fights."

A thousand generations later, a little girl, the boy's distant descendent, strings sea shells. She wonders at her mother's explanation of what makes the skygod angry. "He blows the wind and rain." *What does he want us to do?* "Be good. Show him we will." *How?* "The tribe will pledge at ritual dance. It will last all week until Skygod speaks."

Another thousand generations come and go. A young boy to whom the girl was an ancestor works on a picture with crayons. The Sunday school teacher smiles. "Do you know how much Jesus loves you?" The boy looked up to the woman. *He does?* "Yes, Jesus loves all the little children."

A few generations from now a young girl descended from the boy will sit in a classroom. "Boys and girls, we are going to study a thing called spirituality." *Why*, the girl will ask, *What is it?* "We'll, it's something we inherited. It can be used for good or bad. It can help us reach for the stars, to make this the best of all possible worlds. But if you don't know what to watch out for, it might turn you or your children into a willing slave."

A thousand generations from now a man with long, curly locks and a flowing robe will step to a high spot and raise his hand to quiet the crowd.

I come among you as one of you. I am not a god, but only the son of man. I am here to tell you that God loves you.

The police will read the man his rights and charge him with using mentally-seductive religious rhetoric without checking his listeners for the age of consent or proof that they've received any inoculating knowledge.

The crowd will be asked if they want counseling vouchers. Some wanted them for their under-age children in case they had been religiously affected.

Is man the creator of meaning?

Does existence or being or even the universe have some meaning in its own right or does it only have it because man has a need for such meaning and, therefore, imputes it? That is, does the human species for its own purposes want existence in its totality to have meaning or philosophical implications and so imposes meaning upon the universe? If so, this is a somewhat pitiable condition.

This seems to be the very void that religion and philosophy respond to, in search of the ontologically mythical explanation of being. In some sense, religious myth looks back from where man finds himself and extrapolates to the world's "creation." Equally simplistically, philosophy might consider *being* and extrapolate (forward?) to man. That's somewhat how the book of Genesis functions.

Without his framework of religion or philosophy, man finds himself in a universe without meaning. In a meaningless world, man is the indirect object of its being. If there's a god, man is the direct object of that god's actions. It's not that man had no meaning without a god, it's just that evolution found a way to give man ultra-meaning through religion. Somehow, for us our story comes alive and is infused with meaning via religion.

It seems fairly basic to the makeup of man who re-presents what he finds in his world both internally to himself (within his own mind) and externally to others through speech, writing, art (cave drawings and murals). Perhaps some aspect of Man the Searcher was the differentiator of man from the last non-man (proto-human ape) and so through an aspect of logic or proto-logic—we see implication.

We encounter something—we see fire (and after some experience, after some learning) we imply that it is hot, but to decouple thought from the present time and place and fully consider actors, actions, and events and determine their implications in the abstract—what something meant at another time and place? Have you ever heard someone ask what the moral of a story was? Or *What's the meaning of this story?* There, for us, eons ago, meaning was the end of a *story*, but meaning became the start of our story.

Meaning at depth

What if philosophy finds that the universe has no meaning as its branches, the sciences already have? Further, what if psychology, backed up by the other sciences, finds that man has a basic desire and perhaps a need for the universe to have meaning? Our need for myth (story with special meaning), and our push to fix our origins—may be because we can't start our own myth until we've identified ourselves by our origin myth. Perhaps, a universe without a purposeful origin defeats our myth before we've started it.

One answer might be that, given the above circumstances, we would find ourselves right where we are today, for all of these situations are a part of our reality. That's the easy part. How do we go forward?

The universe has no intrinsic meaning, and man needs his world to have meaning, and both premises are known to us. In the past religion gave meaning to being and bound together those of a common belief. Philosophy doesn't serve that purpose very well, but is more useful in the pursuit of truth for its own sake—or so it says.

We are at a frictional point. Such a point at which philosophy through one of its science branches, and philosophy is the trunk to many, has dispelled religion in the name of truth, and shows there is no meaning to the universe while religion would provide meaning to life but is not based on fact or truth. (Here, one should point out how much greater a gift is a reality that is ours for the making by bringing to it our own purposes rather than having El, Elohim, Yahweh, Jehovah, or I-am-that-I-am's purpose as our cross to bear?)

Was the life of Jesus, an apparently great man, brilliantly lived by one who so loved humankind and sorely knew its need for meaning which would allow it to transcend a suffering world and who saw how to create that meaning (or maybe that was Paul)? Was it a most benevolent fabrication—and one the world desperately needed?

Perhaps this untruth was more beneficial to the world than a truth which would have ended this benevolence?

It may no longer be in print, but a book of interest thirty to forty years ago was entitled, *God Struck Me Dead.* It entails recounted born-again religious experiences and at least one by ex-slaves. They talked of such miserable, spiritually destitute lives. Their hearts aching and sad until God struck them down and they arose with the Spirit in them.

Would you like to undergo this "reawakening?" Perhaps none can be had from general platitudes. How about an emotionally compelling "spiritual" story? If it was apparent today that Jesus was the path to salvation, for instance, if God in a white beard appeared in the sky, or let's say s/he appeared to each person in a form that by seeing him, that person knew it was God. Perhaps God would say something like, "Want to come to heaven? My boy will fix you up. Form a line." If it were this obvious, many or most people might be "saved" rather than the few who seem to have unsoundly based, or insufficiently justified, belief—perhaps that makes it faith—in the whole story.

I would have been more likely to accept a Jesus story in which all who based their lives on the Golden Rule and didn't hurt others and basically followed the Christian beliefs could be "saved" and not left out, or behind, if in good conscience, they found there was not sufficient evidence to believe the Jesus story. What supreme being would condemn them if insufficient information existed?

The most faithful have always been represented to us as the most worthy. This principle would seem to uphold greater and greater belief, based on less and less evidence, as the noblest state. Where's the virtue in believing with insufficient reason?

Perhaps they considered just such a scenario as their own—that otherwise just people would be denied salvation because they did not accept Jesus as their Savior. Is that alone, if a life were otherwise virtuous, exemplary, even Christian-like, such a serious sin as to require eternal damnation?

Why are there Zombies for Jesus?

From *Confessions of a Christian atheist*

A glommed onto religion/creation myth transforms the individual (as if it's some kind of hyper-meme—only now we have a plausible mechanism that explains why it's like a virus). He is faithful to these beliefs alone, through a deep bonding, and thereby rendered no longer susceptible to other religions.

These people aren't particularly dumb. It didn't seem that they were hallucinating or insane—some said deluded? Still, it seemed like they were somewhere between Stepford Wives for Christ and full-blown evangelist zombies.

It just didn't add up. Something was missing. They thought they knew something we others didn't. They spoke of their "truth" with heightened excitement, sometimes whispering about it, sometimes treating it as a special secret—something we others were missing out on. They wanted to reveal it to us as it was revealed to them. The more enthusiastic they became about their beliefs, the more evangelical they became about spreading the word.

There were no obvious explanations for their belief and behavior. They made attempts to explain it and relay their enthusiasm for it. They would be frustrated when their arguments, their ostensible reasons for belief, didn't sway us and we with them for thinking those faulty arguments *would* persuade us.

Historically, only the argument from design and, in a sense, its metaphysical or cosmological underpinnings as expressed in the question, *Why is there something rather than nothing?* weren't totally refuted (though, see *A Universe from Nothing* by Lawrence Krauss, his book, but also video on the web). But even those arguments are far from proving the existence of an Abrahamic god or any deity. These arguments prey on our unanswered questions, but offer no reason why a deity should be inferred. These may have been the default thoughts as best they could be expressed and thereby helped get religion started eons ago.

What should be inferred, I believe, is that people *do* infer a deity or at least a supernatural realm and that's how we've answered the otherwise imponderable questions—complicated by the fact that these religion memes took forms that we allowed (or were helpless to avoid?) to survive and replicate (better answers may not have been so appealing and could not induce, nor reward, us to replicate them). Maybe believers are sensing that primal source within . . .

At any rate, a bit like the fact that the constituents of fire are fuel, heat, and oxygen, a viable religion, too, must have a number of characteristics that fall within favorable parameters. Believers must have the standard gene compliment to enable them to be believers and carriers of belief. The religion must have sufficiently strong beliefs, including sufficiently powerful spiritual content to psychologically reward the believer. Finally, the community must be an enabling substrate as well as a beneficiary of all the community-enhancing behavior of its members.

Great. They found Jesus. It still didn't add up. Yes, it would be great to be immortal, to be loved by the universe or its anthropomorphized, re-apotheosized avatar. But that doesn't fit with the world as we can know it and, in order NOT to know it to that extent, believers of different types deny different amounts of science. Even if their resulting "science-lite" worldview was plausible, the result just doesn't fit the world around us. Science, itself, eventually gets rid of bogus theories or hypotheses, even if the criticism is true that science only advances one funeral at a time. At least, it advances.

Religion, the predatory meme

It's a remarkable human trait that we mine our everyday events for the rich vein, the pure ore, looking for that nugget which once found will allow us to infer, once and for all, a correctly founded worldview and the philosophical trappings that come with it.

We secretly, if not subconsciously, test the many nuggets that come along, our treatment by others, the playing out of relationships, the events that swirl around us—both minute and earth-shaking, the thoughts and moods we have, and the philosophical bobblings that chatter around us, in hopes that we may say, "So *this* is the world."

With unspoken fear we hope to leave undisturbed our long-ago-internalized microcosm of reality—whatever our culture, parents, and minds may have equipped us with—so that it might do whatever we've programmed it to do, whether that's to bloom, to fester, to crystallize, to hunker down, or to lash out. Our tools in this pursuit are denial, cognitive dissonance, and a host of psychological mechanisms pressed into the service of self-preservation at whatever level needed.

And so in our normal course, we regularly fend off the random encroachments that challenge our sweetly biased versions of reality. We use reflexively something that we pull from deep inside ourselves to reject the "new."

Still, the new seeps in. The young and inquiring, the pundit and the professor, they challenge us. They bring in the new no matter how revolting it may be to us.

Once a strong religion is in place, though, we shift from the state of "openness" described above to any in a range of possible levels of closure. For example, extreme fundamentalism's position might be likened to being in a religious, philosophical, or mental "lockdown."

Consider the thought that religion is a sort of prophylactic shield against these haphazard events or other assaults. If a person stumbling across such objects had no "immunity" to them they could cause her to drop what she's doing and might force her to reorient her life around a newly forming set of inferences, that being the next best thing to deflecting the assault altogether.

If it is more serious, though, she might be immobilized thereby upending the basic philosophy of her life. Or is this *la condition humaine*? That is, do we find in modern life that our basic philosophies are under continual assault? If so, then is religion the sort of thing that builds its own bulwark against all challenges?

It seems in this risky business that whatever is being considered, if it came to us fully digested by our culture, then it seems bedrock to it, and as such, it is likely that it was internalized by us at a tender age. This early indoctrination is the way of the modern world (perhaps, cultures that wait until puberty to indoctrinate their young need to use the more elaborate rituals and rites to sufficiently impress their religious beliefs on these slightly less impressionable minds).

We sometimes get a glimpse of such ancient wisdom when a saying or observation rings true to the philosophy or religion previously embedded in us by our culture (or genes, see moral instinct, below) and thereby convinces us by that sympathetic resonance that it is True.

To be clear: the culture and the individuals that have a strong religion in place do have a prophylactic that shields them from significant changes, especially of an unforeseen nature or something that would cause them to abruptly head off in a different direction. Such change can still befall a culture or its members, but the stronger the religion is in the culture, community, and individual, the more resistant to change they are.

Believers can test this hypothesis by attempting to consider these thoughts without any reference to there internalized religion/world view/belief structure. Can you do it?

Such memes, then, steady the individual and the culture and though they may be called ancient wisdom, it may be more accurate to say that they served as a wisdom substitute. It must be admitted, though, that they may contain some wisdom. After all, the lifespan of a major religion can be measured in millennia rather than years. Something of use must have accumulated over time.

There is good evidence that we have an innate moral instinct (See The Faith Instinct by Nicholas Wade). This may suggest itself to the thinkers of the faith who codify what we typically "know." What we think we are intuiting, may just be a resonance of our memes with our genes. These statements, then, resonate with what we "know in our hearts" (or our genetically predisposed neural structures).

As to the meme-like nature of a religion, another analogy might also serve. When a sperm cell enters an ovum and fertilization takes place, the cell membrane of the ovum "hardens" and becomes impervious to other sperm.

Beyond that, prophylactic religion serves important functions that have survival value for the individual and the culture. It saves time; the person isn't immobilized by the daunting task of working out a new philosophy (the culture, in the sense of the person's tribe, has a vested interest in counseling against that). The individual's identity is maintained, his membership in the social unit is intact, as in fact, the social unit itself is, by avoiding the weakness that the flagging fidelity of a few members could cause.

Also, it protects the cultural unit which could be split if a new competing philosophy or belief set were to be developed. These scenarios don't relay how devastating the failure of a religious worldview could be. Like a virus, (See Ray, *The God Virus*) a strong religion, newly introduced to a culture could weaken, divide, and conquer the culture from within. In the malaise, the culture probably wouldn't be able to recover and replace its beliefs and myths immediately. The exposure to danger for a tribe in a shrinking world could easily be catastrophic under the wrong circumstances. (Consider the turmoil in Africa after the early and more fundamentalist missionaries served them. Is it possible that an imposed religion is just as devastating as an imposed regime?)

Religion was a bolstering effect for the small community, but it didn't evolve to cope with globalization. As a global community we are lucky the religions merge as well as they do. This isn't to say the present religions haven't moderated toward each other (See *Toward a True Kinship of Faiths* by the 14th Dalai Lama). Still, the greatest tests lie ahead. Evidently nothing is going to curb the human population growth. Religions have been more a part of the problem than offering any solution. The religions will be measured by how they facilitate the interface of humanity with looming catastrophes. They certainly can't all happen, but what's the chance that none of them will happen?

Religions can be tenacious memes that lock down the human capacity to factor new evidence or occurrences into their understanding of the world. Instinctual reactions come automatically. It is no different with this instinctual drive for religious activity. Believers religiously offended can be as recalcitrant as a snarling dog whose action also comes out of its instincts. Where the individual might be immobilized by viral philosophies and the calculus of their philosophical implications, religion can stand as an intellectual barricade against such incursions.

Closed social groups benefit from strong religions. Just as xenophobia exists because it had survival value, so do strong religions. Religion is a good defense; it is an organizing and preparatory force, and it can be out front of a crisis the way few other things can. Religions can largely be all things to all people. Some are responsive to a changing world; they can also block the way to progress. Instincts change slowly and even though people can moderate their religions themselves, they are not likely to do so fast enough if dire circumstances threaten disaster.

If the religion is weak, if the people have lost interest in their god, they are open. If early men were open to new people, insights, or philosophies they could have been deceived and destroyed. But if the guard is up, then, somewhat like the false positive of the hyperactive agent detection mechanism, the group is wary, it remains intact, it survives. (Dennett says we have an instinct to "attribute *agency*—beliefs, and desires and other mental states—to anything complicated that moves.")

If the village was defeated in battle, if crops were lost, if the hunting party disappeared while on a hunt, it might be time to look for a stronger god. It might have seemed that the next tribe, the neighboring clan, or, say, the city of Rome, had a stronger god. It might not have been the case of the stronger god, just the stronger religion.

The archaic religions, the classical pantheisms of Rome and Greece, at length, had failed. The people had lost interest. But people still carry the genetic code that impels religion forward as a desire and forces the person to seek spiritual fulfillment (or community-wide religious orientation) or suffer for the lack of it.

In the Axial Age (Karen Armstrong) of the modern religions, the older religions faded away. Some of the newer religions are waning or are now in flux. People explain it quite succinctly when they say they are spiritual, but not religious. The drive is still there. They seek spiritual fulfillment. If it isn't forth coming from the traditional religions, they seek elsewhere. Some stay in their faith traditions, some evidence that religion is a social force. They have the drive, the need, the instinct, but nothing calls to them. Alternatively, they see only risk, fear, and regret ahead if they are considering "going it alone," that is, striking out into the spiritual wilderness.

Ultra-Meme: Were we born addicted to religion?

A meme need be little more than an idea, but let's say a religion. When it finds an open (unprotected, susceptible) mind, it may lock into position and bar other religions or even philosophies from being considered as openly. That would seem to be the nature of a meme or at least an aspect of its survival or reproductive strategy. At least this is true for the ultra-meme, religion.

Things that fall to the low end of the meme scale might be belief in the gods of the Greek pantheon. Presumably, what might have once been a successful meme, pantheism, now ranks below belief in the tooth fairy.

Beliefs or ideas start to show up on the meme scale when they show their strength and tenacity within a culture. Christianity has done that in the past. Given the history and breadth and depth of Christianity, it has practically been all things to all people—from the tyranny of the Dark and Middle Ages Church to the highest aspirations for humanity at many peak moments. From the solitude of an introspective individual spirituality to mega-church congregations.

The American Madrassa

What are the strongest memes? Are there just a few? Some examples—Christianity, Nazism, racism—those have bored down to a radical, core depth in the collective consciousness.

Does it take a mind at a certain susceptible age? Certainly, the young mind is the most open. Educational psychologists study this, but it hasn't been wasted on the creationists. If they can keep evolution out of the high schools and pepper the zeitgeist with *it's only a theory* and continue to float the "teach the controversy" rhetoric in the school communities, a large number of kids will come out of the school system with some doubt about how life proliferated on the planet and perhaps the possibility of a fundamentalist or literalist view of God still in their minds and as it dominates the culture, Christianity is the brand that's most widely advertized.

For the children of believers who are already in the fold, a much greater level of indoctrination is assured. Christian and family traditions, a church community, holidays and rituals more or less dominate their lives. All of this, of course, will inoculate the child against defecting from belief—at least without an extremely high cost (loss of time invested, traditions both church and family, relationships, values, and all that the church and parents might choose to scare them with).

For the ultimate immersion in belief, many people are homeschooling their children and keeping them indoctrinated in fundamentalist Christianity. The home school environment can range from a Sunday school-like setting to a Christian madrassa. This defeats the moderating influences that could have come from the input of other teachers, peers and the larger culture—which, for the fundamentalist parents, is exactly what they want to avoid—and for the good of the child and society—exactly what they need.

At the same time, it is exactly what saved a lot of kids from the isolation and domination of a bizarre parent, and brought other ideas and viewpoints forward for consideration. There was some safety, some protection for society in that. The next big terrorist event will be brought to us by a man who was homeschooled by a psychotic fanatical fundamentalist mother who has drilled down into her son's psyche to the depth that only religion can achieve to allow her access to program a fertile sociopathic mind.

If it was anything else but religion, society and its governments would have a right to protect themselves. Christians in congress, its lobbies, and other branches of government have fought hard to give religion free reign in the United States. The only joy left is watching the extreme fringe of the Christian right squirm out of fear that Sharia law could slip in to occupy the same silk pillow they've set up for Christianity. As they've tried to discriminate against that religion in the laws, some of their efforts are getting overturned. It's unconstitutional to legislate against the establishment of religion, remember? (Be careful what you wish for.)

With respect to some sort of locking, blocking mechanism of bedrock beliefs, this would play nicely into Tim LeHaye's (Left Behind series) plans in a Battle for the Minds. And it might have had a boost from natural selection. Say that a tribe has a set of beliefs, origin myths, rituals, etc. They aren't going to want to see those just abandoned when a stranger comes around with a new philosophy or a child has a sleepover at the next tribe and hears about *their* Big Kahuna. Still, to even hear of another set of beliefs raises the question—*Could those beliefs be right and mine wrong?* That's why blasphemy and heresy were punishable by stoning to death.

When we consider the core beliefs of others, we tend to take them lightly, especially if they are contrary or at odds with our own. That helps us fool ourselves into thinking that rather than going radically to the core of that person's reality, their beliefs are something less, almost superficial. We are missing the mark. Those core beliefs are the basis of that person's life. Additionally, the human mind has evolved and is structured to build a worldview, a basis for all other knowledge and beliefs, to be built upon. Haven't you seen someone who's had the shock of having one of their "pillars of belief" destroyed? They are devastated; unable to function. Usually, slowly, s/he is able to assimilate or rationalize away the problem. Or more rarely, s/he might modify they're worldview and maybe those basic beliefs, or rarer still, perhaps s/he'll become an atheist and restructure their internalization of the world.

We all know people that are uncertain of many things. They may not have their world under control. They may move tentatively through life. It is left to the "strong" to grab life by the horns and make it yield to them what they want of it. That comes from confidence in themselves and their worldview, their bedrock beliefs. Sometimes a little less intelligence is an asset to that person or at least an unquestioning acceptance of their core beliefs be that religion or what have you.

And so a strong set of beliefs, a strong religion, a monotheism with strong tenets, time-tested mythic elements, publicly observed holidays—how about a culture-wide acceptance with iconic displays?— widely practiced rituals, invocation of the one true God at public events (the religious equivalent of males marking territory), this and other stimulating features account for Christianity's power, acceptance and spread.

Of course, it wasn't for pleasing the tribal elders that natural selection would cause a "lock-in" of a set of beliefs in a child's mind. It was rather for the added strength to the tribe whose beliefs are held most strongly. Tribal elders since time immemorial have generally approved of religion's hold on their people to the extent that that hold has formed a comfortable handle for those leaders.

The essence of this thesis, then, is that we have been evolutionarily conditioned to lock in such core beliefs. We are spoon fed the lore and origin myths of our culture when we are young. In the days of the hunter-gatherers, there were no competing views, only the clan's own interpretation of the underpinnings of their reality.

By our day, the generic class of such ultra-memes (a capacity for them, for religion) have been fairly cemented in place by a number of things adapted for the purpose: our neural structures and pathways, instincts, e.g., xenophobia, numerous psychological devices, the felt need for spiritual wellbeing, etc. The receiving of special, sacred, revealed knowledge probably elicits the secretion of neurochemicals that reward behaviors performed in the religious mode. Ritual as well as prayer, if done right, probably promotes that, too. If not, the repetition of the behavior is a psychological reinforcement in its own right.

We are initiated into the tribe at puberty and are now responsible to carry on its legends, myths, and lore. We've been inoculated with this revealed ultra-reality and after the implanting of the tribes beliefs, our minds "hardened over" with a level of protection from conflicting ideas or beliefs that we might come in contact with later. We are open to indoctrination early and begin to close to it with the onset of puberty. Along with that closure or hardening, an ultra-strong ultra-meme makes us impervious to new belief systems and ultimately, that harmony and unanimity strengthens the tribe.

Is the person's fate sealed with initiation today? Maybe. A few are always deconverting, some will washout of overzealous congregations/communities/cults while others never see the "light."

All the different devices and psychological factors that various evolutionary psychologists, anthropologists and other scientists and philosopher use to explain the ubiquity and persistence of religion could still be used to explain religion *if* belief and practice and anything else we lump in with what we call religion had a normal distribution, a simple bell curve with say 50% of the population on the nonbeliever side of the curve and 50% on the believer side.

The game was rigged, however, the house doesn't always win, but all other things being equal, it wins the majority of the time— and that's because there's not an equal distribution of the probable outcomes—the house of worship has a higher probability of winning. All sources of statistics support this. Most polls indicate about 85% of the U.S. population are believers. The actual distribution probably conforms to the distribution of genes that predispose us to religious belief (with all the mitigating factors we've discussed allowed their influence, too). That should be a hypothesis that can be tested. Quite convincing evidence is the high degree of similarity in the religious orientation of identical twins reared apart.

Certainly many things can affect the phenotypic expression of religiosity, the existing religions and how they are faring, what's going on within the belief community, the society, the governments, where the civilization is in its life cycle and the educational levels, the work ethic, the zeitgeist—the influences are myriad. And yet, none are as significant as one's own inclination and that brings us back to the question where does that come from? A question which twin studies neatly answer with an answer that cannot be dismissed (See later discussion on twin studies).

A leg up

Religions compete whether they know it or not and they compete even more than a theory of memes might suggest. One of the special adaptations that the "fittest" religions have demonstrated is that they produce a religious "edifice" that provides for our spiritual (as well as other) needs. The best adapted religions are those that CAN trigger our perks (our psychological and spiritual felt rewards) the most.

Religions can fall short, though. They can die out, be replaced, or evolve into another religion. Do those things happen the moment the religion fails to deliver a significant spiritual perk/high/reward to more people than an alternative religion?

No. With the accretion of other benefits such as social, supportive, and ministry functions, religions can become so important to the individual (and the community) that it would make no sense to give it up. Religions can become institutions that are entrenched in society. Still, Europe is showing us that institutions can crumble as Christianity appears to be doing there.

In the U. S. as well, there are plenty of people to whom religion means little. We've discussed how there would be a statistical distribution of nonbelievers, but even in the religious fold, there will be others that may be believers, but not very interested in religion— sort of ambivalent. Too, as has been said, religions have a life cycle. Christianity is in flux; some of it certainly in decline. Society is in the postmodern world. People try to make themselves comfortable with the world through all sorts of means. Religion is becoming less and less one of those means.

Religion refined and redefined

Our definition of religion can now be refined with the benefit of all we've discussed since the earlier definition:

Religion is a multifaceted, meme-like, psycho-socio-spiritual complex or "operating system" that evolved adaptations to serve, protect, and strengthen the group and the individual by fulfilling a number of human needs, some needs that it, in partnership with multi-level selection over deep evolutionary time, created, enhanced, and deepened, while significantly rewarding both individual and group psychologically, socially, and spiritually on a number of levels. One or more needs appear to function as a religious drive.

There is a tendency toward high cost invested membership producing close-knit, committed participants. In addition to concern for each other's earthly welfare, the core beliefs that draw the body together are based on the possibility of each person having a relationship with an envisioned ultimate, transcendent reality of major significance to the world.

Exercising metaphysical caution

We humans tend to over-determine meaning. (Maybe there's a philosophy gene?) It's as if we think answers to the ultimate questions are under every rock and behind every tree. And if not that, we attempt to extrapolate meaning from just about every mundane thing.

We seek those special words and ideas expressed in hush tones. We look for the oracle. We await Neo. We remain aware, hoping to discern special meaning hidden within everyday patterns that the less attuned cannot or will not see.

More often than not, there's a simple material explanation, a common interaction of matter and energy, and there is no cosmicly significant answer waiting in the wings. As we came into the Age of Reason, we understood more and more with ever less attributed to supernatural causes.

Instead of God being revealed when our universe began, it looked like the Big Bang was just whatever matter came together into the singularity that would become fuel for the Big Bang. No metaphysical occurrence, just the physical stuff of reality, matter and energy acting upon itself. [I'm told that this theory is wrong and a newer hypothesis popular today says the membranes of two parallel universes collided or otherwise momentarily joined to spark said Bang].

A cycling universe of Big Crunches and Big Bangs fits my bias and personal agenda better. Perhaps, like me, you feel like you've gotten your head around those ideas. Possibly, they've just been around long enough to get comfortable with them.

Maybe it's fear of the unknown. The frightening prospect is that science gets stranger and stranger the more we know, the upshot being that as basic theories become more esoteric in order to come closer and closer to reality, they will, finally, offer no facet of themselves amenable to the uninitiated, perhaps not even to the otherwise educated mind?

If man is not the measure of all things, and especially not the measurer of meaning, let's take the *human* out of the equation and leave only God and a universe barren of human life. Is there still meaning?

First aspire, then affirm

Can man evolve beyond religion? There is an escape mechanism, but humankind holds strongly to religious beliefs. That served man for a time when we weren't equal to understanding the world. Now, reason rigorously tested gives us an alternative. For it to succeed, it must be incorporated into our beliefs. Some would say it must supplant our beliefs, our religions. Others say it cannot. There is always a middle path (see Siddhartha Gautama, Buddha). The eclectic sampling of the ancient religions is, and has always been, how newer religions have moved forward. New paths, new branches, new denominations do start up and will continue to. Religion evolves. We must participate in that dialogue and be involved in the midwifery of tomorrow's beliefs.

The fundamentalists don't want us to be. And if we act like atheist fundamentalists, the liberal and moderate Christians won't be open to what we say either.

It's a corollary to the theses expressed in this book, given the Homo sapiens we are, that we must plug something into that "who and what we are" slot in our reality—our core belief slot. Will it always need a creator and supernatural entities? Probably not. Will those entities be with us for a while? Evidently so. How should we address that? With tolerance.

Think of it as a major aspect of earlier human life. It's analogous to the disc operating system (DOS) of the early personal computers. As time progresses, the deity, supernatural, and soul aspects will continue to diminish. Consider your pc at startup. DOS flashes by before the start up of Windows or whatever. The deity and other archaic aspects of religion will become like that. Compressed, minimized, but a flash on the screen of tomorrow's super community of minds (faiths).

And this on the way to an operating system of humanity that we must start dreaming of today. Support humanity. First aspire, then affirm. Make the good works programs sing to the world the song of human unity and ascent.

Religion re-Explained

Not in your genes?

In *Religion Explained,* Pascal Boyer says religion is not innate or in the genes. "To explain religion is to explain a particular kind of mental epidemic whereby people develop (on the basis of variable information) rather similar forms of religious concepts and norms."

As one who has used hyperbole or even worse direct criticism of religion, I'm not in a position to be critical over that aspect of Boyer's work. The one observation I'd make is that process of developing similar forms of religious concepts from variable information (different cultural input) is all about that innate instinctive behavior of religiosity. Boyer may be free of the effect of that instinct—a statistical outlier, say, three standard deviations to the left. I'm not. I believe I feel a spiritual need that I think most of us do.

Further on Boyer's behalf, he seems to be one of the few scientists who is willing to mount a rigorously academic effort to prove his point. I disagree with him, but his effort is significant while some of the icons of science represent themselves rather poorly in this regard.

Boyer makes an analogy that, although he may mean it in a more literal fashion than I credit it with, may be useful. Boyer says we have mental *templates* for these concepts somewhat like recipes or formulas that allow us to readily handle them. We have a template, he would say, for the category, "person." That template is what we would use to facilitate our understanding of God or a spirit. Mentally, even subconsciously, we plug "God" into our template for "person" and modify the template by adding special powers or attributes to the concept.

Because we do this, we are then able to draw inferences from our mind about God. Boyer goes on to say these inferences are what make the concept work. For example, God is a person who is eternal, who has special powers, who has a mind like other minds. Boyer suggests

145

that the cognitive underpinnings of religious concepts "are hidden from conscious inspection." In other word, our mental templates aren't readily apparent.

Boyer explains, "The reason religion can become much more serious and important (. . .) is that it activates inference systems that are of vital importance to us: those that govern our most intense emotions, shape our interaction with other people, give us moral feelings, and organize social groups."

Selective evolutionary pressure surely is and was at work in our social milieus—that is, those individuals most adept at handling culture, information, social events, and relationships were more successful and, thereby, "selected" for survival.

Boyer discussed these special capacities for social intelligence, "[A]dvantages (. . .) accrued to individuals who could better predict the behavior of other human agents, since interaction with other human beings is the real milieu of human evolution."

"Religious concepts are those supernatural concepts that matter." Westerners consider religious concepts as the expression of some beliefs about how the world works. But as westerners may see religion as doctrine, they may be surprised to see religion as a practical thing. People interact with these supernatural beings; rather than a contemplative theological reasoning, people interact with religious agents. Again, social intelligence that enables inferences with implications for relationships with the supernatural agents are of ultimate practicality.

Boyer, p. 143, "A common explanation is that we imagine person-like agents who rule our destinies because this produces a reassuring view of our existence and the world around us." "We project human features onto nonhuman aspects of our world because that makes these aspects more familiar and therefore less frightening."

From my perspective, I would say that makes the supernatural something we can relate to. And religion, in part, is an attempt to encourage the supernatural to relate to us. We supplicate, placate, and otherwise act like sycophants in the hope that we might actually have a relationship with the supernatural—that power behind the natural.

People perceive supernatural agents as having minds. This can apply to anything that appears to move of its own accord. People think that they are detecting highly nuanced traces of such agents almost everywhere.

The human "agency detection system" tends to jump to conclusions. We intuit that an agency is around when other interpretations are as plausible. A primitive tribesman today can still think a trickster god has fouled his hunting trip.

It would be the rare person from a modern culture who would attribute anything to a trickster god. Still, most thinkers on this topic say when a person hears a noise they are more likely to ask *Who is it?* Rather than consider *What is it?* This could be a survival strategy carryover from our earlier evolution. Predator detection in the physical plane becomes agent detection in the spiritual plane.

Boyer goes on to say, ". . . but thoughts about gods and spirits are not like that." Gods and spirits are permanent, stable fixtures in their minds and environments. But, Boyer says, "we do not have the cultural concepts we have because they make sense or are useful but because the way our brains are [made] makes it very difficult not to build them."

In discussing ritual, Boyer considers whether the use of ritual could have survival value and decides against it. I would suggest that ritual behavior might have started as a superstitious behavior, to which reality applies a naturally occurring variable reinforcement ratio (df. A desired behavior is randomly rewarded), thus training the believers to use ritual.

"[A] lot of human culture consists of salient, cognitive gadgets that have a great attention-grabbing power and high relevance for the human mind as a side effect of these minds being organized the way they are." Boyer, *Religion Explained*, page 235. "This may be the case for rituals as well."

"[C]hildren assume that kinship terms (aunt, grandmother) refer to something more than the mere fact of living together. They (and adults) seem to guess that some [. . .] internal 'essence' is shared by people with a common genealogy." Boyer p. 251.

"This makes them, like adults, extremely receptive to ideologies that describe a whole group of people as internally, naturally different from others." He goes on, "Both acquire ideologies effortlessly suggesting ideologies that describe a whole group of people as internally, rationally different from others."

Boyer explains on page 253 that groups have a life of their own and won't die with a member. Being a member matters because of how earlier members behaved. If this group fought that group, then in a sense, the intersection transcends the existence of its participants. In other words of Boyer's, the essence of the clan is inside us and our descriptors "are not loose metaphors but show the inexplicable magic we can't explain of the strength of our social group" (and I would add—consider the forerunner of this as it may have originated in early human or primate troupes).

"Rituals like initiations and weddings do seem to have the transcendent effect aimed for, but no one including anthropologists can say why." Boyer says. "They seem to activate some source of causation, some mysterious forces that people can sense but not describe, let alone explain." There seems to be, then, an unknown missing ingredient with a potent effect.

[These potent effects are largely the topic dealt with herein. These "mysterious forces" are the power given to religious activities by our genes in support of our religious drive and resulting psychological and neurochemical rewards for fulfilling them.]

Boyer says, "that, for now, the inadequate explanation of ritual is that they are 'snares for thought' that produce highly salient effects by activating special systems of the mental basement. He says "human minds are made such a way that rituals are a natural performance element, a fit as it were."

Boyer, p. 255, "Not performing or partaking in a ritual when others all have is a defection from cooperation with other members of the group."

I'm going out on a limb with this thought, I know, but with all the mechanisms in place, I think it likely that a species specific behavior exists that causes group members to synchronize their supernatural beliefs (or religion). If some don't, they receive punishment, ostracism, or such as the group sees as fitting for the offense. This belief synchronization may be an unspoken purpose of priest, shaman, or holy man, useful to the group, and functioning below the conscious level. The holy man is the spiritual metronome for the religious group keeping the members harmoniously in sync.

If you simply consider the consensus-forcing effect of being one alone amongst a group expressing coherent beliefs, you can imagine the latent pressure. And, isn't that the way that every tribesman, every

Muslim, every born-again Christian and in deed each of us has to face the monolith of belief?

"People in a group tend to have a similar description of supernatural agents, a local doctrine on gods and spirits. The sharing of this religious ideology and ritual performance "shapes their perception that they are a group with clearly marked boundaries: a community is created." *Religion Explained*, p. 265.

"Worshipping the same gods creates a community and by implication gives that extra edge to the feeling that people with different gods or spirits really are potential enemies."

P. 285, Why do some find it morally compelling to exclude or kill others because they are not members of the "true" religion or do not follow it in the "right" way? Religion seems to create a community. "It seems to go without saying that holding the same concepts and norms as other Christians, for instance, does make people members of a group, with the expectation of a degree of solidarity with other group members and a general distrust toward non-members."

"Humans seem desperate to join some group and demonstrate loyalty to it."

Fundamentalism

Boyer says on page 293, Fundamentalism wants to return to a (possibly non-existent) past. "It is neither religion in excess nor politics in disguise. It is an attempt to preserve a hierarchy faced with defection."

Why do people hold incredible beliefs? What makes them plausible? Boyer p.297, It is the successful activation of a whole variety of mental systems. Boyer says it is a sub-rational, inaccessible process of decision-like effect.

When it comes to belief, human mental systems activate in a certain way and inferences of a special sort occur a little more than others. Say lightening strikes the totem at the center of the village. The physical world impinges on the consciousness; it makes an impression. Time for agonizing reappraisal? New inferences are drawn. The body of belief grows by accretion. Over time this makes a huge difference.

Reflections on Boyer's Religion Explained

Boyer energetically works through most of the inadequately short answers that others typically offer to explain why religion exists and why it is so widespread, nearly universal. Many stock answers to the question use some benefit of religion as their reason. Modern religion's benefits do suggest reasons for its survival or perhaps for one religion to be more popular than another. Early humans didn't puzzle out those benefits and decide to adopt religion. But admittedly, the benefits of religion could reinforce its use without the participants being aware of it.

Boyer says, as was noted elsewhere, that primitive humans did not and do not have religion, but only RTB's: religious thoughts and behavior. Evidently, if they pass on any heritable form of a predisposition to religion, it may be at a most basic level. And, indeed, vis-à-vis their religious thoughts and behavior, their heritable need for religious engagement could be very modest. That suggests that cultural and religious complexities evolved together.

If today's surviving primitives are a look back into religion's evolutionary past, we may be seeing something nearer the beginning state. It may have been much later that music, dance, and trance became attached. And it may have been later still that prayer and meditation came along. Later still for religious epiphanies and mystical experiences? Hallucinogens and trance may have been early encouragement for mystical experiences; they were both seen as ways to get in touch with the supernatural.

Pascal Boyer makes the important point that when early man didn't have the intellectual capacity or the knowledge base to draw on in order to understand his world—and it was beyond him to puzzle it out—he defaulted to speculative thoughts, superstition, and the use of myth to do so.

Proponents of religion have gotten a lot of mileage out of this universal aspect of religion as an argument to prove there's a supernatural basis for religion, that because most people think so, there must be a spiritual realm and souls and gods/spirits. And, in deed, why would we have *religious man* in a secular world?

Boyer points to the fact that not all religions have gods or spirits. That seems to impact on my hypothesis that the primate alpha male hierarchy leads to a godhead religion. I have argued that we have this hierarchical alpha male model: a template from our primate origins. Great apes including man will accept a "strongman" as leader (alpha male), the more legitimate the candidate, the better (The more qualified? The more popular?). This 'template" may impinge on some essence which underlies this concept of legitimacy [It's not lost on me that chimpanzees may sense there is no legitimacy in their leader; that may be why it takes strength and politics to keep an alpha male in place as it invariably does to keep a strongman in place].

"Alphamalism" as a thesis offers some possible explanations and insights into the "religion template." The fact that some religions don't focus on a god, some will allow for one, and some are simply mum on the question, I think, points more to how we should define religion than anything else. At times, we seem to have defined religion from the inside, from the perspective of the believer. The larger view of religion can best be appreciated from the outside.

Also, we may have inherited slightly different templates. Humanity, as it spread over the globe, differentiated into races and ethnicities, environments differed, cultures differed, so did myths and religious experiences. Some of the mental templates like the alpha-male/political template may interact differently with social/religious templates or economic/nationalistic templates in different cultures. (Paired in no particular order, in fact, how do these models and the realities which they represent interact with each other? Probably each alters the other.)

By and large, a godhead was sought and, man, being religious, therefore often found one. Confirmation bias at work? Subsuming the question of a godhead, probably, is some broader plain, perhaps the monolith of the ultimate question. That question manifests in some cultures as *Why are we here?* In others as *Why is there something rather than nothing?*

Lawrence Krauss, in his book mentioned previously, *A Universe from Nothing* says we are really asking the question, *HOW is there something* . . . and he goes about explaining that. Krauss acknowledges that the explanation that quantum fluctuations of virtual particles that pop in and out of existence may not be a philosophically satisfying answer to why we are in a material universe.

With differing interpretations from different perspectives, some cultures may seek an underlying reality or source of all being. Other religions or philosophies may form other questions. They don't all have to be *god* questions. Do they all have to be about transcendence or ultimate reality? (Are there really *religion police* to enforce this?)

Philosophy deals with ultimate questions but it usually isn't considered religion. Maybe for the believer the ultimate questions are necessary for something to be a religion. What else? What makes it different than the typical philosophy?

Do we all know a religion when we see one? Or can that only be appreciated from within? Perhaps there's a "nebulous cloud" of attributes most of which are necessary for something to be a religion. Maybe there are such things as near-religions that don't quite make it. Graceful life philosophies? Mental disciplines such as those in some of the martial arts-philosophy hybrids?

Dennett and others credit the detection of hidden agency as the immediate source of religion. The question arises in such discussions whether language predated anything that could be construed as religion's beginnings.

In fact, our mental templates predate language by quite a bit. Our animalian Threat Response mechanism became our (human) Hidden Agency Detection Device. From that perspective, the world may have taught us that a "hidden agent" was a special thing represented by a known thing, and that's the nature of a symbol.

Is it possible that we might have had an earlier desire to use symbols for representing that unknown power behind the world? Nothing could have been more intrusively in your face than the stark, inhospitable world thwarting you as you face the demands to fill your urgent and continual human needs.

Yet with language every word and sound is symbolic. We are so dexterous at it that it is easy to forget its symbolic, even contrived, nature.

Let's look back around the birth of humankind to the common ancestor of chimps and humans. Chimps today are completely capable of "asking" you for something they want by gesturing and issuing grunts. It doesn't take much imagination to place yourself with a primate whom you can't quite distinguish as ape or human. You, too, are one of his kind. He seems to have his arms loaded down with fruit. He's probably picturing a scene with him, the fruit, and the troupe's females. You haven't eaten anything today. With eyes appropriately downcast and head lowered you put a limp hand out timidly and emit light sounds from the middle of your vocal register. In this instance you are both begging and supplicating. He doesn't respond. In desperation you present your rump for mounting in deference to his dominance. He considers it, but thinking of his bounty and what he can barter for, he walks on by.

Since this could just as easily be a scene involving only modern apes, I submit that this forerunner of language and symbol came earlier than, not the hidden agent detection which many lower animals have, but the application of symbolic thought to that detected agency.

It seems the desire to verbalize a thought must come before the verbalization, the symbol. Can that be generalized to this: *Thought came before language*? Let's look back to the chimpanzee model. They think. Remember Washoe the signing chimp and Kanzi the bonobo who operates a keyboard and display with well over a hundred word symbols? It appears that chimps and bonobos can toe the line right up to the human niche, but not cross it (I think there's been a few million years of human prehistory where the leading hominids pruned back the less competitive branches of the family tree.) They can use a language of symbols, but they don't create it, at least, not an entire system of language symbols from scratch (several of these apes have stretched their limited vocabularies by making compound words they've not been taught, "water-fruit" for watermelon, or experimented with different word orders or phrases)to express ideas o their own).

VI. THE SPIRITUAL EXPERIENCE

Why are we spiritual if this is only a material world?

Would we each feel drawn to a spiritual quest
if it's truly a secular world?

Yes, we look beyond our alphas . . . We look to the night sky with wonder, but I wonder if it isn't as much the look within that leaves us with greater questions. There's as much awe at either end of the equation. We individual units of being are thought of as *soul.* While the *All* of existence, the seemingly infinite, is mystified, then personified and thought of as God.

We ought to have a soul. Taking the Earth for granted, a given world, we are the most miraculous beings on the planet, the most miraculous beings we can imagine, less One. Strangely, we think because we can imagine her, she, too, must exist. Our reach out of the humble dirt toward that One seems insignificant. We fear our basely origins are too mundane. We can't stand that so we make the One care.

Are we not some-thing of the One? Each then is made significant by Her. And by our treatment of each other as part of the One, we, too, become significant. And our destiny isn't to fall into the dirt one day, but to proceed on, on into the All. To be reunited with our source, with Her, to be one with the One.

We may alternatively seek higher purpose or strive to give our lives meaning (which I think we can and we do). Some say that's enough; others say not. Whatever the specifics of our spiritual drive, natural selection came up with it. Religion *can* meet the need when it's adequate to it. It would seem that it can fail, too. Is that cause in our stars or in our genes? Or is it the evermore complex friction of the postmodern world abrading away the protective religious veneer on our hunter-gatherer psyches? Or more directly, is that what happens to spiritual beings in a secular world? Or do they have to know they are in a secular world? Is it paradise lost for the knowing?

Natural selection gave early humankind the spiritual experience; not only has it allowed the faithful extra perks for staying in the fold, it has probably allowed the start of new religions when old ones have played out (It would be interesting to know if a feeling of stronger spiritual reward has led the followers of a dying religion to a new religion. I suspect it did over and over again. Or perhaps, was it nothing more than the promise of spiritual feelings in a new religion when the old one no longer produced any?). That process may be more difficult now. If a religion weakened at any time in the last fifty millennia, a new one might have suggested itself via the god-sick feelings described before. Perhaps, a new and shining charismatic leader would arise with a new vision and the next religion would rise where the last one lay dead.

In all those past millennia, though, no religion in its death throes found itself in the postmodern environment—the world of modern civilization, science, medicine, philosophy. With people of reason and clarity who no longer live in a *Demon Haunted World* (Carl Sagan), are new religions possible?

This is a problem that short sighted only-one-true-religion types don't give any worry to. Why should they? All the gods, spirits, manna— got it wrong throughout human prehistory, then one day God said, *Myeh, I like these Hebrews . . .* and the rest was history—sort of. But now, what spiritual or religious event is going to capture and inspire postmodern humanity?

Mormonism is much newer than western civilization, but it borrowed a god. New Age? Well, not really a new god there either. New religions come from existing ones, many students of religion say. I don't know that it's true that every religion rises like a phoenix from the ruins of the last, but what religion, even among the many new micro-religions, can be said to have formed in the absence of any religion, from a culture free of religious influences? Societies have a sort bedrock or background religion. (Perhaps, that's the source of conflict in societies where there are two religions seriously contending to be that religious undergirding of society. Societies that have no broad agreement are societies troubled.)

Never say never, but it seems unlikely that a new religion could pull people together to the extent that the existing religions did in their heydays. Religions begun post-enlightenment, postmodern may tend to be fragmentary. Of course billions of believers are still reported to belong to the major religions today.

Spiritual drive

What I've been proposing is a hypothesis that has the most explanatory power for the world we see and the minds within it that we can't see. There's a patternicity in those minds with respect to religion and all things that arise in response to the felt spiritual need. That patternicity isn't explained by the dismissive statements that are often used to wave it away. There's an urge to fulfill some spiritual need or desire for religiousness. It seems best described, this need, as a drive of sorts.

For it to be a drive means we feel a need, maybe even suffer a little for the lack of it. I think it might be the sort drive that when unfulfilled could entice us to try drugs, alcohol, tobacco, caffeine—in other words, some people might substitute these other habitual, even addictive, needs that they can fulfill.

I'm speaking in general of a genetic predisposition toward religiosity that wants to be satisfied and rewards us if we satisfy it and perhaps punishes us if we don't. I'm suggesting we are in a general state of spiritual want.

I don't think it is a need or drive for religion, per se—though religion is what's being applied to the need in most cases. (It would be interesting to see a group of people otherwise equipped with the same genes representative of the larger population who have never been exposed to any religion plopped down on an island to see if they developed any religious behavior. No such population is available, though, is it?)

Religion is the default solution—or default product—to the felt need and it fulfills us or not depending on an unknown number of variables. I wonder if a satisfaction survey has ever been conducted to gauge a believer/practitioner's happiness with the workings of her religion with respect to whether it meets her spiritual needs?

I suggest this hypothesis because the rewarding and reinforcement of that behavior, spiritual behavior, by neurochemicals isn't enough to explain its existence. Like the sex drive analogy, our pleasurable experience when we have sex has little to no explanatory power when we seek to understand our urge for, and the effort we expend toward, obtaining sex. (If you doubt that, consider the person who has never had sex. The suffering has little to do with looking forward to the orgasmic reward for having sex as much as the release from the unrelenting drive—that incessantly punishing drive that can power quite an urge.)

If it's not exactly a religious drive, is it a religiosity drive? If we say that a certain religiosity or religiousness is heritable, that approximates it in the broadest of brush strokes. That's what we seem to display behaviorally . . . but it doesn't come very close to what we seem to experience internally. A *spiritual drive* seems as close as any approximation comes. Yet that leaves out entirely anything about our religious activity and orientation. Therefore, it seems more accurate to term the product of our genetic blueprint a religiosity/spirituality drive, cumbersome though that may be.

Ultimately, we may find some neuronal circuitry that came to us pre-wired that can be appeased by ritual or trance-like behaviors, most effectively in a communal setting. Those behaviors will make us feel good (including higher level senses of fulfillment) if we are able to achieve the release of certain of the neurochemicals that reward our thoughts and other special brain activity (not unlike an addictive habit?), and activity that we would think of as spiritual or of a reasonable similitude. We surely must have some preprogramming in this area, though there are almost certainly learned components, too.

Shinzen Young in *The Science of Enlightenment* says we feel a tiny perk, I think he means neurochemical in origin, when we exhale (it was mentioned in the context of a relaxation exercise). I presume that sense of reward comes naturally to us. Even though breathing is under the control of the autonomic nervous system and we don't have to think about it, it can be argued that it is beneficial for an organism to breathe and so there might be a tiny reward for that. (Young's exhale is slightly more pronounced than normal so the reward may rise to the nearly perceptible range.)

I have a daughter who liked arithmetic in school. She was good at it and she obviously felt rewarded for engaging it. Though the mechanism for giving ourselves those little perks may not be immediately accessible to us, it isn't too difficult to imagine that my daughter eventually "learned" to give herself that small neuronal/neurochemical reward for successfully attacking arithmetic problems (consciously, though, as she never had the intent to reward herself by releasing dopamine, serotonin or the like). No doubt this began as others rewarded her for small successes with arithmetic, but following their example of reward which she no doubt internalized, it is a small step to triggering the reward for herself as she went on to face later arithmetic challenges alone.

The spiritual high

Sometimes described as an oceanic feeling, the religious epiphany or transcendent experience is not so much the evidence of an act of grace or some sort of blessed event bestowed by a supernatural being from some spiritual realm as it is a psycho-chemical anointment that produces the feeling of a spiritual experience, perhaps a feeling of euphoria while engaged in spiritual pursuits.

It may function as an internal validation via our feelings that we have achieved a desired or anticipated state or level. That feeling is the effect of an endorphin, dopamine or one of the other positive, mood-boosting, or pleasurable neurochemicals that our mind/body rewards us with for the achievement of certain accomplishments or experiences *that we see as positive* (or things with an added survival advantage that accumulated through natural, sexual, and other selections).

If it isn't apparent, the experience as well as the validation and reward are all internal to us and those positive experiences alone are enough to urge us on for those "feel good" moments. Even beyond that, though, we do have something or a combination of things within our human make up that add up to a drive or felt need for us to seek spiritual fulfillment—fulfillment for how that longing makes us feel. Soul weary discomfiture is perhaps how the former slaves mentioned in the book *God Struck Me Dead* would describe it as might the yet to be born-again of today.

What is that resulting mental state of the religious experience? Rapturous euphoria? Religious intoxication? Piously impaired? Religiously insane? Maybe not quite. These are at the rather far end of the scale. People having a minor religious experience are able to compartmentalize the ebullient mood so that it doesn't incapacitate them in other areas. I wonder if the daily experience of the faithful isn't some what subliminal?

Actually, the typical mood of today's believer may range between subliminal to somewhat elevated, but probably not quite as high as when the "initial sale" was first made, when the believer became a believer or, perhaps, had a born-again experience. That initial threshold, at least for the adult convert must be a little higher in order to move them from nonbelief. The religious experience for an individual in the ancestral human population may have been quite different. That, too, is in dispute as we shall see.

It seems there is a *felt* need for spiritual fulfillment not unlike the sex drive in its dogged urgency. Where does that urge come from? Is it instinctual?

INSPIRED BY *Start Your Own Religion* by Colin Morris

This might seem like a funny source to quote, but these passages from Morris' book capture the essence of religion and hints at the evolutionarily created "sweet spot" for belief within us.

Morris explains that the believer sets up as desirable a spiritual goal such as being saved or enlightened within a culture of being saved or enlightened and seeks the experience of the same as the highest good. I drew from Morris's writing the thought that the internal psycho-physical warm and fuzzy feeling rewards the achiever of the spiritual quest for both low and high level spiritual activity—choral singing, communal prayer, feeling touched by God.

"[R]eligion seems to bring into focus the mingled motives and cravings of an unfulfilled life." (Page 31, *Start Your Own Religion*.) I would reframe and expand on this to say: Every person, when they become fully sentient and worldly-aware, find themselves in the middle of several narratives which seem to have no beginning and no end. What we known and learn seem to fall far short of what we wish to or need to know. The creation myths give our narratives a beginning and perhaps an end or a vague hint at an aspirational destiny.

(Paraphrased from p.33 ibid.) Religion answers the human hunger for explanation by ascribing a meaning to life that may go far beyond the available evidence, and so is a matter of faith, but it seems to work for those who accept it as a source of inspiration and a means of support.

". . . [S]omething else at work . . . not a specific appetite . . . but a vague longing . . . To be human is to have a feeling of dissatisfaction with our existence as it is, an almost indignant sense that there has got to be something more which is better than anything we presently possess." P.33.

"This strange longing . . . suggests there is something some where that can satisfy it. Some religions say that satisfaction can come from within us. Others say it must come from something that transcends us." (P. 34 ibid)

Where does this longing come from? I think we'll find proof some day in genomic research that we have this previously mentioned need for spiritual fulfillment that's like the sex drive. It's weaker, no doubt, but enough to be deniable? This is an idea that's something of an orphan. So far the religious haven't taken to it. For the fundamentalist it's a nonstarter. It makes religion a product of human evolution—that dirty business that significant numbers of Christians have already denied or tried to ignore. Even the more moderate believer has no particular reason to embrace the idea. It's a stretch for them to believe that evolution would be God's chosen way to put humanity on Earth, but to have given us religion as an evolutionary adaptation via natural selection . . . ?

I think for the religious, that's a little like the exhortation in the Wizard of Oz, "Pay no attention to the man behind the curtain."

That spiritual feeling

The length of the religious or spiritual experience seems short in duration like a sexual orgasm, but the effects can be life changing (See Quantum Change). Both the religious epiphany and the sexual orgasm appear to be good for the individual while 'peak" experiences induced by an outside drug are not or, at best, appear to also take a drag on the individual, i.e., a stress trade off is the necessary baggage exchanged for the high (caffeine, marijuana, etc.). Epinephrine (adrenalin) may be neutral to slightly positive (highly positive if it saves the organism's life in a fight or flight response, but we are talking more of the felt positive experience of the individual in response to her spiritual experience).

Peak mystical experiences or ecstatic religious experiences also tap into these psycho/neurochemical rewards in the brain of the participant creating something like a spiritual high. Also, specific areas of the brain activate or de-activate to produce other states seen when the person has what they define as a transcendent experience—the feeling of oneness with everything, for example.

Spiritual beliefs can reduce stress. Positive spiritual experiences, perhaps even the thoughts that we are having a positive spiritual experience, reward us (believers only, I suppose) both cognitively and neurochemically. This is where some would say believers and nonbelievers are different. Nonbelievers, they say, lack something—a spiritual gene or some spiritual equipment that keeps us from having the experience. I, for one, think I have at least some of the "faculty" (susceptibility?) but that doesn't make the promises of any specific religion come true for me. It remains to be seen who has what faculties or innate equipment. Genomic research may eventually clear this up for us.

Others might say that believers have a God virus or a meme that has infected them. Still others might say the full-blown mystical experience is diagnostic of a pathology such as temporal lobe epilepsy. Heaven knows, I'm a critic of religion, but those earlier critics who cited some pathology as the sole source of mystical experiences were a little more critical than even I would be. I suppose it seemed more plausible at the time—looking at a person as a blank slate who is having a religious experience—that pathology was the cause that made sense rather than most of us having a predisposition toward religious experiences.

While there is nothing in a hypothetical Venn diagram of, let's say, *Temporal lobe epilepsy Intersects Mystical Experience* that rules out any such intersection of the two and it is possible that, while a pathology could conceivably produce a religious vision, I don't think it is reasonable to expect every mystical experience to have at its base some mental pathology. (The reason for this is elsewhere tied to a thesis in this book.)

I ask for your indulgence for mentioning this as I haven't been able to verify this, but there is a story of a nun who had orgasms when she prayed. Prurient interest aside, the purpose for mentioning the story is that there would be something instructive about her neural wiring along the lines of neurons that "wire together, fire together."

Surely, the nun's neural structures or the neurochemistry at work could shed some light on the relationship of neurochemistry and synaptic routing in the religious experience. In that ever so slight misrouting of similar neuronal responses to vastly different brain states lies proof that while prayer stimulates the rewards of religious experiences, sex stimulates the rewards of sexual pleasure—and they are not so very dissimilar in result.

Belief that brings with it a neuronal boost or perk is a (positive) net sum game—like the caffeine in your coffee or the nicotine in tobacco—or so says your brain, anyway. This direct response of the brain, serendipitously bypassing the rational centers, can form an addiction to those seeming perks. In other words, the brain perceives a net sum benefit that the rational mind might reject for greater overriding concerns. The pleasure centers of the brain might enjoy, for instance, eating the third chocolate bar. While, rationally, the mind knows it's an excess that would sooner or later have negative consequences for the whole person.)

We might know how we would respond to some spiritually charged words or deeds, but do we have to be especially prepared or readied to have a significant spiritual experience? Born-again evangelicals who proselytize as well as recruit potential believers ask the would-be prospects the same exciting questions they were asked, *Can you feel the love of Jesus?* As that idea elicits positive feelings and the initiates experience an upsweeping joyously positive emotion, they are asked, in effect, if they feel as if they are saved.

In his book *Born Again* (1976 and 2008), Chuck Colson describes his spiritual experience:

". . . while I sat alone staring at the sea I love, words I had not been certain I could understand or say fell from my lips: "Lord Jesus, I believe in You. I accept You. Please come into my life. I commit it to You." With these few words . . . came a sureness of mind that matched the depth of feeling in my heart. There came something more: strength and serenity, a wonderful new assurance about life, a fresh perception of myself in the world around me."

Up until now, we've not really been invested in what the born-again experience consists of. It has been assumed to include what believers would call a confirmative spiritual experience. If that is not what believers mean when they say they are born-again, so be it.

Colson doesn't actually say he felt the spirit of Jesus moving within him. He appears to have come right up to that threshold and stopped. Neither does Colson clear up for us whether the source of his experience was outside himself or not. He may have left that open for his larger reader audience—Christians on both sides of the divide—those whose experience had the input of a divine component and those whose experience was totally of themselves alone.

My intent wasn't to judge this aspect of the born-again experience. Rather, it was to have a benchmark experience that was common enough for most people to understand and appreciate, at least to some extent. For that reason only, every use of the term "born-again" in this writing means an experience which the believer initiates and is met by what the believer feels as some form of divine or supernatural input.

Must we be trained—or train ourselves—to produce the feeling that we interpret as spiritual stirrings within us? To at least some minimal extent, this must be necessary, but not sufficient, to cause the experience or many more nonbelievers would have such experiences.

Or would we have to accept some of the premises of religious belief as a prerequisite of "experiences deemed religious?" Must we believe religious experiences *can* happen? I believe this and other preliminaries to an experience are generally necessary. In the anecdotal first person accounts of those who profess significant religious experiences in *Quantum Change*, most or all of them felt overwhelmed and swept away by the experience. The person is all at once so taken by surprise and this, even though they have typically been dwelling on a weighty religious issue of very high significance to them or, alternatively, they have maintained an intense and rising focus on their personal religio-spiritual issues.

This fits with the thesis that the neurophysiology of religious experiences is one in which the person's neurochemicals create for them a positive reward "at the edge" of a thought or feeling and that contributes to a rising mood and emotional state suggesting that the person is having a significant and especially *real* experience. That possibility is exciting and stimulating and the person is having greater and greater neurophysical experiences confirming it. These folks often consider this the most important experience of their lives.

We've consider the lowest spiritual experience and the highest, the question arises, *What is the upper limit to such experiences?* It is evidently somewhat short of these people being spirited away to heaven. Obtaining enlightenment might be argued to be a realistic maximum (there is cottage industry surrounding enlightenment; the namesake magazine sums up the state of the enterprise, *What is Enlightenment? [now EnlightenNext].* Enlightenment certainly has a number of varied meanings.). Other spiritual quests might entail a sense of communing with a god, feeling the oneness of all, achieving salvation or inner peace. But the experience, even an ecstatic and beautiful one, is produced totally within the person's brain and body—no outside influence is necessary.

To anyone seeking spiritual relief from tragedy, a downtrodden existence or any other depressing negative life experience, a spiritual relief or an even more positive spiritual fulfillment certainly has something to offer just as any stimulant (or feel good drug) might, only with no apparent drag on your physiology, in fact, your mood or psychological wellbeing may be more than enhanced, it might positively be turned around.

To the extent that such a spiritual boost is seen as natural, it offers an avenue that doesn't have the stigma or legal repercussions of illegal drug use or the negative or addictive side effects of, say, alcohol. Although, few believers would be able to verbalize their attraction to the neurochemical high of belief, the subtle effect may be known to them as that "spiritual" feeling. Back in the day, they termed this feeling *the spirit of the Lord move within them.*

Can all that—religious epiphanies, mystical experiences, feeling "saved"—really occur only "in your head?" The enjoyment of most pleasures begins in the brain as wishes, plans, fantasies. Don't we relish the anticipation of an event? Isn't that part of the enjoyment? Are neuronal chemicals at work in these instances, too? Count on it.

All the more so for the believer who belongs to a group bound by common religious beliefs, and more so yet if that group reigns supreme, and even more so if contrary groups are nonexistent or not ascendant (dehumanizing or denigrating the out-group or not giving them a place at the table may serve that end).

It is within this range of evermore ascendant states that believers can experience the greatest serotonin, dopamine, oxytocin, or other neurochemical releases. Even those heights are simply points on the scale with that religious utopia or nirvana that their trained brains and juiced neurons seem to point them toward with promise—the promise of perpetual religious rapture—while the underlying mechanism, out of sight of their vision, is their neural circuitry and neurochemistry making it all possible.

This internal rewarding may train us to seek similar situations. We all have low points or tests of the human spirit. Through our days of dealing with this, we may sense when thoughts or actions would lead to a more successful handling of those "lows," something that nurtures the spirit.

If a religion is in place, it may meet that need. For those who see religion as a purposeless spandrel, this points out yet another overlooked benefit—no apologist for religion am I, that's just the reality of it. At its best, it serves the spiritual need. At its worst, religion subverts the need to subject humanity to a yoke of oppression while actually repressing the human spirit it should be championing.

The ecstatic experience

The pre-pinnacle build up begins with the subtlety of an imperceptible spark. That spark suggests a possibility that rapidly ignites the person's anticipation. The person (who may not yet be a believer or who is a believer under stress) is pleasantly surprised by an upsweeping emotion surrounding thoughts or feelings she's having that touch on the spiritual. The believer or potential believer senses she's in the grip of a significant spiritual experience (a false positive for it), one that engages neurochemical releases and specific neural paths. The person's emotional sense of wellbeing is rapidly rising. This might be the conclusion of a born-again experience.

Alternatively, the event may catapult the would-be-believer to yet a higher plane of spiritual epiphany; it is akin to being carried away by your emotions.

The believer may continue to be surprised by the joy of ever higher levels of spiritual obtainment somewhat analogous to the climber who, due to the mountain's immensity, can only see the next part of the mountain as it's revealed at each new height she achieves. In fact, it seems that the higher the level of spiritual rapture that the believer is open to, the higher level she may achieve.

As this ecstatic joy feeds the rising crescendo of the spiritual experience, it is the believer's sense of the experience that gives her her impression of the nature and magnitude of it. That's the case, whether it's the born-again experience, the touch of an angel, a word from God, a mystical experience, or a pre-rapture rapture.

The born-again experience, again, seems to be the benchmark experience. It is not only the most common spiritual experience, it is above the subliminal or lowest level experience—that warm and fuzzy believer feeling. It is the only acceptable spiritual experience to the mainstream of Christian believers (other than the unrecognized, minimal experience above. By born-again, though, some believers mean

171

making an all out commitment to Jesus—without any supernatural input). Overall, then it is, perhaps, the most valid example of spiritual experiences.

I think many believers could either produce the born-again experience at will with sufficient prepping—or surprise themselves as described in the detailed discussion of spiritual experiences—or be guided by an adept prompting them into an experience. (As a skeptic, I must add that those who've had a spiritual experience crowned with a divine confirmation are fooling themselves and others.)

That cascading flood of emotions of an even greater spiritual epiphany must surely feed energy to the entire experience not only enhancing it, perhaps enlarging it—making an impression on the person that lasts a lifetime.

Without a doubt, there's no physical evidence or any external proof that the event took place. Even though the believer may have felt she was perceiving another world, a spiritual plane, or attention of some supernatural being, it was all internal to her mind.

Just as a particularly moving violin piece or angelic choral voices might bring tears, touching personal sacrifices or accomplishments against all odds can bring flooding emotions of warmth and overwhelming goodwill. These kinds of peak emotions can pull us toward a flood of feelings that might induce unknown thoughts and beliefs. It was postulated earlier that there might be a type of synesthesia at work in some spiritual experiences.

It has been said by believers and nonbelievers that we nonbelievers lack something that makes us spiritual. That may be. Or it may be that while believers learned to be rewarded for their particular set of religious trappings, such learning just didn't *take* with us. Therefore, we simply didn't learn to be rewarded by the same things the believers did. (Many nonbelievers would say we dodged a bullet there and that they are just as happy not to be Stepford Wives for Jesus.) Is it possible that we learned to be *negatively* rewarded by religion or its real world shortcomings?

Failing to learn to be rewarded by religion doesn't mean we don't still experience the felt need, the religio-spiritual drive. At the risk of redundancy, the thesis here is that the spiritual need is inborn and so is genetically encoded in our DNA.

There are some analogies that roughly fit this case. Addictions to minor drugs, caffeine, alcohol, tobacco, inculcate needs within the individual. These felt needs may crudely approximate the religiosity need, aka the spiritual drive.

The other category of needs or drives are of the inborn type. Thirst and hunger are of a very basic sort. Most organisms have needs of this sort that are necessary to stay alive. Nature and natural selection have made the sex drive very strong. It makes a person feel as if it is a matter of life and death. What does the individual need it for? Satisfying the very need that the individual has inherited. The individual may suffer in the absence of satisfaction, but that suffering is in relation to a need fully created by our genes to pester us into the procreative act or a reasonable facsimile thereof. (Well, that and any peer pressure, guilt trips, or "You can go to hell for that!" type warnings from those on the righteous side of the divide.)

The spiritual drive for most people is felt at a lower level of need or urgency, but that may be because there are numerous significant benefits to help it survive as an adaptation (very much under-played in the theories that reject religion as an evolutionary adaptation).

The belief benefit

The sparsest assessment possible of a believer is that she has an idea and a feeling about that idea. The idea may be a belief, a visualization, a myth or part of it, its hero, its moral, the aspirations it holds for its believers. These are things that the believer has learned to hold sacred. Perhaps only things that are held sacred, certainly ritual objects, (but here we are considering ideas, beliefs, and visualizations) can be used for the attainment of a spiritual sense of whatever magnitude.

Would anything that duplicates the same spiritual feeling be equal to or as good as those beliefs? (This does assume that a believer is equipped to have a positive reaction to belief even if that reaction is subliminal—below the believer's sensory threshold to detect. There are, certainly, many who find themselves [trapped] in the pews and who choose to go along, but have no positive experience of the religion, subliminal or otherwise.)

Perhaps, with the exception of sex, there is no greater psychical peak or enjoyment than the belief that we, at our core, are aligned with the ultimate source of all being and not trivially so, but relevantly and significantly so. This can be reduced to a simple thought or concept that has little or no spiritual feeling associated with it (spiritual in the context of this writing means: a sense of the positive, enjoyable feeling created, enhanced, enlarged by the neural network or a neurochemical reward for thoughts, beliefs, feelings, and behaviors which can produce, or are closely associated with a sense of wellbeing, be it from experiencing the sacred or the divine, having a mystical experience, or such secular or intellectual experiences that might produce spiritual feelings as described above.)

Why would this be a most pleasurable or most positive experience? This goes to the heart of the thesis: *Whether religion is in the genes.* It seems that those who think there's not an inborn drive downplay the strength of religion by citing the weaker examples.

The quest for a stronger god, for a stronger religion, was touched on a few pages earlier. (Actually, the seekers for a greater god may have been stopped in their tracks when a stronger religion took hold of them. What's in the heart of the beholder may be slave to what's in the genes of the believer.)

The more superlative divine attributes of omniscience, omnipotence, and so on may be necessary to maximize the beneficial feeling. A minor trickster god simply won't do (Did these RTB's—see Pascal Boyer—sideline the primitives who found themselves on this path?). One of those polytheistic religions with diverse deistic personalities, say the god of thunder, obviously can't stimulate the believer to the same extent as the person who thinks they are in communion with the creator of the universe (though it might have had a significant effect back in its day). Nor can a person get much more connected than a personal relationship with God in which they think the deity is responsive to them.

The Spiritual Spectrum

In describing the feelings of the spiritual kind, there is a spectrum of responses to these neurochemical perks from the subtle, like, say, the pick-me-up that drinking a soda might give you all the way to the peak spiritual "orgasm" or ecstatic state like the rapture Ekhardt Tolle describes from his own experience in *The Power of Now*. (By the way, Tolle implies that his was a spiritual experience, but cites no supernatural beings. Does this leave open the possibility that his might have been a peak secular spiritual experience?)

Then, there are all the experiences in between, God-struck-me-dead, born-again Christian, and others described as mystical and religious experiences (though this latter seems like a misnomer that should be termed "spiritual experiences." You can experience an awful lot that's religious without experiencing anything spiritual.) All of them serve the purpose of validating the person's behavior, actions, or thoughts that brought her to this level. On the face of it, it doesn't really matter what religion one is practicing, does it?

Wake up and smell the lotus blossoms

The typical churchgoer isn't having pinnacle experiences or even ecstatic epiphanies. Possibly not even the minimal spiritual buzz that some have in the pew. Statistically, the two most common types of day in and day out experiences are no feeling at all and an occasional minimal even miniscule nebulous something, a certain warmth of spirit.

Given the lower level of the spiritual life of the typical church attending individual, perhaps, the afterlife trumps a present day spiritual experience. Maybe it replaces it in the believer or potential believer's spiritual outlook. Life after death would really be something. It's immortality. That's monumental. What earthly religious experience, especially, the average joe's, can rival that?

Perhaps, if one is "spiritual," this same belief in an afterlife can be a springboard into the chain of spiritual assent setting up the believer to some new or higher base level spirituality as well as giving the average joe more of a spiritually fulfilling experience than he's had. This could be another way to the ecstatic spiritual experience. As an everyday reality, though, it could be a maintenance dose of spiritual feelings. We need it; we seek it. If we find it, we'll probably stay with it.

It is a legitimate question whether the high spiritual experience is something to be pursued. What is its value to believers or nonbelievers? It offers a major, possibly life changing experience—depending on how it is received and interpreted.

Still, the tamer version of spiritual experiences, something that believers and religious practitioners may encounter perhaps once for the greater experiences, perhaps, occasionally for the minimal experiences, these may be of more value than the swept away peak experience.

The mystical experience may be the crossover—potentially generated by a religious ascetic, it would seem to be the result of a legitimate spiritual practice and yet shares, at least in reputation, some of the greater intensity of the higher level spiritual experiences.

Even though believers set themselves up for those pinnacle experiences, they are far from under control. I can't say for other religions, but Christians that have that meteoric, rockstar-ish, religious epiphany are going to be treated with skepticism from their fellow believers.

Spiritual but not religious

Spirituality, in all but a few denominations (Pentecostal for one, born-again evangelicals are another), is all but gone from the Christian American scene. There are no doubt many individual exceptions, but religious or spiritual experiences are so far removed from the typical churchgoer's experience that even the born-again Christian's experience causes the rolling of eyes in many a pew.

Those disillusioned by mainstream Christianity have removed themselves from that population. This would seem to cut them off from any chance to have significant spiritual experiences (although they may seek and find in other religions, congregations or even cults, an outlet for their spirituality). Further, it seems highly likely that with them, they will pull out their peers, friends, and acquaintances.

Some of those disaffected infuse the zeitgeist and collective consciousness with an atmosphere largely inhospitable to the spiritual person and so banishes them from the public discourse. Strangely enough, the majority of these folks still default to Christianity in the voting booth, on holidays, and in public displays no doubt largely attributable to having grown up in or around the Christian traditions. The slender portion of the disaffected that consider themselves atheists are still largely denigrated by all the others in the spirit of the Old Testament.

It's a sad commentary on present society that perfunctory religion is the default. It is what's defended—the civil religion, supported politically and shoved at us by our culture and government while what's missing is everyone's spirituality. The religious achieve little if any spiritual satisfaction and the nonbelievers achieve less—often blocked by the under-satisfied but rigidly dogmatic fundamentalists who in turn blame the nonbelievers for their (the fundamentalist's) failure to launch . . . spiritually.

The explanation that a person is *Spiritual, but not religious* is an oft stated phrase that is an open, telling statement supportive of the thesis that a predisposition to religious behavior is genetic and heritable. (See twin studies, cited below. Identical twins reared apart have similar religio-spiritual resumes. That is, the depth to which they are involved in religious pursuits is strikingly similar while the particular religion or path is of course not.) In fact, that is the way the predisposition would be heritable: Being spiritual is genetically supported, but a specific religion is not.

Adhering to a religion? That may be genetically supported—look at all the heated rhetoric and violence coming from all directions. Religion-on-religion hate may not come from the spokespeople for the religions but rather the random believer whose testimony is a statistical sampling of his religiosity—and representative to some extent of his ilk—the phenotypic expression of his devotion, depth of belief, in short, all displays of religiosity.

Humanity has easily been exploited over time because we're programmed to respond positively to religio-spiritual stimuli. (Discussed elsewhere, it seems once a religion is adopted by the individual, the susceptibility to other religions is greatly reduced and perhaps even blocked. The xenophobia preached in the Old Testament and other early religious writings may reveal cultural adaptations, if not also genetic ones, to avoid exposure to interloping religions that may come on the scene from time to time.)

Certain religions and perhaps many rulers have more or less subjugated humankind through this need. Yes, the religions, and sometimes the state, offer a channel for fulfillment of the spiritual urge, but, once the state religion is in place, those holding the reigns of power, hold the power over all the people all the more tightly. Then conformance to god/state is judged, deviation from dogma/law chastised. (These intertwined religions and rulers fall far short of full-blown theocracies which can become all the more iron fisted.)

The unappealing institutions that the mainstream religions have become, as well as the disappointing "results" that people draw from their experiences have numbers of the disenchanted heading for all points on the religious compass—Buddhism, New Age, Humanism, Wiccan and others—as well as just dropping out of the religious scene.

Twin studies

Recent twin studies show, as did earlier studies, that one twin's religiosity is the best indicator of the other twin's religiosity.

Time and again, twin studies, especially of identical twins, show that religiousness, religiosity, and/or spirituality are heritable. The most recent is Koenig et al; U. of Minn: "Twin Study finds Adult Religiosity Heritable." Most famous is the older study of Bouchard & McGue. This study included twins raised apart so any significant correlation of religiousness would most likely be attributable to genetic causes.

Buried in the polls, interviews, and studies was one account in which a girl within her own biological family described her amazement at why her adopted sister was so interested in religion and spirituality when she herself still went to church but had no interest in any aspect of religion. This points up that the parental input, though perhaps supportive of the church attendance, wasn't all-important to formation of the child's degree of involvement or interest in religious or spiritual pursuits.

The influence of parental input could have been the basis of an argument against heritability if parental influence could be shown as all important in forming the child's receptivity to religion. Even though the above scenario is only anecdotal, the weight of a few million anecdotes could be related by children who are now adults as to how parental influence, for instance, making sure the child got to church, may have negatively correlated with one's religiosity.

There may be some validity to the effect of parental influence and the child's larger environment as well, but if the child has no interest, his or her own make up is going to be the greater influence in his or her pursuit of religious or spiritual values.

If twins raised apart show equal religiousness, and parental and other environmental influences are equal or accounted for, then religiosity is heritable. Does heritability equal adaptation? Yes, heritability is the mechanism of adaptation. Interestingly, heritability seems to raise the level of the discourse. It may not be fully one's choice how religious or how spiritual they are. (Though the debate about freewill could be tied into this question, we are more interested in the individual and their genes.)

Religiosity and spirituality may simply conform to the distribution of a few genes throughout the population. Some of the genes that would have to be included in that list would be the neurochemicals such as the DrD4 mentioned at the beginning of this work where that influences mood to the extent that even skeptics will consider explanations for things that show a definite shift toward the mystical.

Could that single gene be the extent of what we have been calling heritable religiosity? As suggested earlier, it's possibly a suite of genes or even some loose, eclectic aggregation of genes and epi-genes. It may well be that unconnected genes contribute to what we may collectively refer to when we say religiosity is heritable. Certainly, if a piecemeal association of genes functioned to give the individual the religiosity advantage, so be it. It doesn't make the complex of religiosity/spirituality any less of an evolutionary adaptation, no matter how it is selected, transmitted, or expressed.

In the real world, there will certainly be room for variability in such genes strung together in this fashion. Certainly, such a mishmash of heritability will leave some with a greater genetically founded affinity for religiosity than others. If these genes take on the characteristics of a statistical array, the outliers will inherit either the most or the least of the gene compliment. That there are people in the middle (of the statistical curve) attests to the fact that there is not an on/off switch for the genes of religiosity.

No one true religion?

Following their own paths, the Buddhist experiences enlightenment, the Christian feels born-again.

Can all religious people can get there? We can't say. Some percentage, the majority, let's say, may be minimally psychically rewarded whether they are aware of it or not. They are somewhere on the scale, maybe near the bottom, or more charitably, at the point of average—the center of the bell shaped curve—but they're not having the transcendent experience that fervent believers like the born-again may achieve. And they definitely are not having the peak, ecstatic or mystical experience. Nowhere near it for most of them. And, even then, only achieving that once, if at all.

Related to the argument that atheists don't feel the spiritual fulfillment because we don't have the equipment, the thought has occurred to me that maybe radical Fundies aren't reaching it either due to some low level of neurochemicals, or low receptivity to them, or maybe not having specialized neural circuitry that typically predisposes people to religious activity.

Fundies typically blame humanists, atheists, or humanity itself for thwarting their spiritual goals. It would be ironic if they can't reach any level of psycho-spiritual reward because of their own "equipment," their own make up, or their personal mindset. Certainly, plenty of believers fail to reach anything like the peak. There must have been some who did, maybe at the basis of a faith, some special people, and some statistically random others? Is there a "social effect" that can allow a sharing (or spread) of a charismatic leader's mystical experience?

Has a fundamentalist ever had a spiritual experience? We're not quibbling with the well-meaning, happy believer who happens to hold to the literal truth of Biblical scripture. We're talking the more hateful extremist, but not so rare that they can't find other like minded fundamentalists. I hope we don't share the same reason with the

Fundies that they don't achieve any spiritual experiences—an overload of negativity (their low levels of dopamine or serotonin?). For us, I hope, it is a keenness of our analytical ability that puts us here.

Do you remember this statement from the beginning of this book?

> Silver also cited Peter Brugger who gave the L-dopa drug to skeptics, who with a dopamine high, showed a new found tendency to accept mystical explanations for unexplained phenomena.

Combine that with this earlier quote from the Barna Goup's president about the 2005 to 2007 study:

> "one quarter of atheists and agnostics said "deeply spiritual" describes them."

> It seems possible that many of us nonbelievers with an increase in our own internal source of dopamine might be, if not believers, at least shifting even more toward the mystical and spiritual. It might be reading too much into these statements to infer a shift toward traditional belief, though.

It's a self-confirming religious experience

The spiritual experience builds-in its own confirmation bias. Or more precisely, one is built into our psychology. What you are feeling makes you think that it *is* what you'd feel if you were having a religious epiphany. What we are talking about is a rapturously, ecstatic, joyous state. It may be neural, mental, psychical, but it *feels* spiritual or so we assume. You'll see it elsewhere described as a rising spiral of emotion, an overwhelmingly positive, even pleasurable, experience.

Is there anything in the perception of the sublime spiritual experience that is apart from the typical neurochemical rewards we have been discussing? Andrew Newburg's work with religious practitioners has shown areas of activity within our brains that become particularly active or conspicuously inactive in the service of spiritual pursuits.

The description of the results may sound familiar. The sense that the self has diffused into a greater oneness. A sense of wellbeing. Finding a place of peace and serenity. These experiences may be less profound than the fireworks peaks we've been discussing. They seem to be of a more contemplative if not meditative bent. The difference seems to be that the practitioner has gained a certain aptitude for achieving these more modest states after many hours of engagement in the practice. (Perhaps they are happy to leave the spectacular experiences to those who may haphazardly or serendipitously have them.)

I'm going to say, for the sake of argument, that little or no orientation is necessary as a forerunner to a petit experience of neurochemical releases which produce buoyant, pleasant feelings, aka, spiritual stirrings. This is the experience possible for the human mind au naturel.

This petit experience is above the baseline for believers who have that warm and fuzzy feeling as they attend church but can't point to a greater experience than that. Even this is above the zero point on the scale—the point at which the perfunctory churchgoer functions and probably a number of nonbelievers assume, rightly or wrongly, that their "spirit meter" rests.

Across some line of demarcation, lies the born-again experience. With preparation and staging, the person is readied to have something more. With the proper coaching, that person's experience is teased out to one of experiencing Jesus' love for them and a neurochemically validated sense that they are "saved."

Is religion nothing more than Richard Dawkins' memes?

Any viable religion strings together a number of things, stimulating ideas, the believer's beliefs, the believer's neurochemicals and their receptors, a portion of the person's neural network either dedicated to, or borrowed by, religio-spiritual pursuits—the good stuff—all the time-tested religious epiphany-achieving stuff.

Each religion has its own code: ostensibly it teaches us what's spiritual so that when we experience it, it will be spiritual—God's love, forgiveness, our immortal souls, and a personal savior in God's own son. To those who have been taught that these are spiritual things, these beliefs and any manifestation or experience of them will typically result in some corresponding level of "spiritual" stimulation of those believers.

If those ideas, or experiences are more stimulating than some other religion (tired old Greek gods; Norse gods like Thor)—think, rather, in terms of your soul living on in eternity saved by your personal god who loves you and with whom you have an intimate, caring relationship—now, wouldn't that religion be the stronger, the more moving, the more compelling faith?

And mightn't the neutral outsider—the guest, the prospective initiate—feel that she might have started on the road to a peak transcendent experience starting with a whole spectrum of lesser experiences that have helped her on her way? Admittedly, this initiate may think of it in less technical terms, more likely she wants to get closer to God. She may seek the born-again experience for that closeness, maybe not the spiritual high, although, there's something that beckons—the need, the drive. Her predisposition to spiritual activity answers that call and shapes her quest and her outcome.

If a meme can wield this power, if a meme can imply and generate all these things, then perhaps religion is only a meme. Stay tuned.

Did religion give us language?

Depending on what you take as evidence, we've been under religion's spell for fifty to, perhaps, approaching a hundred thousand years, though if we didn't have language until 40,000 ybp as some say, our religions would necessarily have been extremely rudimentary—if possible at all. (Some anthropologists say we've had language for 100,000 years, a few say more.) Some say our involvement with budding religion may be how we came to know the world and that perhaps once we apotheosized the hidden agents behind our world we struggled to speak to them—we could only handle them symbolically so we developed our methods in that direction.

It would seem unlikely that religion could have come before language, as some argue, but could it have been the midwife of greater language? Religion could have fostered the development of language as that symbolic handling of the world with language as the tool. It seems overreaching even then to give that idea much weight, but we must remain open to it.

The primate need-to-know which of the next of fifty kinds of fruits will be ripe and when has been suggested as equipping the brain with enough complexity to handle symbolic thought. The hunt of the hunter-gatherers certainly required split second coordination not only to save the clan from starvation, but to bring (most of) the hunters back from the hunt. The intricacies of game, its habits, travels, and ability to defend itself, would be even more complex than monitoring fruit and nut trees.

Strong religion was and perhaps still might be a very competitive adaptation. It was a cultural element that was sooner or later supported by genetic or epi-genetic factors. Religion may even have been integral in how we became behaviorally modern humans.

Religion/language parallel

Religion can be likened to language with respect to the genetics of it as an evolutionary adaptation. Those who argue that groups don't have genes and therefore aren't subject to natural selection might say that language is a cultural adaptation.

It's true that specific languages evolved within a culture and only within a culture. But the same argument that groups don't have genes can be applied to cultures.

Some of that confusion can be cleared up when we consider the capacity for language separately from a specific language. A specific language can evolve only in a cultural setting, but the physical capacity for language evolved earlier. Did a single person or a series of individuals evolve this capacity alone? Or was it a group "adaptation?"

Either way, the capacity for religion must have evolved similarly to language. It improved the chances for individual reproductive success. Maybe not a runaway, but a slow statistical superiority to out reproduce the less genetically endowed—probably the same way increasing language skills and abilities would have accrued. The more skilled individuals out-reproduced the lesser. Could it have been sexual selection? It could have been. Does one avenue of selection rule out another? David Sloan Wilson says *no* with respect to what he calls multi-level selection and that selection pressure from multiple sources can be in effect.

The missionary position

If we negate all spiritual claims, souls, afterlife, and gods of the believers, have we dashed all their hopes? I hope not, but I worry we might have. Consider the countries of Africa and the political and social disasters that its humanity is left with after the native religions were taken away by western missionaries who substituted Christianity.

That and worse happened to Native Americans, too. At a pre-revolutionary southern Atlantic coastal mission off the Carolinas they were enslaved by the Church. As forced labor, the Native Americans were given only corn for food. (As a result they developed iron-deficiency anemia as archeologists found from studying the bones of their remains.)

And still today, humanity's potential has never been so bright. As a species, humans are virtuosos of dexterity and motion and the human mind, a citadel. Human cultural, its Excalibur and, sorry for the shock, religion had been its cutting edge. I think this points to the original source of the friction. Maybe there *is* a little overlap of these two magisteria (see Stephen J. Gould; religion and science, he said, deal with two *non*-overlapping magisteria or realms).

Largely, now there is a truce, but there is no buffer zone. Religion was the first to be offended and lash out as an institution. There have always been those skeptical of religion (Don't we know!), but the institution most likely to be confronting any religion was another religion (Though there have been lovers' spats between religions and their host governments as well. The Church of England is an example as well as an interesting story. There are others.)

Infinite possibilities

Why is the human potential so great? Think back a few million years . . . to a third chimp species. It seems there were a number of hominid species or at least broadly different varieties on the scene. It's difficult to be certain whether they were contemporaries. (At this writing there is news that some of the gorilla genome is more closely related to Homo sapiens and, yet, part of the chimpanzee genome is, likewise more closely related. The explication of that interesting twist promises to be exciting.)

Some slight advantage of the mind, neuroplasticity, greater brain mass, the advent of parallel processing, or whatever, gave early proto-humans a culture-handling problem-solving advantage. Along with that, we can all appreciate what an advantageous adaptation culture is. Its power is evident everywhere. Consider the culture clash between Native Americans and the European settlers. With no judgment as to one culture being "better" than another, the Europeans had cultural advances in weaponry that the Native Americans couldn't overcome. The European culture as an adaptation had greater survival value and yet, a European would have been hard pressed to best his Native American counterpart in the absence of the native's cultural adaptations.

Likewise, competition among the early hominid varieties must have been fierce. Only the strong survived. Those who found themselves too close to the niche of man without being equal to it, soon found themselves extinct. This, over and over again, pruned the great ape branch of the tree of life back to the apes with a healthy no man's land giving a wide berth to the top hominid.

The niche at the top has ever since seen fierce competition. The berth grew wider as the hominids ascended to humankind. The nimble, omnivorous, street smart human, adept at language, culturally sophisticated, was well equipped with these battle-bred armaments.

What role religion?

Its binding power is evident. That's one of its greatest strengths. Its social and communal strengths are grossly underrated. Religion offers identity and unity through its creation myths, a certain reverence for life and nature, and it may honor the questions, if not answer them, "Why are we here?" and "What will become of us?"

For early humans, these questions went to the group's purpose and destiny. When answered with strong identity elements, survival was more likely. Evidently, it mattered more that there were answers rather than what the specific answers were. All totaled, the clan, tribe, or village with all the benefits and by-products of religion would have been much stronger than a group where these were absent.

Aren't there other powerful types of group identities, allegiances, political loyalties? Sure, but add religion to any group and their organizational strengths and you have a more tightly bound, stronger entity with religion than without. So much so that it answers the question, or more correctly forces us to reframe it, *Why is religion so universal among the many races of humankind?*

Reframe the question how?

As we know, most if not all humans are closely related—not much genetic variability across the entire species—with Mitochondrial Eve and Y-chromosomal Adam being ancestral to most living humans, and perhaps the winnowing effect of multiple population bottlenecks further limiting the genetic diversity. So as to the question, *Why is religion so universal?* As the evidence shows, on top of Homo sapiens' other skills, religion was a further adaptive advantage that enabled those with it to thrive—and may have made the difference between survival and extinction.

Recognize that once spread, primitive religion, say, traditional hunter gatherer religion or that of agriculturalists, was how life was lived. It was practical, daily, and ongoing. It was their way of knowing their world. Ritual was where the individual met the sacred, the spiritual aspect of reality. It was more than acknowledgement of the sacred, it was participation in it. It was the person reaching out to that aspect of the world that made sense of all the seemingly senseless aspects demonstrated everyday in the mundane world.

The great unknown became sacred and the sacred was anthropomorphized, humanized such that a mysterious persona-likeness, an ultimate being, could lock into reality and make it behave as the believer found it in daily practice. Liken this concept to the whims of Providence at work. It was an interface between believer and reality buffered with just enough metaphoric latitude (a so-called minimally counterintuitive world) to say the hand of the divine is evident.

Ritual may have been the earliest acts of religion. Initially, a superstitious response to the Great Unknown, ritual was the habitual act that our confirmation bias told us would work I we could only perform it just so. Families and the clan had to look on attentively out of respect for the Great Unknown and the hope that the ritual act would be efficacioius.

Ritual was also a social act. These folks weren't like some single person alone out in nature. They were social groups typically based on one or more extended family making up a clan. They all attended the same "church," too. There was no UU congregation as an alternative. Their religion encompassed the entire village. There may have been the occasional nonbeliever, but typically the individual would conform to group beliefs just because they were the group's beliefs. Isolation from competing religious concepts would have kept the ancient wisdom safe and largely unchallenged. Someone within the tribe could hardly come up with a wholly different origin myth. What would he gain? Most likely trouble.

From that point on, religion was here to stay. If it wasn't a top successful survival mechanism, show us the successful societies without it. This isn't to say that a strong religion wouldn't have been part of a "package deal" combining the most bellicose, the most technically advanced cultures—and that an indication that the people were the premier culture-handlers—probably the most linguistically advanced, probably the most intelligent. If you throw in the most political and territorial, you've got the local conquerors. The troupe that dominated the fruit trees. The tribe that took control of the watering hole. The clan that controlled the mammoth herd. The feudal lord that claimed title to the land. They came warring into history as modern man.

VII. Out of Africa: 50K ybp

Western civilization and indeed all humankind have these things that were individual and group assets such as aggression and religion but that became "baggage" with respect to humanity. The ancestral human population evidently brought that baggage with them out of Africa 50,000 years ago. Or did it come out before with the Neanderthals? If Neanderthals didn't have these instinctual assets, it's little wonder they disappeared or were assimilated into behaviorally modern human populations. (Some archeologists have said, of flowers and other grave goods found in Neanderthal burials, that those are signs of religion. The grave goods might be evidence of preparing the departed for travel to the next life, if they had any reason to think there was a next life, but the flowers could be the sign of an aching heart expressing love and loss.)

Behaviorally modern humans, were, or maybe are, bellicose believers, as they are us and we are they. On top of the other social bonding factors, including even xenophobia (a survival strategy) as it binds you if you're part of the in-group, religion is a shared experience that goes to a more radical level than most. It's what bound the early human group together, or is at least one of the strong cohesive forces, perhaps rivaling, if not surpassing, the strength of kinship.

There were some significant tests of early humankind's resolve and ability to survive. A few may have left their mark. The Mount Toba super-eruption of 75,000 years ago and the one thousand year volcanic winter that followed may have contributed to the later glacial maximums. Climate change, especially in Africa as jungle gave way to savannah and savannah, in part, to arid desert, molded early humans.

Major population bottlenecks linked to causes like those mentioned above help explain why modern humans are so narrowly constrained genetically (Why the genetic variability is low—the genes are very similar across all living humans—with the exception of just a few tribal populations). Estimates of the surviving populations are stated over a range as low as five hundred breeding age females and as high as two thousand after all the effects of the Mount Toba super-eruption settled in.

Perhaps a few of the strongest clans or tribes survived to populate the world; the strongest religion may have determined who that was. Although, it's certainly possible that there could have been some luck in where food or shelter was available or maybe weather or climate protected the few remaining tribes. If populations in a single region survived, say western Africa, they may have been related clans. If they branched from a single trunk, an ancestral population, a single religion might have prevailed. No viable hypothesis can ignore the widespread presence of religion.

If religion and its genetic underpinnings are everywhere on the globe, then it either spread with that diaspora that eventually populated the world or it arose independently over and over again in later cultures after they separately branched out. The latter proposition is the sort that is typically rejected in evolutionary thought while occurrences of the former type are considered strong evidence that the characteristic was common before a point of separation or divergence. That puts us at 50K ybp as a minimum for having religion in our genes.

What better to be xenophobic about than religion?

It might be the remnants of xenophobic religions that we are seeing in radical Islam and the Old Testament Bible—they tell their adherents how to dispense with unbelievers. Most who follow the Judeo-Christian traditions today aren't going to stone the adulterer or follow any of the other violent suggestions for dealing with transgressors.

Germaine to our argument, there's an isolated hunter gather people, the Andaman Islanders, that put all visitors to death (See *The Faith Instinct*, Nicholas Wade). A tradition that's very likely to trace back to their religion. As a cultural adaptation that certainly has survival value for their troupe in light of the fact that infectious disease has decimated many an indigenous population. I'm not faulting religion here. It's likely that the Andaman carry in the collective memory of their myths the injunction to kill strangers. Just like the false positive that comes from our hidden agent detection equipment (ascribing a noise heard in the dark to someone) that can be selected for, all sorts of xenophobic behaviors could and have been selected for.

Of course, evolution doesn't have to answer to anyone, but its human products may. Consider how fiction likes to show us simple, naïve people who trust too much. The novelists only vary the iterations of how much loss and destruction the innocents are to face.

In other words, there's a warning that may be difficult to discern. *Trust others at your own peril.* Religion can make us xenophobes, but it can make us gullible innocents, too. Jesus said love thy neighbor as you love thyself, though it's been said, he was only talking about neighbors in the Hebrew 'hood.

Which of thy neighbors is worthy of love? Our same religion, our economic class? Those who *go green* with us? Christianity says man is redeemable. We all know populations we have our doubts about and would like to turn to our way of thinking.

Attempts at redeeming humanity have abounded in fact and fiction. I'm thinking of one novel where consumers are the object of redemption. It may be more than western civilization, perhaps all of mankind or at least Ishmael's takers (*Ishmael* is Daniel Quinn's dialogue novel)—meaning modern man since the agricultural revolution—those who live a lifestyle of unlimited growth and consumption in a limited world with limited resources.

The Spell

People have a drive toward religion. A need that's fulfilled—or not—by the oriented activities of ritual, song, reverence, special knowledge, community loyalty, identity, and participation—or lip service to all the above and, more or less, full participation set in a societal group of people very much like themselves.

Dennett and others have tried to explain the source and staying power of religion with cogent arguments, but short of allowing that it might be an evolutionary adaptation. And short of that, their explanations just don't seem to fully capture the power of religion's grip on mankind.

It really does seem like humanity is under a spell, that of religion—and not entirely unwillingly. Man's enthusiasm is far greater than mere acquiescence; some are coconspirators and pursue their faith with a vengeance. (Professor Dennett explains this is not the *spell* he means in *Breaking the Spell*, but rather that a deep studying of religion has been taboo and he's calling that at an end.)

I think there are lesser, but still rewarding experiences that say to the searcher, *You're on the right path* (regardless of the path). Perhaps, a more common way of describing the state is as a validating glow from within, neurochemical or not, rather than a flash of enlightenment.

That's how it feels, even the low level of reward, somewhere between the nearly subliminal intuitively sensed validation on the low side to the feeling of a rising mood at the moderate level. I think that's why they believe their faith statements are true even in the absence of objective facts. That level of reinforcement is somewhat like the sense of good fortune one experiences with a "win" of a minor sort, say a free soda, or like an intellectual "aha" moment when someone achieves an insight.

For those people raised within a religious tradition they're getting reinforcement from all directions, home, school, peers, the media, society. Although, this external reinforcement is of another sort, it still is reinforcing of the all encompassing milieu of the religion. Some of this is proportional to how mainstream their religion is, to how immersed in religion their culture is.

Anthropology of belief

(Though not the cultural or social anthropology of religion)

In our dimmest days of primate ascension, we looked first to our alphas. As higher primates radiating into the spectrum of the great apes, we varied that theme. Then as early man, did a strong alpha lead the hunt and the raids? If it's true that we had no leaders in the purported equanimity of the hunter-gatherer's life, we must have sorely yearned for an alpha from the yawning abyss of our deep evolutionary time.

In the stark in-your-face realities that a thinking animal faces in an animal world, cause-and-effect thinking in the face of danger and want would necessarily be constant and maddening. Though we may have modeled our ultimate questions, our worldview, our cosmology without alpha leaders during our rising consciousness of the last 100,000 years or so, we might all the more have sought to fill the void of leadership in its absence. Survival rewarded that behavior by making it ingrained, and ever since, our innate nature urges us toward the cluster of behaviors that relate to the sacred or supernatural.

And with leaders? We still look for answers and that quest draws us to our leaders for leadership in the absence of knowledge. To our elders for wisdom, even if they have none. To our holy men, even if they aren't.

And, so, in ignorance we stand, we've tried out answers, we've honor the questions, the process, and over steep cultural time, we eventually became religious about it—and that served . . . for a time.

I've said elsewhere that I believe the need for religion was initially borne of the quest for the legitimate alpha male—the search for the rightful one who would lead us. Though that quest can be seen as a symbol for our worldview or an even a greater platform, something we haven't yet named, something more broadly based, more inclusive, something that contains and anticipates all of reality to it's furthest extents.

Alternatively, that need was at least hung on the bones of a social skeleton—the hierarchical form of society—and that society, our society, has countless iterations of interplay with the process which is never complete, no matter how weary we become—unless we find the ultimate alpha male who can quiet all the discordance of life and bring us to our spiritual home once and for all.

That pursuit and that form urge us on to seek the most legitimate alpha male, and for religions so inspired, we end up with a deity at the head, a heavenly father, an ultimately authentic father, where our earthly ones are so inadequate.

For religions without a head, that body allows us a supernatural realm reminiscent of a perfected social order. In whatever form we visualize that transcendent reality, it is surely visualized with the aid of the living experience and a certain amount of natural disappointment in the hierarchy of human society—as we seek the right form of that, religion offers to guide us in our socio-spiritual efforts.

Earlier, on the pithecoid's side of the divide (think *chimpanzee troupe* for the sake of argument), brute strength, with some rudimentary efforts in the social and political areas of their lives, could produce a more or less legitimate alpha male for the apes. He was, of course, subject to being overthrown at anytime and replaced by the next alpha male.

Earliest man, and certainly the earlier australopithecines, must have started out with similar alpha males and similar challenges to their right to power. Could questioning whether the alpha male was worthy have begun on the pithecoid side of the line? Chimpanzees have complex social and political interactions with nuanced calculation and scheming just below the surface. Or did it take being able to voice the challenge of the alpha male for it to be given serious consideration?

It should be apparent that finding the alpha male lacking could have occurred in the earliest human societies over and over again. Could it have been much later that the politico first courted the shaman? These early (religious) representatives of social institutions could do much to shore up or tear down the defensive wall between their subjects, aka the laity, and their leaders.

It is an accurate criticism, here, to say that I'm being vague—that I'm blurring the lines. When I'm talking about legitimate alpha males of some early model human troupe, do I mean political leaders or religious leaders? The line is blurry. I mean whatever that human troupe "meant" in their quest for that ideal alpha male and whatever entities they saw him serving. I think this is part of the reason why "God & Country" are linked today in an entangled manor. We moderns visualize and define both *God & Country* as very distinctly different, but I wonder if our primate brain (monkey mind?) doesn't conflate the two more than we consciously acknowledge or even understand? (And this along the lines above and elsewhere in this writing.)

Further, I think *country* now fills the void (or shares it) where the believer's group stood. Remember, religion *binds* together . . . . I'm continually surprised by those critics of various writers in this area who think the writer has erred in citing a significant strengthening of the believer's community as the pinnacle reason religion exists. It's not to justify our various theories and hypotheses about religion as some critics and reviewers say. It's what we see when we delve deeply into this subject, religion.

The critics may be considering the believer's reasons for being part of the community and determining the believer isn't joining to strengthen the community. Agreed. It's not the believer's purpose that perpetuates the community, it's the community's. And it's not that communities strive to strengthen themselves, though they might, it is rather, the result that counts. Communities that survive had been strengthened whether by themselves or by whom or what.

It is necessary to say that there is possible evidence, as well as proponents of the theory, that hunter—gatherer tribes were egalitarian (Nicholas Wade, *The Faith Instinct*) and free of alpha male influences except that such strongmen when they had the support of others may have grabbed power (that sort of rule today may be a flashback to a rejected animalian precursor).

My first question would be, if this was the case, how far back into human ancestry would it go? Secondly, could it be that higher primate, then hominid evolution for millions of years had an alpha male at the top of a societal organizational chart only to drop it in the hunter-gatherer period and pick it back up for modern man? Maybe that's possible. Bonobos have the female hierarchy that seems to function diametrically opposed to the functioning of a male hierarchy like the chimpanzees and it has borne most of the implications of a role reversal.

The gist of the argument advanced is that hunter gatherers had to live with equanimity because no one could accumulate more than another—they were limit to what they could carry with them. No accumulating surpluses, no wealth. That changed with settled agricultural societies . . . wealth could be amassed, then the wealthy could be chieftains (alpha males), lords, kings.

Counter to that, I would say that if hunter-gatherers had little to no leadership, they may, all the more, have carried an imbedded desire for it—a collective memory buried in their genes—to seek the legitimate alpha male. That may be us experiencing our need for that alpha as we look longingly up our social organizational chart. How much more we would feel that need if we went 100,000 to 200,000 years without our alphas?

(I couldn't resist using the line, above, ". . . a collective memory buried in their genes . . ." as a metaphor for the phrase in the earlier line, ". . . carried an imbedded desire for it . . ." I do that in part, for the spiritual content it offers the reader. Just as writers in other spiritualities might. Have you felt other points of spiritual stimulation throughout the writing?)

Religion's Practical Side

Again, for religion to have flourished, it must have or have had something, a survival value, a benefit that made the member more fit than others would be without it. I think it is, at least in part, the settled nature of the ultimate (or perhaps, faux ultimate) questions as they appeared in practical terms in daily life. With the complex that is religion, early humans knew who they were, knew where they came from, knew what their purposes and goals were. Life might have been a bitch, but at least it was a world with intentional order—and they knew the big Kahuna and that, in his world, he would let them win some of the time. If only they could get a little *"Closer, my God, to Thee"* and thereby improve their odds.

The stronger their beliefs, the stronger their community. Perhaps, this is why doubt about belief, publically expressed, was (and maybe still is) taken as the worst form of attack on the community? The medieval remedy for this was to burn the heretic at the stake. If there is a more cruel form of torture and death, I can't think of it.

With these questions settled, even if somewhat unsatisfyingly, a person could go about daily life without having to rethink his philosophies before every move. The argument could be made that we function today without the ultimate questions being settled and so we may be exposed to suffering through continual re-analysis. Are we? Society does suffer from lack of certainty as well as the friction between differing worldviews. We do benefit from the social fabric being richer, but we suffer from it being weaker at the same time.

We like not having to rethink our worldview at every turn. Our lives can be stable, our society can be stable. Social groupings that develop this adaptation for internal cohesion and strength tend to last longer. At least in western societies, this may explain much about why the existing cultures are still around. If any and every religion fills this need, it may not take an unattainable goal or quest to satisfy. Something, anything that fills the hole—a placeholder—even a placebo . . . as long as we don't know it's a placebo. (Given a reality with no supernatural realm or beings, aren't all religions a placebo?) . . . Something we accept as a religion, something that we think gives us purpose, unites us, grounds us, yet shows us some shiny orb, a figurative salvation or enlightenment that may do.

If it's too weak of a shiny thing, though, we wander off, in spite of our need and due to our insufficient (psycho-neurochemical) spiritual fulfillment. (Perhaps, we are known to wander and this is why all the heavy handedness from the Old Testament writers and their dogma. For the heretic to be stoned for religious disloyalty, is similar to the adulterer being stoned for marital infidelity. Both fates are prescribed in the Old Testament.) This is the way of the Greeks and Romans were with their gods—at length, the gods didn't hold the interest of the people. Yet the people still had their need. So they searched, so we search.

Is religiosity an innate drive or need? Many nonbelievers would say not, that life can be happily lived without it . . . but, and I'm not calling atheism a religion, nonbelievers have certain worldviews that fulfill part of this need. Then, too, nonbelievers may engage more in ultimate-question-pondering (as we're doing here) than typical believers do, thereby demonstrating the thesis.

Heritable religiosity versus religious dead ends

Pascal Boyer says primitive humans existing today have his RTB's, Religious Thoughts and Behavior but have nothing like a true religion. They may know a deity, but he bedevils them. There's no religious practice directed toward this trickster god—and therefore, Boyer says, religion isn't ubiquitous—isn't universal through out all human cultures and that undermines the universality of religion as strong evidence that religion is heritable.

It's true enough that some of today's primitives don't have full-blown religions. It may be a fuzzy line that divides religion from RTB's. Some of today's primitives like the African Zande (aka the Azande) people have a worldview that revolves around their belief in witchcraft. For the Merina people, their king became a god and ancestor worship is their form of practice. The Kham-Magar of Nepal and the Beti of the Congo see animism at work behind nature. The Baku pygmies of Cameroon ply the forest spirit with rituals of song and dance. The Kwaio of the Solomon Islands are also ancestor worshippers.

(Ancestor worship doesn't seem to fit the alpha male schema of religion. It's an iteration of that hierarchical scheme where family lineage teased out to be more important. It's a variation on the theme (of alphamalism) and it is one that's easier to see extending from a clan—leading from individual through the patriarch (the ruler, usually the oldest living male member of the clan [an ultra-extended family living as a sociopolitical unit])—and on up into the ancestors of the family tree. The father figure could serve as alpha male as well as patriarch. The similarity of the "heavenly father" with the earthly father is perhaps the most used metaphor in Christianity. When these align with alpha male and patriarch, it's a powerful arrangement for the human psyche. This jump is not a large one, but a natural one.)

These examples, above, of religious behavior of modern primitives, may fall short of being true religions. Isn't it likely, that some hunter-gatherers, circa 50K ybp, also were religious dead ends. The impoverished existence and minimal cultures of today's primitives who have something short of religion, though it may be the same as it was fifty thousand years ago, could be the best evidence that "religion-lite" of their type *didn't* lead anywhere.

There were reportedly one or a few cultures in Africa that budded off the ancestral family tree early in human history and remained relatively unchanged. Perhaps, it was before religion had fully developed into the significant adaptation it became, and arguably before the main diaspora out of Africa, again, 50K ybp.

It could be that the primitives in those early days were on the extreme fringe of the early populations who had the "religion" genes and it might have been that isolated tribes like these primitives that only have Boyer's RTB's, didn't need the adaptation of a strong religion to survive. Or if their isolation was a newer occurrence, they then, might not have needed the religion adaptation so their genetics drifted away from it. At length, whatever the case, it hardly seems much of an argument for the nonuniversality of religion to point out that a few primitive tribes don't practice religion like the rest of humanity's cultures everywhere in the world.

Even with the more obvious reasons for religion—people are still typically born into it, children are indoctrinated into it, their cultures are saturated with it—their family and society are more or less fully invested in it. This may make a religion appear more of a casual arrangement than it typically is (though there are people and families whose relationship with religion is casual and not very important to them.)

Such a "faculty," a predisposition to something in the way of religious behavior, would hardly have to entail belief in a deity, and possibly little, if any, belief at all. All that would really have to be selected for might be no more than an imbedded need or drive—a nagging need for spiritual satisfaction—and these little perks of neurochemical rewards for the activity, both mental and physical, with the addition of supported behaviors of ritual chant, dance, and ultimately trance in a religio-social setting.

Why else would these physical religious behaviors earn the participant rather higher level spiritual experiences when viewed from the participant's perspective? (Perhaps going through the motions of habitual practice, standard rituals, group singing, sermons, etc. keep those who might stray from the flock in line. Repetition keeps behavior consistent which in turn keeps belief simple, conforming, and on message.)

Remember how pews were put in the churches to stop the parishioners from dancing? It evidently wasn't a Christian dance that was blocked. It seems probable that it was a dance from their folk religion from the days when the individual could seek and perhaps achieve his own spiritual fulfillment.

Our religious professionals probably wanted to get away from any spiritual pursuit in which the individual could achieve anything on their own. And, if they could achieve it on their own, it would most certainly be a greater spiritual achievement than what the religious professional could deliver, and therefore, it was the *one* path to greater spiritual satisfaction.

What would be the extent of heritable religiosity?

Eventually, genomic research may correlate the genes and epi-genes that produce a defined set of universally common religious elements. The result may not be pretty. Selection constructed our DNA and it's typical for scattered genes to affect an inherited characteristic. I think it's said that thirty genes affect the inheritance of height. Consider also the current thinking that some characteristics, say like intelligence, may not be a heritable trait and therefore there are no known genes for intelligence.

Bear in mind, too, religion may only be the blacksmith to our spiritual steel. Across time and cultures unrelated religions and proto-religions aren't going to contain any specific dogma in common, per se, and almost certainly not any specific belief.

Of the estimated ten thousand religions in the world, the diversity and varied content of belief supports the thesis that religion is an adaptation that is selected for its environment just as skin color or any other refined adaptation is. A much less likely thesis is that one or a few deities exist who have inspired these thousands of religions.

The simplest, most primitive proto-religions, as alluded to before, may or may not prove to be the forerunners of modern religions, perhaps nothing more than a branch on the tree of religion that dead-ended (much as the Neanderthals don't appear to be our ancestors). Still, any theory of the heritability of religiousness or spiritual propensity should endeavor to address them.

As close as we may come to a heritable belief in the supernatural may be the sensing of the hidden agent pointed to by our Hyperactive Agent Detection Device combined with deactivation of neural area of the brain that let's us feel we've diffused into a oneness with everything, add in a rising sense of well being for good measure. Perhaps the psychology of belief is only a unique sequencing of brain modules like attachment, neuronal circuitry, and neurochemicals playing one type of concerto pulled from our repertoire of special mental functions.

That's an example of the kind of piecing together that selection might have done and the kind of thoughts and behavior that early man might have naturally fallen into, that could have become somewhat habitual like the false positive of thinking there's a hidden agent behind every rock and tree. The hypersensitive, those prone to confirmation bias (perhaps spiritual synesthetes?), over time came to be rewarded for the behavior. The loosey-goosey, happy-go-luckies were eaten by the cave bear and were the first to become the hapless examples in a Sunday morning sermon.

Eventually, *"propitiate the hidden agent"* became the watchword, the word to the wise. It had survival value—about fifty percent of the time. Earlier, this psychological term was defined—a variable reinforcement ratio—as the random rewarding of a desired behavior. These random rewards would seem to result from beseeching the hidden power for some desired thing. Prayers are seemingly answered randomly. The occasional win—or seemingly answered prayer—keeps you in the game.

Such a powerful hidden agent as the nature god would be paid homage in a superstitious way. Magic is the action the hidden agent takes in the world so "magic" action would be the way to communicate with that spirit. Those methods that seemed to work would become ritualized and repeated just so each time. The "answered" prayers or rituals would seem like a reward. While a neural reward for ritual and other behavior would feel like a reward for the related beliefs about the hidden spirit or deity.

For these ancients, as for believers today, these little neurochemical perks could get them over the rough spots, the dips and downs of doubt. Serotonin, dopamine, buoy the spirit, and make you more positive. Inspiration must surely build based upon some interplay of the mind with these neurochemicals of the spirit. With their help, the believer is able to leap neural junctions or synapses that he had heretofore not even imagined. Each level of reward would feed the next until some level of spiritual experience has been obtained. And that is the nature of belief and the secret of its evolution as meme or more.

Evolutionary theology

Consider how a cultural adaptation like religion must have originally begun. Our ancestors must have been driven to more than distraction by awe and even angst—rivaled only by their fear—of the calamitous world they found themselves in.

How daunting the realization that they'd been thrust into a highly inhospitable environment, a bizarre world, dangerous to be afoot in, and yet, they had all the acutely pressing human needs—and that they had to brave this new world in all circumstance and all kinds of weather—especially if you consider an ice age, supervolcanic eruptions, and meteor strikes extreme "weather." It was something of a nightmare for the ill-equipped humans who may have recently become *aware that they were aware*, so much so that they tried to do something about their wholly unsatisfactory interface with the world.

Perhaps, around that time, our ancestors got decoupled thought and that allowed imagination. That and their other brain modules and some well perceived data (with poorly inferred causes) from the world around us started chugging around in those glimmering brains. Immense forces were being wielded in the natural world, but there was no understanding of what was driving them, or should we say *who*?

Well, probably we shouldn't have said *who*, but we did (see hyperactive hidden agent detection device). Our ancestors took to improving that interface with the world. Guided by superstition, they tried lots of things. Some of those things were rewarded by false positives—something happened, randomly, after a bit of magic or ritual that seemed to confirm their belief. God only knows everything they tried. Perhaps killing chickens to study their intestines to see what that would portend about the future, manipulating the animals of the hunt by depicting them in cave art and holding ceremonies over them, looking for signs in the sky and the weather to tell them what to do.

Over the eons, the trials and errors would be endless. Nothing was too extreme for prehistoric humanity to try in order to gain influence over the forces shaping their world. Sacrificing virgins or goats, shaking out a sack of special bones, dancing beyond exhaustion to reach a trance state, fasting until they'd hallucinate, hallucinating via magic mushrooms.

Strength, among other things, in numbers

The social and communal aspect of religion should not be given short shrift. Nicholas Wade in the faith instinct shows the strength of marching in unison, for instance, and the generation of true esprit de corps that such training necessarily generates. The powerful effect of being part of a group that acts as a single whole has to be experienced to be believed.

Similarly, the peer pressure to conform to group beliefs about the radical and basic sacred truths of the community would be immense. If you're in the Stone Age, there is only one truth, one history. There are no alternative theories or science. No other theology. One and only one truth.

What about us nonbelievers? How did we get here? The occurrence of a few negative statistical outliers in the form of a few nonreligious folks isn't an invalidation of the hypothesis, only a factor to understand. It may be a normal distribution of varying degrees of religiosity and any genes that underlie them. It could be a mutation or gene variant. Is there a believer gene that only a percentage of the population has—and the rest of us have let them scare, bully, and cajole us into suffering their overbearing assertiveness as they dominate the culture and shame those into silence who might voice a degree of difference?

The family tree of religion

Today's surviving primitive peoples are cited as an example of how hunter-gatherer religions may have functioned. There's an assumption made here, and supported by the modern taboo on ethnocentrism, that all cultures (and with them their religions) are just as valid a way of life as western civilization and that we shouldn't look down on the primitives and their way of life. Granted. Moreover, I don't for a moment take the position that modern western culture, with its love of war, colonialism, and aggressive diplomacy, strong to overbearing religions, compulsive economic activity and mandatory growth are superior. Far from it.

As I said before, it's an open question whether what we see today in the few remaining primitive cultures is the same proto-religion or pre-religion that gave rise to the strong religions present in the world today. This may be analogous to pointing to the stringing of beads by the earliest humans and stating that it led to industrialization. (Then, again, maybe they both did.) Since these living primitives, now many millennia removed from the time hunter-gatherers were the majority, still raid the neighboring tribe and continue to make their bead or shell necklaces, maybe *that and only that* is what those sorts of things lead to.

The only thing we can be sure of when looking at primitive tribes is that their cultural aspects have brought them to where *they* are. We might agree that their proto-religion (if nothing more than Boyer's RTB's: religious thoughts and behavior) might not have led to the existing religions of today. That simply may mean we might need to look for a religion model and a path of evolution that would.

Is such a family tree of religion so unlikely? Or might we expect that if we could turn back the clock on the evolution of religion that we'd find simpler and simpler examples of religion until we arrived at nothing more than religious thoughts and behavior? (I'm not accusing

Boyer of saying this couldn't happen.) Alternatively, the present day primitives (rapidly disappearing), seem stuck in time. Their isolation that protected them from influences of outside cultures, kept them from all sorts of cultural exchanges that an ethnocentrist might have called advancement. Anything in the religio-spiritual sector of their culture would have been equally rudimentary. Moreover, their isolation may have barred a more complete inheritance of the religious adaptation that interbreeding cultures may have enjoyed, or alternatively the tribe initially had received a full compliment of the suite of gene/epi-genes in question, but in isolation the aspects of religion (attributable to genes) that didn't prove to be an advantageous adaption in that environment would drift away. Perhaps only vestigial components of such religions would linger on as dead ends.

Perhaps Boyer's criticism that religion isn't universal due to the primitives who have only RTB's may be overlooking another possibility. If these primitive peoples who don't have full-blown religions neither have the full compliment of the genes of religious inheritance, it is hardly a disproof of the thesis that religiosity is heritable. It, in fact, may be a proof that religiosity is inherited by a certain robust gene compliment while RTB's may have little or no genetic support.

In whatever way that religion was passed down to us, it is certain that the cultures that gave birth to civilization had somewhat more complex religious urges and faculties to pass on. Like all the other highly nuanced aspects of human life and culture, it's no less likely that the evolution of religion and the life cycle of a religion are the product of a complex interplay of culture with psychological, sociological, and anthropological forces.

Survival of the fittest meme

The idea of religion as a meme takes on new significance if the religious urge and predisposition, as described herein, are considered. If humanity knew it had these in place it might have gone looking for the meme.

Religion tells man it is above question and he believes it! By survival of the fittest, stronger and stronger memes have each supplanted weaker ones—and the grip on humankind grows ever stronger for it.

In the above observations, throughout this book, and everywhere in human life, it seems that there are clues to what gives religion its staying power. In today's post-modern world, humanity still searches for spiritual fulfillment. It seems prior to or perhaps coeval with the Axial Age of religion (several of the major religions began between 1500 and 2500 years ago), the search for the stronger god, or the one true religion was ever present, but was especially keen in this period.

The extant religions may not fully satisfy, but like the ubiquitous McDonald's, there's one on every corner. Your local culture tells you *this* religion is true while none of the others are. Yes, some believers may say, *There are many paths to God*, but they pity those other folks who haven't quite got it right. Not all; there are more enlightened people, more enlightened faiths and faith communities.

Neurotheology: Your brain on God?

Some efforts in neurotheology are more scientific than others and in that more scientific portion of neurotheology, under SPECT scans, the areas of the brain "on belief" light up with activity via a radioactive tracer. And they light up similarly for the believer in prayer and the practitioner in meditation—for the Carmelite nun and the Buddhist alike—with some individual differences.

Here's another one of those clues. Andrew Newberg, a researcher in neurotheology, said that believers and atheists alike thanked him for his work. It confirmed their beliefs. AND it confirmed the beliefs of both groups even though those beliefs were polar opposites. That's our confirmation bias acting out. Steven Pinker is right, we're no blank slates. We inherit the human brain with all sorts of pre-wiring, as they say, for language and much more (a baby's clinging response and urge to suckle are two).

[The term instinct when applied to human behavior was out of favor for many years. Freud called many human behaviors "instinctual" and he may have been right, but as he has fallen into well deserved disfavor, much of what he'd said is looked on with doubt. Then E. O. Wilson's book and new field of science, *Sociobiology,* was an insightful breakthrough that was trounced unnecessarily for sociopolitical reasons. A perhaps similar thread can be picked up today with the work of Steven Pinker in the renamed field of evolutionary psychology.

Then come the neurochemicals, those little perks that mean so much, preprogrammed by our genes, a part of our NON-blank slates. They drive brain functions quite powerfully. Dopamine, the so-called love drug, comes into play in a number of our peak experiences. (I wonder if a little dopamine release into the brain might not, itself, support further release of dopamine or the other neurochemicals under the right circumstances. And, mightn't those right circumstances be solely determined by our brains—those hardwired, predetermined, instinctual, neural structures with billions of ready to be wired synaptic connections with enough neural plasticity to facilitate amazing cognitive dexterity.

It suggests itself that we could compare, let's say, a "religious mind" with a "nonreligious" mind, but we might not be able to find any that are fully free of the benefit of evolving toward religion as all our minds have (except for the primitives?). Even if there is a difference between believers' brains and nonbelievers', today's nonbeliever may have carried along many aspects of the earlier believer's brain. It might take going back a hundred thousand years to find a mind free of all such influences.

There may be other reasons for being nonbelievers. Enough negative experiences with religion may do it. It could have been a certain coincidence or perhaps other random events. Or maybe there is a difference in a few of our genes. Could nonbelief be a recessive trait? Unlikely. What if most of us nonbelievers are "missing" some mutation that caught on during our human ancestry's early days of flirting with religion, some thing that made them more spiritual? Are we lacking or deficient because we don't have that particular mutation? Or are we superior because we weren't born addicted to religion?

Well, as I've said, I think I have some spiritual feelings or sensibilities. You'll note that my definition of religion hinges on the mind/body's spiritual reactions and feelings. As there is no spiritual realm or supernatural beings, those who are having experiences of such things are being manipulated by our evolutionary adaptation that has pulled together a number of psychological mechanisms, perhaps various schemes of neural programming, a few different brain states, some neurochemical releases, and who knows what else.

This matrix or complex gives the "prepared" mind experiences that many call spiritual or religious. As stated repeatedly, this includes experiences of the lowest spiritual sense, perhaps, a warm and fuzzy feeling when we (well, they) think of Jesus or go to church. Or for me, and perhaps, for you, we feel something for the goodwill of humankind, and more for the aspirations of humanity and perhaps more yet for ennobling the human spirit.

Better living through neurochemistry

Epinephrine, serotonin, oxytocin, dopamine and other specialized neurochemicals affect mood, thought, belief, optimism, love and more. With the benefit of inside and outside influences, our brains more or less automatically determine what's appropriate at the moment. Some of that determination, is hardwired, some learned, some we've chosen or programmed our own minds with, more or less consciously.

Those "Eureka" moments are brought home to us by the neurochemical soup we steep our brains in—as are our moments when we are swept away by love. So too is the pleasure of the sexual orgasm. Likewise, are our false-positive confirmation biases. So also are our religious experiences from that subliminal nudge that says *this is right* to that ecstatically joyous rapture of the near-god experience.

How "high" can that rapturous joy of the divine kind go before it crosses a line? A line into . . . what? Schizophrenia? Temporal lobe epilepsy? Well, you do the neurophysiology. I'm not going to say it's madness of the clinical variety even if the mystical experience and some special case of pathology are identical (I'm not saying there are any that are). The former is an atypical, temporary peak, something of an overstimulation, if you will. The latter, well, we haven't really defined it, but generically I would say, even if it, too, has peaks, that it probably carries other symptoms that are diagnostic of neuropathology.

This is purely speculative, but the upshot may be that the ecstatic peak may push the "god delusion" into the realm we call mental illness, ever so briefly, yet not be mental illness. I'll suggest that this perhaps, highly stimulated mental peak known as a spiritual experience may bring together, may in fact, tie together, neural circuitry that would be pathology if it weren't for the fact that these brain regions and chemical releases were pulled together for and by this specific function, for this experience. In short, if it functions, if it developed as an adaptation, it's a benefit, not pathology (and, yes, perhaps it could be both).

As a further illustration, perhaps you've heard of the Jewish gentleman who when he saw a vision of St. Thomas fairly well knew it was his temporal lobe epilepsy—he was Jewish after all. But a divinity student, let's say, who sees St. Thomas after a series of sweeping peaks of rising spiritual epiphanies probably isn't pathological.

All the foregoing gave me a non-hallucinatory epiphany—here <u>was</u> the missing puzzle piece! Here was the reason religion was universal! We *evolved* a propensity for spirituality (religiosity). Nothing short of this had sufficient explanatory power to explain why people can seem zombie-like in belief. Internally their brains reward them with neurochemical perks, like it does everyone of us, for certain behaviors, certain thoughts, though some believers seem to achieve levels the rest of us can only imagine—or maybe can't quite imagine.

If you add to that our ability to retrain our brains to make specific responses to specific thoughts or events, our brains could produce significant religious experiences and perhaps experiences of other kinds. Mystical experiences (meaning the highest or pinnacle experiences in contrast to the lowest level religious experience)? Assuming religious practitioners of that type are honest, hasn't that already happened? (Remember, I'm not saying they've contacted any spiritual realm or spiritual beings, only that they've had the neurophysical correlates that make them think they are having a mystical experience.)

Could a person be trained, and then be certain, to have a peak spiritual experience? Does it take a certain mental makeup? Curiously, the question that seems most relevant is this: Could a person who knows that the goal she seeks is made of neurochemicals, certain genetic predispositions, training, and practice, under those circumstances could she still achieve that religious or mystical experience?

Would the average religious person still want the seeming transcendence of the ultimate mystical experience if she knew it might not be from "on high?" I would vote that I would still want it. I doubt that most believers would, though, due to the artificiality of it. Richard Dawkins had hoped he might have some sort of experience when he donned Persinger's God helmet.

It might be interesting to know how those who participate in the Navaho peyote ceremony feel about using that strong assist in reaching the divine. From what I understand, they accept it as part of the path to understanding.

What if there was a chance that a religious/mystical experience might change you, change your mind literally into a "believing machine?" Michael Shirmer says that's what we already have in his book *Why People Believe Weird Things*. This raises the interesting question, Is there out there such an experience that it would make a believer out of *you*?

Symbols of transcendence

Daniel Dennett said in *Breaking the Spell, Religion as a Natural Phenomenon* in 2006, ". . . lacking language, animal brains have not had a way of inundating themselves with an explosion of combinations not found in the natural environment." (I take it that he meant that humanity does have symbolic representations to a sufficient extent that we can overwhelm ourselves with them to culminate in a transcendental experience.)

By and large that's probably right and Dennett may also consider chimpanzees, bonobos and maybe the other great apes as exceptions to the rule. If not, I'd like to draw his attention to them. (Not that they are having any religious experiences.)

To illustrate, consider Roger Fouts who has Washoe the chimp who was the first to learn to sign. Fouts' story includes telling that Washoe taught other chimps she lived with (limited) sign language. Fouts goes on to explain that he has hours of video tape showing these chimps engaged in signing conversations in the absence of any humans even a cameraman as the camera was a stationary fixture, the clincher being that when the chimps are angered or agitated with one another *they continue to sign.*

Obviously they have internalized the symbols of language and that suggests at the very least a mental image or some other mental symbol over which multiple minds can have common agreement.

I wouldn't rule out and would suggest that where chimps have heard and learned associated words, they may "hear" those words in their minds and see an image. (See elsewhere, the discussion that the existing apes may come right up to, but not cross over, the borderline of the human niche, e.g., they can't create language, but they can be given it. Once the line is crossed, the apes would be in direct competition with humans—and would lose.)

Kanzi, a bonobo, now at the Great Ape Conservation Center at Des Moines, Iowa, was taught symbols at a specialized keyboard. The first lessons accidently took hold when Sue Savage Rumbaugh tried to teach the symbols to Kanzi's mother and she wasn't interested. Kanzi had learned just from onlooking and has been learning symbols and the meaning of spoken words ever since. As a mature adult, he understands and uses over 300 keyboard symbols for those words at present.

VIII. RELIGIOUS MAN WON OUT

Perhaps, the old fundamental texts of the religions that call for killing the apostate are a vestigial holdover from early man, perhaps even the great apes, natural selection codified into dogma, yet represented as the inspired Word exhorting us to follow the extermination of the genes of, say, the third standard deviation to the left—the nonbeliever. The tribe's that did this would enrich the believer genes in the gene pool. But before we extrapolate, let's consider the milieu.

Drop in on an earlier human tribe for a week of dancing to achieve the trance state (See: The Faith Instinct, Nicholas Wade), with feasting and libation, perhaps ritual hallucinogens and you may find yourself in a culture vibrant with religion. No, they aren't going door to door extolling the religious life, they're living it.

Excitement during the times of religious fervor described above added a zest to life. Calling it a carnival atmosphere would be a gross understatement. Possibly, this level of activity and excitement got teased out simply from trial and error, action and reward, the tribespeople (reportedly mostly men) dabbled with rhythmic music, drums especially, and typically hours of repetitive dance that seemed to put them in trance (Some dispute whether this is possible—whether a trance state really exists. If it's real, I see its place as one in a continuum of religious experiences, i.e., a number of possible brain states, neurochemicals, and wired neural pathways).

On the face of it, this seems to be a little bit of a cheat, reaching a religious experience by teasing it out of a purposely stressed mind and body with behavior known to produce the intended state. This has obvious parallels with the Navaho peyote ceremony where the drug forces a transcendental experience of sorts upon the mind. Fasting in the desert or in a cave was the method of choice for Old Testament

Hebrews to commune with the divine. Passive as the activity is, it would seem fairly easy to set up. All you'd have to do would be to run out of food while grazing the herd, sit or lie down, and wait.

No, evolution didn't give us communion, it probably came closer to giving us Zulu drums. We may have had drumming and ritual dance for tens of thousands of years. Perhaps that's why music is "in your soul." It seems likely that a cultural activity with a performance goal, if pursued on an evolutionary time scale would be "rewarded" with adaptations in the direction of the cultural activity (cultural adaptation.)

What cultural activity? Ritual practice, drumming, dancing, trance as a communication with the divine, the spirit world. At the very least, it is a message from the supplicant: *If you're there God . . . , I hope you're there . . . , I'm assuming you're there . . . , I need you to be there. Of course you're there. Here, I offer something of value in a sacrificial offering to you. I am your dutiful, attentive servant acknowledging your presence."*

Ritual and all forms of communication with the spiritual realm are the practice that affirms that the attention of the supernatural being or object of worship is on the believer or practitioner. The activity isn't one where you let the number ring three times and hang up if there's no answer. The practice or ritual proceeds without interruption and doesn't look for a confirmative response from the deity or spirit world. (Of course, there'd be none.) It assumes it and goes right on.

Where we find drug-inspired religious experiences or other ritualistic practices, these didn't form over night. Primitive people had to be receiving some benefit (or psychological reward) for pursuing the activity and perhaps they were slowly "trained" in this direction by benefits and rewards. It's true that they may have been fooling themselves in this respect. They may have perceived a reward where none existed: after the rain dance to the gods, it rained, and therefore they felt a reward. They've made an invalid inference that the rain dance was the indirect cause of the rain.

Was this a replay of how the neurochemical rewards for religion first evolved? Maybe. Natural selection tends to reward action and, as above, those who acted and felt rewarded for it would not only tend to act in similar fashion in similar situations, they may have "learned" the (false) efficacy of their actions. Along with that, they learned the fallacy of thought about the rain dance, above.

In some respects, all of the foregoing discussion shows the value humans place on the religious experience. It is worth having at the price of using these methods of reaching it. I would suggest that this valuing of religious experiences is some evidence, again, that we both have a need for it and we enjoy various levels of achievement in it.

Many suggest that music and dance originated for worship. Music still seems to be associated with it; dance, too, in numerous cultures, but you'll remember that pews were reportedly put in the churches to discourage the dancing that may have been a hold over from earlier folk religions.

For the sake of argument, let's say the path for the evolution of religion as an adaptation could have employed some existing mental "templates" and wouldn't have to have included reinventing all of the neural wiring, or say, the neurochemicals that were already in place to reward us, for example, for sex, our food choices, or some lofty accomplishment. The process could have, and probably did, coop various different existing systems of psychological mechanisms, neural pathways and, regional brain activity. This may have been the time when a few genetic components supporting the reward for religious behavior were combined, linked, or perhaps even a looser association that may have been tightened up slightly over time as selection refined the adaptation.

The new genetic prescription, rather than being a rewrite of already existing psychological mechanisms—attachment (such as to mother), dopamine for that ebullient feeling, extra activity in some areas of the brain to create the sense of a felt presence and lessened activity in other brain regions for that feeling of oneness with everything—might be a neural nexus, a wired path of neurons that uniquely connects portions of the above brain functions or other devices to support our seemingly voluntary spiritual pursuits.

As stated before, there could have been numerous facets of individual religiosity that might have be selected for and that we might have thought at first was group selection (selection at the level of the group—so the argument goes, there's no such thing as group genes, so there can be no natural selection at group level).

This may be an unfair judgment of all group level selection. Consider barbarian warfare. The attackers kill the men, often the boys, rape the women and abduct the young women and girls and so the entire population is disbursed. There is a genetic result. Shaped by selection? At what level? Only the individual? Or do wholesale changes in the group's population that target the whole group or specific factions constitute selection at the group level?

What about more random deletions of members from the breeding population if they still have significant effects on the future of the group? David Sloan Wilson in *Darwin's Cathedral* says we should think of the group as a larger organism. Perhaps, then we should consider the entire gene pool as the genes of that larger organism.

Whether we think of organisms or organizations, are strong social units possible if there is no group selection? It seems to me that the detractors of group selection, need to explain how strong groups could form.

It certainly seems that a mass extinction event could cause selection at the level of the group—be that group the clan, the gene pool, or the culture. A population bottleneck or even severe times could have winnowed away all but the strongest communities with the most superior survival skills. Even being in the wrong place when a meteorite strike or a super volcano erupts might arbitrarily spare or wipe out a related set of genes.

As a result of that 50,000 ybp diaspora out of Africa, you Cro-Magnon types moved in on the Neanderthal's territory. We don't know the details, but in the kindest possible scenario, Cro-Magnons, or behaviorally modern humans, may have assimilated them. There's a little of them that lives on gene-wise in us, but they're long gone as a culture, a population and a gene pool. There was an individual story behind every Neanderthal's ancestry and descendants; were all these individuals naturally deselected or was it at the level of the group?

The same fate as the Neanderthals has almost come to fruition for the Native Americans. They were "unnaturally deselected" at the hands of the US government, many died, though a few were assimilated, some live on remnants of reservation lands. Was this extended genocide a group level selection? Their treatment as inferior people, instances of enslavement, and loss of their homeland seems reminiscent of the Biblical Hebrews. Perhaps a son of *their* god will inspire us to a new religion.

In a very different time and place, Genghis Kahn forced sex on a whole host of captured women from his plundering campaigns. Estimates place his fecundity at 10,000 offspring. Gene researchers have found something like ten percent of the present population in the affected areas to be his descendents. This is similar to the exclusive breeding rights that the alpha males of some primate species command. The effect on these respective gene pools is underlined for us by Kahn's "survival strategy."

The alpha males in the primate species that have that sort of social structure may be the only males contributing genes to the gene pool. Consider that effect generation after generation. When such males control the mating habits it is their behavioral traits (and mental and physical characteristics) that lead to such matings that are rewarded with successful reproduction (placing their genes in the next generation). In chimps this has made aggression, power, and control supreme. Where sexual selection by females is the norm, other factors that appeal to their psychology, as shaped by their genetically dictated criteria, reigns supreme above all else.

The religious thread

It has been recently reported that evangelism is attracting more people than any other form of religion in the U.S. (Recent Pew polls, however, show evangelicals' numbers to be stable.) Atheists think they are growing, too. Europe has wholesale numbers leaving the Christian religion altogether. Is that the future path for the U.S.? The vocal religious here say no. Some of them scoff at humanism for thinking it could replace religion. Still, the number of "nones," those of no religious affiliation, are growing.

The Middle Way: the Road More Travelled

People seem to naturally want a taste of transcendence—normal life with just enough added flavor that they don't feel that unfulfilled spiritual want. They don't want to snort ebene with the medicine man, but just to smell the coffee and feel God's hand on their shoulder or see a glimpse of the oneness of all being. Modern life, though, seems to be skimming too near the bottom. Most people now nearly shun the seriously religious—the person more religious than the preacher (or more correctly, more *spiritual* than the preacher. More religious than the preacher might mean even more dogmatic, but not spiritual). Perfunctory ritual, nominal faith, it's enough for some, but for many, it doesn't seem quite enough.

The *crisis of faith* that the postmodern world has been experiencing must in part be due to the loss of energy many in the Christian faith seem to have been feeling. Modern times have certainly abraded Christianity's surface if not cut it more deeply. It has lost followers in Europe and America. Too, Christianity is aging and in some quarters is in obvious decline. That evangelicals (and Pentecostals) are holding their own, if not growing, speaks to the loss of energy in broader Christianity as well as to the thesis here. While the run of the mill Christian is feeling insufficiently rewarded for her faith practice, the evangelicals and Pentecostals are putting in and getting back greater psychical and spiritual rewards.

I would suggest that evangelicals have approached their religious practice in a way in which they expect more and invest more and therefore receive more—more neurochemical rewards and perhaps a greater sense of wellbeing or other psychological benefits from all aspects of their religion, e.g., their groups are social and gregarious as well as interactive and supportive of the pursuit of a religious life.

One of the most challenging questions that can be put to nonbelievers is, *Why are we spiritual if this is only a secular world*? That will be taken up in the Spiritual Atheist section, but in a larger sense it can be said that this entire book deals with this question.

God of the Greater Ape

From religion modeled on the alpha male primate hierarchy many inspirations can be drawn, as well as much metaphysics, justice, and human rights.

There are other strengths, survival strategies, and adaptations at work in the human line. Perhaps the lineages of man had to have the whole checklist of attributes to survive, to people the world: the most advanced of each of these: language, religion, technology/industry, warfare, politics, as well as great social and economic skills. No (or few) communities would have existed in a void. Though there could have existed trade and cooperation with neighboring villages, competition would have been the bedrock undergirding all.

To the point that not all religions focus on a god, consider that early human troupe, say, post-australopithecine (post ape-like creatures = earliest members of the genus *Homo*) but pre-Cro-Magnon (pre-behaviorally modern = anatomically modern humans). We have on the one hand, at the oldest, most apish end of human ancestry, the alpha male and the primate troupe structure, the "hardwiring" of our human reality, a positional hierarchy of social organization (see below), the law of the troupe. We have on the other hand, the criteria for the alpha male, and an internal paradigm of our social reality—if that becomes symbolized by our near ancestors, is it the source of our other reality, our supernatural realm, and the religion of the greater ape? It may certainly bear a relationship to it. More likely for the great apes, though, it may serve as a basis for their crude sense of justice however rudimentary that may be. For humans, it could be both as well as the foundation for our world view or cosmology.

I'm saying that the human lineage, as the great apes before us, has long had a fuzzy mental image, inherited, like any other instinct, that confirms the hierarchical form of their social structure with the alpha male (or female in matriarchal troupes) at the head. [Is this, their social hierarchy, at the same time, their political hierarchy? (The organizational chart—and more—could be inspired by the same subconscious paradigm. The glass ceiling women found in corporate structures most certainly was/is that way because it was a patriarchal chart with an alpha male at the top.)

The specific social hierarchy consists of each individual in his or her status or power position. The orthomorphic (true to form) structure is the general organizational chart of these positions—or however the troupe members see them, internalize them, and pass them on genetically—the posts of alpha male, their lieutenants, consorts, kin, mate—whatever the position might be.]

Generic structure of Human/Chimp troupes

Alpha male

Primary supporters/lieutenants/dauphins/sycophants

Potential aids / Potential rivals

High ranking females

Young potential rivals

Other special rankings

Rank & File Members

Juveniles/ Charges-in-care

Hangers on/Near outcasts

—

The crude outline above is only a suggestion of how a primate socio-political structure might be envisioned. Some aspects of it may be more chimpanzee than human or vice versa. Commonality was sought rather than specificity.

It's not this general paradigm or template that I'm referring to as the religion of the troupe, but rather the (human) troupe's projection of it into the realm of the hidden (supernatural) agency perhaps as the forerunner of religion or Religious Thoughts and Behavior (Boyer's RTB's). The individuals do use decoupled cognition [as explained by Andy Thomson, *Why We Believe in God(s)* and others] to consider their troupe structure with its implications when projected outward— into the unknown—the hidden reality that underlies all and what that greater reality means and what that greater reality informs us about what our reality means. This may be one source of the impetus for philosophy (and political and social theory?) that seems to spring organically from within us.

What about the hunter-gatherer bands that have a trickster god, or a lackadaisical god or a minimally effective god? Are those the more common gods of hunter-gatherers? People can invent or imagine any kind of god or other reality they can dream up—and dream them up, they will. After all, there have been cargo cults in the islands and Heaven's Gate in California.

Somehow, though, modern humans, at least in historic times (See the Axial Age) have sorted religions to find the ones they think offer them the greatest benefits for becoming followers. Is it more power for the follower, a more powerful god, or a more powerful religion? Is it the greatest sense of spirituality? That may vary. Autonomous sociopolitical groups (self-governing like a tribe, village, city or country) have gravitated toward religions that do have some power and that typically proceed from a god or spiritual realm that is perceived to have power.

When the religion has some strength for whatever reason and can be successfully aligned with the powers that be, again, tribe, village, city, or country, each seems to be reinforcing of the other. God & Country, remember? Those who use the phrase treat it as if the parts are inseparable. Something of the two merges within many human minds. An alloy is formed that is stronger than either of the constituents. Not all patriots think there's a conflation here, but all the religious who do, seem to be Christian. See George H. W. Bush, elsewhere.

The alpha male hierarchy as represented by the orthomorphic chart, repeated above may be the source of the unitary allegiance to God & Country. The allegiance is inseparable in the minds of those believers, because the hierarchy represented by the orthomorphic chart is a unit. God & Country are iterations of Alpha male and tribe. The allegiance is to the unit as a whole.

It would seem that not all religions have this religious conflation of God & Country, nor did Christianity always have it. Again, it seems likely to be something that "bubbles up" from the sociopolitical boilerplate that is the alphamalism hierarchy or chart. Perhaps a certain mutuality between national identity and religion has to take hold before the mysterious synergy of God & Country arises. Or perhaps, there are roadblocks between God on the one hand, and Country on the other that keep that deep mutuality from taking hold.

Give me (the benefits of) that Old Time Religion

There couldn't be a much "older time religion" than what the early hunter-gatherers and perhaps Neanderthals had. Somehow I doubt that today's fundamentalist believer who aspires to the religion of old would want it quite that old.

Homo "religiosus" enjoyed his stronger group cohesion, heightened sense of purpose, and greater responsiveness to each other that ever more compelling religions would bring thus giving his troupe/community an advantage—a survival advantage—that bestowed on every individual a survival advantage to the extent that she was able to maximize her membership benefits.

Would this have been prior to the diaspora out of Africa? The recent spread—estimated at fifty thousand years ago—that powered the modern human population to cover the globe? Or is the ubiquitous nature of religion, proof that it was integral to that spread? Could it have powered, even empowered, the spread?

Let's delve deeper into this. Say that early man found himself gifted with a curious, inquiring intellect—but more—a conscious self-awareness. Chimpanzees have that, too, a conscious self-awareness, all the great apes do—signaled by their self-recognition when furnished with a mirror. (They may not be aware that they are aware. That's a quality of mind that proves elusive to us at times.)

Man when he first took off was minimally, incrementally above the chimp. He could ask the question, *Why?* Or at least he could wonder. What did he know? He had more questions—more fears—than anything else (fears can be questions that can hurt you if you don't get the correct answer). He had his tribe and his tribe had him. He knew his group, clan, community and he knew its hierarchical structure.

Man is the hominid that has a need to define who "I" is. Budding self-consciousness could have been the spark that ignited this need. We may have been *the first animal who was aware that he was aware* . . . An evolution of religion could have been triggered by the incipient knowledge of the self.

For man, as generalist, cooperation became his great strength. After culture and the intellect to handle it, cooperation was supported by his sociopolitical unit—the troupe or clan hierarchy. Things that served to strengthen the group added to its survival. Groups or communities with religious practices had many of these: shared ideas, beliefs, sense of group identity and by extension the individual has an enhanced identity as a group member.

Perhaps, our hardwiring for religion is simply a variation on the hardwired organizational chart of the human/ape troupe and maybe it inspired or generated a godhead or spiritual realm in the minds of men. We must allow that there would certainly be some variants of the theme.

Whether a god is imagined or not isn't of much consequence to the troupe. It's the religion's benefits to both the individual and the community that the whole process is about. It is the adaptation, almost a tool, for creating a cultural reality that is most meaningful to the troupe.

That cultural reality tells the troupe who they are, where they come from, it points to their purpose, puts in place their values and (purportedly) it frames their morality. Further still, this cultural reality is an adaptation that allows the troupe and the individual to handle the larger reality of a difficult world and tame its harshness to a degree.

Through their belongingness and mutuality they raise their value to each other (It's hard to turn your back on the people who value you the most highly. This is akin to your most important and valuable family relationship.). They are not just believers, not just members of the same group, they are sharing their most basic spiritual experiences, co-travelers on the most meaningful journey they can have. (A local church expresses this in a statement they display as a tagline with the name of the church, "It's all about the journey.")

This doesn't hint at the depth at which these believers can bond. The believers are vulnerable and exposed to the radical depth that only religio-spiritual interaction can reach. Their mutual faith is a shelter for them and all this vulnerable sharing can forge a strong bond between believers. It is often the choice of believers to testify to their belief, first to each other, then to the world. Evangelical missions have sprung from this sort of spiritual practice.

Their religion and the cultural reality they create with it are a buffer against that outer world—it is their way to become outfitted for their journey. It is their *cultural reality adaptation*—an informed, responsive, viable worldview, but more than that. It informs and infuses their aggrandized worldview with the reality they want to live in, if not their best of all possible worlds, rather their best interpretation of that possible world merged with the world they find themselves in. So to defend that faith is to support their whole cultural reality, their enhanced worldview. They can make that worldview a way to cope; when that is threatened, they don't cope too well.

To attack that faith is to threaten to leave the followers without an adaptation or an understanding of reality, to leave them with only a greatly diminished worldview or perhaps none at all. This isn't easily done of course. This particular cultural adaptation, religion, has such a hold on humankind that we have evolved to conform to it, to extol its virtues, to defend it. That isn't as rare or as preposterous as it might seem, though. We have evolved to accommodate our spoken transmission of culture, our language, too.

If someone could threaten to take away our language and culture we would probably have quite a reaction to that. Not possible? Consider the schools that Native American children were uprooted and sent to that forced them to give up their language, culture, and heritage.

The "software" that is our culture does adapt and evolve though our religions don't acknowledge it because they seldom want to evolve. For some religions (most?), it is their claim to having it *right* upon which their reputation rests. That is, the religious leaders would prefer that their statements of belief aren't flagrantly contrary to readily known facts. Both the current pope in Rome and the Dalai Lama have acknowledged the need to conform to reality, at least, when it is apparent that they have it wrong. More of a departure it would seem for the Christian tradition than for Tibetan Buddhism.

Still, religions don't want to admit that they could evolve, though evolve they do and evolve they must or they will be left behind, deleted, a recipient of the Darwin Award.

Speaking of language

What was termed Cro-magnon man has been generally subsumed under the title behaviorally modern humans. They became differentiated from an earlier population which only looked like us, anatomically modern humans, about 100,000 ybp. The diaspora of the ancestral human population—some place it as far back as 75,000 ybp, say that it was spread over that time period from 75,000 to 50,000 ybp. In addition to that timeframe, nascent religion and the other major cultural adaptations, e.g., the mind grappling with symbols, probably had to have time to "percolate." (The DrD4 mutation allowing much more dopamine to be released—making poets, prophets, and painters out of us—remember, is dated at about 30K to 45K ybp. Note the reminder, below, about the time period when language began.)

Let's go back further. For the sake of argument, let's say anatomically modern humans perked for 100,000 years. The general estimate places them in the time slot from 200,000 ybp to 100,000 ybp when behaviorally modern humans came on the scene. (Quibbling with this designation, if BMH didn't have speech until the 45,000 ybp estimate, it doesn't seem like they could be behaviorally modern until then. Although, some anthropologists date language to be older than 45K ybp and as much as 75K ybp (rare estimates top 100K ybp).

It seems likely that if 45K ybp is when the FoxP2 physical adaptation in the larynx [a mutation in the hyoid bone] came along, we were certainly doing some near-language noises by then—the ability to communicate prior to language would certainly have been rewarded by selection, probably multilevel. (See David Sloan Wilson's *Darwin's Cathedral*.) I would guess that the selective pressure on any improvements in language would have been immense.

Washoe the signing chimp as well as at least one individual from each of the other great ape species have learned the ability to manipulate symbols. As it was said earlier, Washoe showed this ability to manipulate sign language into an original arrangement when she asked for watermelon by the combination "water fruit" in the absence of a symbol known to her for watermelon. If the great apes bump up against the niche of man, but short of crossing into it, then at their best they could use symbols, while creating symbols would be rare and creating a language beyond their ken. How much less adept at symbol manipulation could anatomically modern humans have been than today's great apes?

If apes today can be given symbols and can manipulate symbols and we diverged from them about 7 million years ago, then there were at least 6.5 million years give or take a couple hundred millennia for us (the human lineage) to create and manipulate our first symbols (although, there is no evidence that apes 7 million ybp could manipulate symbols like the apes today—today's apes are also the product of 7 million years of evolution since they diverged from our line. It's a somewhat disconcerting thought as to how and why today's great apes can sign. Were they nearer to us once, then repelled back to their present niche?). At 50K ybp (and probably before) we could create the symbols of language. Humans surely must have felt significant need to express their thoughts and a burning frustration when they could not.

The need and desire to express a thought probably pre-dated true speech and language by quite a bit. Any improvement, even the shaping of guttural noises to make the communication better would be refined to the furthest reach of the individual's (limited) vocal equipment. An outstretched hand and an imploring, "Uh-Uh" might rate a begrudged ration of food, but a, "My but you're looking handsome today. Might I get just a taste of that leg of Wooly Mammoth?" could earn a fat reward.

Perhaps, language and symbolic thought grew organically together. There may have been individual *Eureka!* moments, but thought, symbols, language and speech may have evolved gradually in the beginning, though any significant level of improvement would have been rewarded swiftly in the cases of cultural and sexual selection while somewhat less swiftly with natural selection.

Things in nature could suggest a symbol; fingers above the head could become a signal during the hunt that herbivore prey with antlers was grazing ahead. Natural noises could be imitated—both to lure or to describe an animal. During the hunt for large, dangerous animals (mega-fauna) split second coordination could mean the difference between feast or famine or death. The desire to communicate between individuals would have been paramount and certainly must have found expression no matter how crude.

Certainly, efforts to direct another's attention would have resulted in some success. Pointing at something in the distance could focus another's attention where it's needed. Hand gestures and grunts would have followed naturally.

Symbols could have evolved out of tool use as well. In a crude sense, a tool is a symbol for its function.

Tool use

Apes like to manipulate things with their hands. As they played with rocks, twigs, perhaps even mud or clay they might eventually realize the shapes they were dealing with could be used to accomplish something. For example, chimps stick a twig into a termite mound and pull it back out loaded with a termite snack. In lab experiments, apes, monkeys and lower animals can solve problems to get a reward. In the wild, chimps use rocks to crack nuts. Even intelligent birds have used one object in lab experiments to get another object.

Prior to behaviorally modern man, Homo habilis, the tool maker, was making stone hammers and other stone tools which became more refined over (evolutionary) time. It's been noted however by archeologists that one of these early tool makers used the same type of stone hammer for over a million years, so one tool does not a Renaissance man make.

Artistic expression, too, could have come out of the manipulation of things found in the environment. Naturally, shells and other things roiling in the surf along a beach would catch an eye. Such a thing collected that had a hole in it might be laced on a rawhide necklace. The artistic arrangement of found objects would suggest other art forms, other things. Symbols can stream from art and from the artistic mind in the flow of creation.

A number of significant salient events occurred in more recent times in the ancestral human population. Consider the possible juxtaposing of the language-enabled vocal equipment with a mind to refining that in a continual feedback loop of communication with other minds. Add to that the higher calling, the inspiration-coaxing release of the transcendental *medication* of dopamine.

Humanity's final ascent enabled

Fox P2 gene mutated	enabled	Modern speech
Vocal expression of language	stimulates	Complex symbolic thought
DrD4 gene mutated	enabled	Dopamine release—upswing of moods, positive feelings, flights of fancy

Upswinging moods and symbolic thought (verging on decoupled thought) may have helped turn religious thoughts and behavior toward hidden agents into something like the common low grade religious experience believers have everyday. That experience, besides being boosted by DRD4 dopamine, is a false-positive confirmation of that hidden agent as well (a believer bias that exasperates nonbelievers today).

Religion being universal, with the exception of a few primitive cultures that have Religious Thoughts (or thoughts of witchcraft or superstitious thoughts) or Behavior, supports the thesis that religion was carried by the diaspora out of Africa ~50K ybp. Genomic research, it appears, will be needed to explain the connection between "true" religions and Religious Thoughts and Behavior.

Culture and narrative

As our ancestors shifted toward modern behavior, their nascent symbolic thought, decoupled cognition, stone technology and various crafts gave birth to a culture that strove to encompass their lives and understand their world.

Among other things, the culture would have developed, even if unstated, a narrative which would set the tribe in its rightful place in the world and tie the individual into his tribe and to the religion. (God & Country are of this sort—somehow a complex whole of religion, narrative, and group. Perhaps this was something only the ancestral mind of that time could behold). Myths tell stories that illuminate the nature of their reality, a rather karmic reality in which heroes perform morally exemplary acts. Lesser mortals fail in their behavior and receive their comeuppance.

In the field of fiction, they say we must maintain the willing suspension of our disbelief in order to enjoy the narrative. Our tribal narrative evolved to tell, if not what our story was, what our story should have been. Our suspension of disbelief had to continue ad infinitum for the accumulating sacred stories in such a way that we no longer acknowledged it. These tales are where we learned to suspend our disbelief. As the myths were sorted into the sacred and the profane, we learned to revere the sacred. We treated it as special knowledge—a greater truth that transcends this world. When we introduce someone to it, when we have chosen them to share in our deepest truths, we speak of this sacred knowledge in reverent hushed tones.

What besides religion could make men bond so deeply to a myth?

Something pretty amazing seems to have driven Christianity in its early years. On the one hand, it's surprising it didn't end with Jesus' death (before Christianity ever began). Yet it ensnared the Greeks, the Roman Empire, and ultimately western civilization.

It doesn't seem sufficient to attribute it to the four stories of the apostle's (or even the other nineteen versions of the life of Jesus considered by Constantine at the Nicean Council) or the Old Testament. Perhaps, Paul (and certainly Constantine) was a hell of a salesman. At a minimum, it was largely their efforts that gave Christianity its impetus to conquer the western world.

Evolutionarily, we men and women, unlike our ape brethren, can obtain the freedom to choose an alpha male (or alpha person). It is the quest for legitimate authority in our lives. Unlike our ape relatives, we seek a narrative—or a narrative enables us to accept an authority— perhaps this is the *why* of fiction and drama's successes in our world. Not that they allow rule to be imposed upon us, though they might, but that they are metaphors for our myth and through that channel they allow us to see the actions of an everyman and the implications of our morality and justice play out.

We are always looking out for something that will inform, but hopefully not invalidate our mythic narrative, perhaps this looking is a species-specific behavior trait. Too always be looking, testing new myths, is a competitive advantage that is of survival value. This might superficially be the attraction of a good story to us. When the heroine achieves justice we test the moral of the story with our own value system—and society. A certain resonance internal to our minds or hearts confirms some level of truth for us. This explains how a fictional story can be said to be important for us.

255

This isn't to say that we would throw over our sacred myths for the next one to come along. Probably we hope we won't find a superior religion (maybe that wish became genetically codified in us by selection *and* religion; I would think the typical believer wouldn't be open to finding a "superior" religion, maybe curious, though). We will certainly defend the one we have . . . as if our lives depended on it.

Religion, the pinnacle of man's evolutionary adaptations?

"There is grandeur in this view of life . . ." Charles Darwin

Evolution outdid itself with the human race. It gave humanity the capacity to select the path of its own evolution. Eons ago the tiny, scurrying primates were the beneficiaries of the reptilian demise; the passing of the dinosaurs left a void. Naturally, predation eased up on the diminutive arboreal primates.

This allowed for the evolution of larger primates, then the apes. With their strong social units they became invincible to the few predators who dared challenge them. And their social units were not only a powerful defense but also a formidable offense. The precursors of man had the strongest social units, the presages of culture, intellect, and language, as well as the will and aggression to prevail.

Whenever and wherever there are enough humans to differentiate *us* from *them*, there will be competition. That competition may have been keener a couple hundred thousand years ago. Given approximately equivalent human physiology, culture was the venue of that competition, or more correctly it was culture versus culture. Cultural advances were the stock in trade. Think the wheel, the bow, clothing, etc. Next add strategy, deception, and symbolic thought.

Advances in culture were dramatic—and devastating to the tribes on the losing end of these original culture wars. Even more dramatic was the human mind driving the cultural advances. With increasing complexity and the handling of symbolic thought, a human mind was on the scene that had serious questions. *Who are we and why don't we know?* It's probable that the question became ever more serious as the nascent minds arose that were concerned with asking.

We are the Clan of the Cave Bear may have been a sufficient answer at one time. At least, until another culture came along with a better answer. *We are the chosen people of Yahweh and he will smite our enemies.* I've jumped ahead of our story a little bit to demonstrate the contrast. Let's back up to see what might have happened between these two extremes.

Sometime in the last 200,000 years religion became a method of dealing with the big imponderables that cluster around the mystery of existence. Elsewhere in this book and in many other books, writers have imagined for us some first religion springing up out of fear of the Prime Mover, the *mana* behind nature.

Medicine men, shamans, holy men stepped forward to help out as go-betweens. Somewhere along the line, the Great Unknown got connected with all the baggage of being and its points of transcendence. Birth and death got pulled together to fall under the same metaphysical job description.

As religions evolved, there was friction between two schools of thought: One, from the grass roots, that says the individual can commune directly with the divine, and Two, from the mushrooming dynasty of religious professionals that say, *No you can't. It takes one of us who are tuned in to the Big Kahuna's wavelength to do it for you. Who are you to think you're up to dealing with God?* (SBNR, spiritual but not religious—those believers who reject mainstream religions. Strangely enough the seemingly oxymoronic category called spiritual atheists might belong in those numbers, but I wonder if any believers would think so. See the later sections on those topics.)

As a result of the challenge by the religious professionals, the individual upon introspection may have felt him—or herself to be inadequate to talk to the gods. Besides, in her face is this guy who claims to have a hot line directly to the creator of the universe . . . so, maybe he does.

When one considers that evolution is the more successful reproduction of the better adapted, it seems more likely that the individual pursuit in quest of the supernatural would lead, over at least tens of thousands of years, to something heritable rather than the passive role of being ministered to by someone else. In other words, religion as a reality in a cultural environment would be exerting an influence on human selection. That's one more reason why I believe it did.

As noted before, chant, dance and trance as a cultural behavior may have arisen in order to reach the "other world" and garner its favor.

The important thing to keep in mind is this: it isn't necessary to reach a spiritual plane; it is only necessary that one has the "experience" of contacting that realm (That is, think it and feel it).

That's the validation end of religious behavior. Now segue to prayer. Built into the Judeo-Christian tradition, and possibly common to all attempts at getting favors from the supernatural, is a form of operant conditioning also at work in gambling houses and known to Skinnerian psychologists as a variable reinforcement ratio. To wit, God answers some prayers, but not others. As alluded to earlier, it's the most difficult psychological training and reward schedule to extinguish. "Sometimes you win; sometimes you lose." Once the gambler is used to that, losing is expected as part of the experience and it's built into our expectancy for God's seemingly random interventions—the random event that a believer construes as God's answer to a prayer, it's the occasional "hit" that keeps us interested or strings us along . . . and so the house ultimately wins!

The measure of success. What's the improved rate of reproductive success of the religious participant? The survival strategies are encoded or implied in holy scripture and range from *The holier thou art, the more likely thou art to find a bride* (social introduction to potential mates, "He's one of us."), to *Be fruitful and multiply*. The latter are the two easiest survival strategies to achieve: 1. Reproduce and 2. Reproduce a lot. This exhortation is embedded in several world religions and therefore extends into governmental policies—note how the religious bans against contraception translate into governments not promoting it.

Sheer numbers of followers are one form of success: Darwinian. Where growing populations are not equivalent to mass suicide or self-genocide, producing more offspring is a strong survival strategy. Right to Life positions reject abortion and can come down against contraception also. All of these factors tend to increase the believer population and that is a success at the expense of those who don't know there is a competition with and among religions.

At the evolutionary end, as alluded to, these several rewards effect the population like a mini-selection at work, sort of on the micro-scale. Many are criticized because they seem to suggest group selection over individual selection—it is after all the individual that carries the genes. In short, the argument is, *How can the nonexistent genes of a group be selected?*

Right. Everything would have to result in an effect on the individual's genes. Perhaps the one area of agreement would be when a group is devastated in battle or even weakened and absorbed into another population, those genes are largely deleted at least as an intact gene pool.

But, you might say, that's the survival value of religion versus no religion. If religion is universal, that's not how it is. True, but even in the competition of religion versus religion the relative strength of each is tested. Religion can be universal in every culture, but that doesn't make it unanimous to the last person in today's society. We nonbelievers are proof that there is at least a statistical slice of the population here that are not religious and more disaffected numbers in Europe where their percentage of the population is much higher.

This is simply my take on it, but when one hears about all the religions formed in the Axial Age, it seems like there must have been a great void of religions. Perhaps a reluctant enlightenment took place as populations rejected the unbelievable gods of classical antiquity. One gets the sense that people had cast about for some connection to the supernatural that was satisfying. The Abrahamic monotheisms were one result . . . well, all right, three.

Even then religion is only one aspect of a culture which has other components that can make it more or less competitive. When the religion is strong it can give an entirely new structure to the culture going to the very root of the culture, revitalizing and recasting the entire social reality such as a "Christian nation."

Religions and governments both at different times have enjoyed sticking their iron hand into the silk glove of the other to achieve their ends. Religions have from time to time enjoyed usurping governmental and political power to make their morals and dogma the law of the land while governments like to borrow the legitimacy and moral rectitude that religions seem to enjoy.

Political forces too can influence the spread of religion by championing one religion over another, but even then the strength of the religion can add or detract from the political will and military might—and the sense that military aggression can be on the side of right, the side God is on. This is probably why the U.S. military had long pushed its troops toward worship.

Try looking back to the early days of anatomically modern humans, again, roughly 200,000 ybp. (Not conceding, though, that the fates of modern governments and civilizations are beyond the above influences, it's simply that this helps us to visualize a simpler social unit for our thought experiments.) The consensus is that tribes, troupes, or clans above 150 members would tend to break up and form new groups. In the short run, certain alliances and kinships might be retained, of course, c.f., certain Native American Indian nations were able to pull together when necessary.

They were somewhat different than the hunter-gatherers who were offered to us as an example of the egalitarian society in which every person is autonomous and there is no hierarchy and no alpha male. The Native Americans had chiefs (the alpha male primate structure I allude to throughout, though tribal councils and other houses of government aren't on the charts) while the typical hunter-gatherer band is said to have been egalitarian or without higher status individuals or leaders. Most or all Native Americans may have dabbled with agriculture, but most also gathered and hunted or fished as they could. So this isn't a pure test of whether a socio-political hierarchy (alphamalism) can exist in a hunter-gatherer economy.

It is curious how that might be, when you consider the fact that the social primates lower on the evolutionary path but up to humans as well as most human units since the hunter-gatherers seem to have political and social hierarchies and something like an alpha male at the head. As stated earlier, it may have been that in a society where you only own what you can carry, everyone's status may have been equal.

There are existing primitives who appear to function with equanimity as the rule (though they appear to be mostly or totally settled societies, not hunter-gatherers). Modern political states and protected borders as well as the lure of modern economies have pretty well ended the hunter-gatherer lifestyle. While that economy existed, perhaps it provided a level of cooperation that bestowed benefits on small populations . . . or maybe it was an evolutionary dead end.

I think it's wise to consider both structures as possibilities. Especially since it is somewhere in the literature that the hunter-gatherers were thought to be exposed to the risk of strongman rule when such individuals were able to enforce it. This might illuminate the nature of the alpha males' rule in chimp societies—the alphas are not always seen so much as legitimate, as a tolerated reality or circumstance.

Over the eons, though, old ties would be lost especially in the low literacy, low technology and low to no transportation realities of early hunter-gatherers, so small units of autonomous populations such as these would dot the landscape.

Each would, even if amiably, compete against all others—for food from the hunt, the woods, the stream and the meadow. There would be territorial real estate disputes, especially given that their hunter-gatherer past could have been largely nomadic and that they might naturally range for food, for prized territories near streams, flint outcroppings, or the most defensible habitations.

I'm suggesting that the small societies were experiments in group competition. Strengths that added to competition and survival were the sort of thing that differentiated one group from another. It seems likely that the individual lived his life immersed in the reality of the mundane gods that seemed to represent every force which was beyond his control. His world and his deity's were seamlessly enmeshed not disparate like modern Christianity, say. The archaic religion would have been about everything that presented itself in the hunter-gatherer's world.

Picture the individuals toward the end of a weeklong celebration of the fertility god that would climax in an eight hour dance to rhythmic drums. Chants, rhythm, ceaselessly repetitious dance, perhaps aided by a hallucinogenic drug, and you too might see God.

Over time, some techniques, some gods, would fall into disfavor. A stronger, more efficacious god would be sought. A stronger god might require more serious worship entailing more significant costs (see various writers' articles about freeloaders in faith communities) of membership.

These and other various "strong faith" aspects would arise as cultural variations first. In the long run, though, evolution can't help but reward the survivors however they got that way. That reward (of successful reproduction) not only supports their entire genetic makeup—it all survives as an entity—but it rewards their behavior if it can be preserved or recreated by their genes.

Group selection

A more selfish gene

Religion, it is purported, cannot be in our genes as it could only come to be there through selection at the group level. At the risk of redundancy, this is cited as the reason that religion can't be an adaptation—because it would be necessary for selection to take place at the level of the group and groups don't have genes.

They do have members, though, that are full of genes—selfish genes. The most selfish genes—those that could multiply their success times the number of members in a group and defeat another competing gene times the members in its group—would seem to be likely to have much more reproductive success. Yet a number of scenarios show that what might appear to be group selection may actually be selection at the individual level.

To put something of a face on both the individual and the group, let's pick a young man who belongs to a denomination of evangelical Christians. Let's use the young man who was quoted elsewhere as having said he wanted his neighbor's life to be better because a Christian was in it. (The scenario from here on is fictional, but not unlikely.)

He became a committed believer as a teenager. He reports he felt the spirit of Christ moving him, he felt a swelling, overwhelming joy that he took as the sign that he was *saved*, and he now describes himself as a born-again Christian. His church is congregational, meaning they are an autonomous group who answers to no higher level of power or organization (save Jesus Christ).

The young man's church is a supportive social network, a community of like-minded believers of similar faith. Simply belonging to a supportive social group has psychological and health benefits. Then there's the benefit of each other actively caring for the members, checking on the elderly, the sick, and simply having a heightened sense of concern for each other.

There's a "value added" aspect to belonging to a faith community, especially one where God values you. "God doesn't make no junk." "We are all precious in his sight." These concepts are supported by the belief that God somehow infuses each of us with an immortal soul. All this serves to make each member ultra relevant to each other and themselves. There is a not inconsiderable bond formed with those who value you the most.

In response to all this, our self esteem rises as does our respect for each other. Our young man will enjoy this boost to his own self image as well as appreciating those who value him more highly. (I would even go so far as to suggest that the pervasive social trust and general goodwill in the United States throughout much of the twentieth century may have been, at least in part, to the credit of Christianity as it was practiced here at the time. I think the same was often acknowledged as creating a platform of social, moral, and business exchanges. The failings to achieve this aspirational benchmark were legion, but it was generally accepted to be the level playing field everyone should be operating on.)

Among other benefits of membership in a congregation is the social introduction to all other members. That makes every member eligible for all kinds of benefits. Help in lean times, support in times of personal crisis, and mutual care in times of catastrophe. As cited before—be fruitful and multiply—Introductions of the young men and women of the church will take place at some point in the activities of the church.

A long standing imperative in religious traditions is the aspiration of having a pure society consisting only of members of their own faith, so becoming a greater slice of the demographic pie is a move in the right direction and a competition with other religions is an unacknowledged goal. This may have roots in the early religions of the ancestral human populations.

Paramount among the benefits that accrue from a religion is a heightened esprit de corps. Perhaps to such an extent that only a trained and disciplined cadre could match. That would have survival value for the individual and the group. The objection to this is that it would be selection at both the individual and group level. Church members may participate in wide ranging activities. This participation and working beside other members builds a camaraderie that one has to experience to appreciate. This creates strong bonds between our young man and a wide range of other members. (Their high esprit de corps is why the US military establishment is struggling internally, as cited above, over wanting to continue their support of religion-versus-none because it is such a tremendous alignment tool instilling God & Country allegiance as it does. [Note that God always has top billing in that identity/loyalty statement.)

In an alternative scenario, let's consider a small community whose members are not all members of the local religion similar to how members of our society are not all Christians. The individuals of the "in" group enjoy the benefits, longer life, better health, a greater sense of well being, finding a spouse who is philosophically (religiously) in sync with them, and on and on.

The individuals who become members of the local religion are more likely to survive to reproduce and have more successful reproduction. That slowly increases the percentage of the tribe that's in the religion. Groups with the stronger religion may have come through tough times better than those of weak or no religion, but ultimately it is because it was able to bring through more individuals.

This may sound like an unfair example at first, but consider the likelihood of survival of a trained military company versus a random selection of the same number of people, say the people waiting to board a plane, all faced with a natural disaster. Your criticism might be directed at the unfairness of the choice given the preparedness of the military unit. A similar "unfairness" or advantage can be obtained by a religious community if its esprit de corps and other ideals of commonality and "love of the other for the love of God" are maximized.

There is a competition among religions even though some like the Shakers don't participate. Religions that don't add members lose members. It's in the care and feeding, how they recruit, and conserve, how they reproduce members. No, groups don't have genes, but they know someone who does.

Not just the group, but the individual as well in the archaic tribes could have benefited from that more supportive network (not your ladies' coffee klatch, granted, but it was the camaraderie of rhythm dancing with your tribe until numbness set in, or perhaps initiation rites so painful you'd weave in and out of consciousness, ancient handed-down wisdom with insights into the unfathomable).

Doubtless there were myriad and sundry ways to bond together in allegiance to the great gods and as fellows in a special troupe. Some of these bonds would see you through the pinch points of life, especially such things as the population bottlenecks brought on by climate change—those mile thick glaciers in front of your cave stretching as far as the eye could see. Or population bottlenecks—supervolcanic eruptions and volcano winter. What tribes were bound together enough for each person to lead another by hand through choking volcanic ash? To press on past the point where they'd have given up on their own lives to care for the other.

That care and mutuality mentioned above would have been present in the archaic hunter gatherer tribes. I think those who don't believe that belonging to a faith community gives one certain advantages underrate or don't fully understand the benefits that religion can offer (as opposed to what in reality the current ones do offer. That has dwindled further in present day Europe than in the US. Possibly the "religious genes" may be more present here—whatever genetic predisposition that sets us up to feel rewarded for spirituality, perhaps to form radically focused groups. More likely, European society may be in a different place with respect to the life cycle of its civilization or its religion. America is much younger than Europe. That allows more idealism, more investment in our myths.)

The arguably most important benefit of religion is that it meets, more or less, that need, that spiritual craving we have. It drives us toward spiritual fulfillment (yet very often leaves us unfulfilled, even frustrated with no clear way to be fulfilled. Writers are accused of writing as a form of psychological self-therapy. [See the spiritual section, please. No "woo-woo," just reality]).

I'll suggest crudely that this religio-spiritual drive is weaker than our sex drive, weaker than, say, a tobacco addiction, (obviously this would vary across the spectrum of, say, all church attendees, but I'm thinking of it spread or averaged over all typical believers) but stronger than bonds of friendship, or, say, a camaraderie with a favored coworker. I think believers might feel the spiritual urge to approximate the craving for chocolate, support for the local sport franchise, perhaps, the love of family. I have more than once heard a believer express their loyalty in this order, God, country, family . . .

In present day Christianity, the individual perks of being part of a religious community are many. In general, people care more about you and your wellbeing on all levels. The most welcoming communities bring too many social services to their members to readily list, in part, because church members are moved to reach out to other members in need outside of any official channels within their congregations. Once it becomes apparent that the members and church community as a whole value you highly, it's easy to cultivate a positive attitude and to swap positive affirmations with fellow believers. Surely, these enrichments add to life expectancy and fecundity. Some of these are also the perks of belonging to other social groups. The more such groups are devoted to mutual benefits the more they resemble religious communities. It would be difficult to believe, though, that there are voluntary social organizations that can bring as much to its members as the best of the religious communities regularly do.

Dance 'til you trance

Finally, consider this cultural adaption of hunter-gatherers of the African savannah about 80,000 ybp. These aboriginals have drumming and rhythmic dancing night after night during their religious observances in order to achieve a trance-like state in which they will be in the presence of the supernatural.

Over many centuries, people have experimented with all sorts of spiritual aids or boosters on a trial and error basis to commune with their nature spirits or deities. They may use hallucinogens gleaned from local plant sources. These help quicken the achievement of trance (or a drug induced trance-like state) which may also be facilitated through music and dance.

Eons pass, over this time those who participate in the religion and achieve a trance or other "satisfying" spiritual experience enjoy a slightly enriched genome equipping them with easier release of neurochemicals thereby creating pleasure and other experiences considered spiritually significant. If those that participate in the ceremonies are the "in" group; those that do not may be an "out" group or more likely, individual outcasts.

This unenviable position could entail few to no wives, less veneration, lower status, a person with whom others would be less emotionally invested at best, and possibly being outcast and shunned, and therefore, to whom fewer benefits would flow. These individuals are the most likely to have an early deletion of their genes from the gene pool.

If the group would continue to tolerate their presence within the group, there would be less camaraderie and mutual defense would suffer in the parent organization so long as they remain a part of it. Such might be the underlying cause why sacred texts say stone the bastards . . . well, the apostate or the infidel, anyway.

IX. You Say You Want An Evolution . . . ? Deeper In . . .

A number of writers and scientists think like Stephen J. Gould that religion is a spandrel, a gratuitous product of evolution that has no specific purpose but rather was a curious consequence of some other adaptation that did. If you're like me, that just doesn't do it for you. The explanatory power of the hypothesis that religion was an adaptation is too great.

When religion came along—however that took place—it may have been by a figurative extension of the primate social structure from the individual up through the social hierarchy to the alpha male and beyond into metaphorical, metaphysical heavenly beings. Or it may have been humanly devised and begun as origin and identity myths that, when put into the form that religion can take, was characterized by the primate "organizational" chart along with cosmic components and spiritual trappings, and, eventually for the believer, over evolutionary time, it led to the inbreeding of a spiritual need and a programmed release of neurochemicals rewarding spiritual achievement. Once this opportunistic ultra-meme locks into position over humankind's internalized social hierarchy structure (See chart), it becomes virtually impossible to dislodge.

Man with a Plan

Evolution isn't really a plan with a purpose. Separate that image, if you have one—of evolution with goals and a purpose—from your image of the living biosphere and cast it away. These living things, plants and animals, alive here and now, that's all there really is. That's all there ever really is.

Evolution isn't a presence in the world like, for instance, they say God is. It's just the name we've applied to what happens to living things over the eons in much the way archaic humans came to name those unknown forces that seemed to them to imply a purpose behind nature—once again, God.

Evolution isn't a force, it's just the name of a result. Life is the force; evolution is, over time, what happened to the survivors, and why they survived. The headline is *Evolution Can't Plan for the Future*. Evolution equipped the survivors with how to better deal with the past and hopefully the present, but that only incidentally equips them for the future, _if_ the future remains like the past.

Is humankind's future going to be like its past, is the biosphere's future going to be like its past? It seems fairly certain that that answer is *No*.

What's Driving Evolution?

It seems that the most important and most basic factor (after the existence of life itself) adapted by natural selection was the ability to evolve. It seems obvious that the propensity to mutate was selected for, and more basic still, that mutation, by any and all means, is an enabling, if not, a driving force. In other words, the fuel of the evolution machine, the rate of mutation, was the key. A super stable genetic structure would have been doomed.

Say the first living cell was based on something other than DNA and that it was a rock hard "powerhouse" that didn't and couldn't change. Suppose its distant relative, a puny little cell with DNA got knocked around by the environment and a single basepair of nucleotides was struck by radiation, a gamma ray, let's say, and that part of the molecule was changed.

From then on the hapless little cell mutates at the drop of a hat. After a few thousand generations, though, one of the little mutant offspring bumps into the big immutable cell. The big cell pays no attention, why should it? The puny little cell cuddles up to the big cell who has all this room inside. The puny cell sort of pokes inside, likes what it finds, and lets go of its DNA which replicates repeatedly until the strong, stoic cell bursts from the overload. All the new puny little cells go off in search of another of those big strong immutable cells.

Mutation as a characteristic of DNA was not only selected as a sort of propensity, a potentiality, it was self-selective. DNA, the amazing replicator, is also the perpetual experimenter. Any and all factors that affect gene variation are all part of a more robust class which subsumes mutation—all of which contribute to gene variability.

Can you see the genes and genetic variability of an organism as just the present summation of the viable dabblings of evolution? What didn't work (well enough) isn't around any more. The future will belong to the yet unknown, untested adaptation that tomorrow's genes will demonstrate in tomorrow's environment.

Life that would evolve, life that was prone to mutate and vary and evolve, was not only very much selected for, it was unabashedly self-nominating for selection. I don't know how we could prove that, but the rate of the occurrence of mutation may correlate with life at the higher end of the scale, or alternatively, a highly adapted or super successful species. Proving that would certainly be supporting evidence. But isn't all life and its evolutionary history evidence enough?

At some point back in the early history of life, if there were organisms that wouldn't evolve they must have found themselves uncompetitive—and soon to be extinct—like the puny cell's robust friend, above, might have been.

The answer to the question, what type of life evolves? is: that life with genes of the type we're most familiar with, the double helix of DNA. It is the life that has the capacity to mutate often (relatively speaking), but not so often as to seriously affect the viability of the species.

The Dark Side

As a lifelong captive student of the human animal, it's difficult to escape the many lessons that life among the natives can foist upon oneself. Among mankind's foibles is his "economic compulsion." Man in most quarters must always be engaged in economic activity; that is, he is driven to be productive all the time. Among modern man's traits which allow him to dominate the world, this one seems more benign than his aggressive militarism or extreme politics. The political and military realities of the world are such that nations must have politicians and armies to fight off the politicians and armies of the other nations.

It is this trait of economic compulsion, however, that drives mankind toward its most appalling manifest destiny: to fully consume the world. There is no limit to mankind's economic drive or unchecked population growth. Man has become steadily more efficient at getting all the "good" out of the environment, at wringing every cent of value out of every piece of land—and once wasted moving on. Humankind is writing its biography as we speak. The course of our actions, or perhaps our inactions, will determine whether life is an opportunistic infection upon the Earth or the greatest self-expression of the universe yet known.

The potential for humankind's future has shifted radically over time as has its prognosis.

In the early 1800's there were concerns about the predictions of Malthus that the human population could outgrow the food supply. In the twentieth century the stakes went up. It became apparent that civilization could destroy or decimate itself by following any of several paths: Global warming could melt the polar caps and flood low coastal areas or might, paradoxically, precipitate another ice age. Nuclear destruction still is possible. Ozone depletion could result in allowing dangerous radiation to reach the Earth's surface while environmental poisoning of all sorts including terrorist initiated events could lead to the destruction of the biosphere and eventually all life.

What year will it be when the growing water shortage comes home to all of us? The free market will be the alternative to rationing. Water, it will be said, isn't a right, so allowing free market distribution is the most fair way. (It's likely the poor still won't have much of a lobby in Congress or with the other governments of the world. Isn't it their own fault if they won't buy safe drinking water? Will Ann Coulter say, *Let them drink wine!*)

As the oceans die, will trash and sewage dumping become more acceptable? When the rain forests (called the lungs of the Earth) are gone, will carbon dioxide in the atmosphere begin to increase more rapidly in the atmosphere while oxygen production dwindles. Will oxygen or oxygen-enriched air become a viable product in the marketplace?

Other potential dooms include a reversal of Earth's magnetic field (No, it's not tied to the Mayan calendar; the calendar would have to span 750,000 years to be certain to catch a reversal. And, no, we're not going to float away even then. We're not magnetic nor do we contain enough iron to be attracted by magnetism; it's gravity that holds us down, remember? However, gamma and other radiation from the sun are not deflected during polar reversals and that will be serious enough. There is no effective shield against the sterilizing effect of gamma rays).

The polar reversal is due anytime, so is Yellowstone Park's supervolcano which also erupts roughly ever 750,000 years also. (Those two events make me speculate that we probably have some sort of extra iron "lobe" somewhere between the Earth's crust and its core that's moving somewhat independently of the tectonic or continental plates and the core. Could it be some part, or even the core, of that Mars-sized object—that hit the earth and caused our large moon to be formed—that may have penetrated the earth's crust and lodged there, perhaps, could it even be responsible for the Earth's wobble on its axis? Does it cancel the true core's magnetic field? Or cause it to spiral until a reversal is complete?)

There are other potential events higher up the scale: The solar system—asteroid impacts and asteroid winter. Galactic magnitude— Supernovae and unavoidable gamma radiation or a rogue black hole?

Cosmic magnitude—Some unimagined effect spreading wide through the multiverse—a singularity flirting with infinity in another universe—opening into ours?

Even in the absence of any of these scenarios, biodiversity will decline at an increasing rate (because it already is). When will it be only man, and his companion and domesticated animals (all three becoming very expensive to maintain) and of course, their hardiest parasites?

There have been "minor" human disasters before. Millions dying from the plague, starvation, malaria, or the Spanish flu. Will mankind hang on, proving to be a fat tick on the life blood of the Earth until it's gone? Or will we somehow finally take control?

Populations, overall, will continue to swell, more birth control will be needed, countervailing religions be damned. The current paths that would save the biosphere are already known—mankind just isn't willing to forego population growth or hard path economics and its high production and high consumption ways.

On a geological time scale mankind's recorded history is like the blink of an eye. During that brief time there have been no cataclysmic planetary or even biospheric events of significance. If you go back 10,000 to 20,000 years into the last ice age, though, that's significant and that's extremely recent in geological time. Did that last ice age separate the men from the throwbacks? There were earlier glaciations and interglacial periods, humanity just wasn't ready to blossom like this before. And yet, what population bottlenecks might those earlier glacial periods have produced and to what effect on our earlier ancestors?

No record beyond limited artifacts and cave drawings survives to tell us what living in that ice age was like. Perhaps of more pressing interest, though, is whether we are just in another interglacial period that might yet cycle into another ice age any time soon. It's difficult for humans to fully grasp all the workings of this planet, let alone, the interplay of planets, comets, asteroids and other unknown objects or events that will affect the solar system, the galaxy, or even the universe.

Evolutionary ascent to humanity

Like the creationists say, we modern human beings are no accident of evolution—three billion years of trial and error perhaps. Even with that lengthy opportunity, the earth hadn't evolved intelligent life in the western hemisphere, not even a great ape species. Had the Earth only had two western hemispheres, so to speak, there would be no great apes—or humans. Prior to that, the dinosaurs had a hundred and fifty million years and evolved no intelligence that we know of.

Somewhere in our more recent ascent we were slowly designed by an ever more critical eye—our own, or what would evolve into our own. Evolution got us to the chimp stage. There are no longer missing links (in the sense of intermediates between apes and men, a number of species have been found in the fossil record and more will be found, but the chain is more than sufficient to show humanity's connection to all life on Earth), but like any "cold case" the fossils can only yield so much. Various speculations as to what gave us a little boost are being debated.

Isn't it obvious that we—through sexual selection and other numerous cultural and social pressures that are brought to bear on one's ability, if not agility, to handle the assets of our culture—have exerted more intensive pressure, as well as a more selective pressure over the recent millennia and in much greater amounts with much finer judgments that have nuanced our genetic results? Congratulations! We went from ape to man in 7 million years. The dinosaurs didn't do it in 150 million years—that we know of. What was our secret? We couldn't have done it without us.

Consider the scrutiny of prospective brides and mothers-in-law over the last 75,000 years. Could there be a greater selective pressure brought to bear on man than that? Too fine of a point, perhaps, but let it serve to symbolize the nuanced nature of selective pressure that humanity and its culture could bring to bear on itself.

With respect to a supposed boost we got about 25,000 to 50,000 years ago that brought on language, civilization, and the blossoming of our culture, it's a scenario that can be likened to the last two centuries in light of the last 15,000 years of agriculture and industry. The accomplishments of the two most recent centuries aren't really due to something recent (yes, the efficient causes were recent). We should, rather, look at it in light of those 15,000 years of preparation.

Similarly, that seeming blossoming of our intelligence 25,000 to 50,000 years ago was, what, 100,000 years in the making? We worked our way to it. When you're sitting around your workshop and you get an idea, it's a little tough to do anything about it if all you have in your shop are rocks. That's especially true if you don't know that there could be something more than rocks (though by 50K ybp we most certainly had more—besides the stone tool kit, there would have been numerous bone, sinew, and wood or forest-related items as well as small art objects, craft items, pots and simple cooking utensils).

The apes today show us the boundary of humankind's niche, or more succinctly, the border between them and us. Apes can use symbols and some language, but they are short of creating it. In the past, if they crossed that line, the human line, they got pruned back to the ape side. Where we've left the surviving apes, there is a profile in sharp relief that shows the niche carved out by early man.

Our paltry culture on our early hominid side of that line was barely superior to that of the other chimps of the day. Chimps, today, exhibit some very limited tool making and tool use. That's where our ancestors began. A point in the debate, above, has been made that early man, Homo habilis used the same stone hammer (the same design, not the actual rock) for about a million years. This, some believe, indicates man wasn't progressing—but was in a state of equilibrium. (See Stephen J. Gould's thesis of punctuated equilibrium.)

When the only evidence is hard artifacts like stone and bone-turned-to-stone, the fine tuning of incremental advancement is difficult to discern. Again, when rocks are all you have in your workshop, it's difficult to advance much technologically (Granted they eventually advanced quite far in the art of crafting fine stone tools). Bear in mind we were at a smaller brain capacity at the start of that run (Homo habilis and contemporaries).

Were we free of natural selection? Hunting wooly mammoths, avoiding lions and mega-fauna? I think not. Surely pressure was on, as well, within social and cultural contexts. Even the ability to communicate with other hunters and especially with prospective mates would have survival value. Outsmarting game and rival clans—when scarce resources threatened—all these demands would have kept selective pressure keen for any incremental improvements.

Consider, though, how much overkill in the advancement of cognitive skills must be necessary to push a stone culture to the next higher level. If, say, 100,000 years ago, all you knew were the rocks in front of you and neither you nor anyone around you even knew there could be technological advancement, how long would it take you to start the Iron Age? There's a high threshold for that level of accomplishment. Incremental intellectual advancement could continue for hundreds of millennia before it could achieve a level that would force a significant difference (And yet cranial capacity wouldn't have grown if it didn't pay its way. It's been said to increase by a tablespoon every hundred thousand years).

Did *illogic* become an adaptation?

Our earliest attempts at logic were poor compared to any standard except the logic of the animal world. We default to what seems like logical fallacies in the realm of reason, but like our Hidden Agent Detection Device we default to the best action for the animal which means erring on the side of caution.

Take the early example of our domestication of the dog. If you're familiar with dogs, they are a living, breathing alarm system that "goes off" at the slightest provocation: any thump or bump, a foreign voice, an unusual sound and the dog reports it with an alarmed reaction as an energetic bark.

The typical dog owner today may wish for their pet to desensitize somewhat. As they are, though, such a hair triggered Hidden Agent Detection Devise would have largely warned of any approaching danger well before the dog's master would know of it and that undoubtedly helped our ancestors avoid harm. Humans would have selected for this behavior which early dogs and wolves before them no doubt exhibited on their own. It has been said that humans, also, were naturally selected for their affinity for, and use of, dogs.

How do humans exhibit their logic? Erring on the side of caution in this instance means assuming that a noise in the night is a *who* and that behind nature, reality, and the world is the supernatural. We err to God.

Is there another human fallacy that's equivalent to an animal psychological template or device? Yes, it's the *post hoc, ergo propter hoc* fallacy and it's basic to the formation of our superstitions: *after this, therefore, because of this*. There's an example in *The Faith Instinct*. One of the remaining primitive peoples in the world believe that watching dogs mate angers their god and that they may suffer his retribution for it. Obviously, someone had watched dogs mate and something occurred after that which they ultimately attributed to their deity as his punishment.

Is there an induction we treat like a deduction and therefore rush to fallacious judgment, though all the while that rushed judgment may have survival value? Yeah, all the time. The Hidden Agent Detection Device makes us, and our best friends, our dogs, "deduce" someone is there making that thing go bump in the night even when the correct assessment is that it's a low probability induction. It's not the dysfunction of false identification that's of interest (except that no matter how often we and our dogs get it wrong, the very next nocturnal knock has us jumping to the conclusion that someone is there again).

Natural selection coped with inductive probabilities by converting them to the deduction that a threatening agent was there in the dark because that was the reaction that had survival value, and that was the reaction that could be made heritable. In short, we inherited deduction; we have to learn induction.

Similar to erring on the side of caution like the HADD (in the example above of ourselves and our dogs), early humans with little or no language and limited thought processes may have erred on the side of superstitious thinking. It is common for primitive people to make logical fallacies in reasoning about the natural world. These errors are the logical foundation stones of superstitious thinking.

Superstitious thinking in the response to an event that occurs after a human act is to assume the human act caused the event. So, a propitiating act to counter that precipitating action, a ritual prescribed by the superstition, must be carried out just so, or it will be a waste and fail to gain any favor or have the desired effect. It is critical to the superstitious mind that the action is performed ritualistically the same way every time, such as throwing salt over the left shoulder.

Fear is an often suggested motivator that pushed, and maybe still pushes, people toward both superstition and religion. Fear didn't have to be invented; it came naturally in an overabundant supply. A lightening flash nearby and a deafening thunder clap—and early man could surely have been provoked to comment, "Now why is that ___ (early expletive deleted) in our world?"

For that matter, do many of the named logical fallacies, when they're committed, add to survival value? I think they do. Take for example, the *Ad hominem* fallacy. It is loosely the fallacy of attacking the argument or proposition by denigrating the person who advanced it. Crudely, this and other xenophobic reasoning would have survival value in the same way that assuming an entire class of actors would do the same bad act or have a similar negative characteristic as a single member of the class. (It is also the source of prejudice and racism.)

No, justice, egalitarianism, brotherhood, nor any virtue would come from the seemingly animalistic commission of logical fallacies in moral or pre-moral behavior—typically, they are diametrically opposed—but they would have survival value so they accreted at the direction of natural selection.

The Evolutionary End

The argument is often advanced, as stated above, that human evolution is over—that it more or less ended when civilization began, or when modern medicine made up for our frailties like correcting our vision with glasses or contact lenses. As we look back into *deep time*, it took life quite a while to bring us to this point, but the duration of human evolution is the blink of an eye compared to where *steep time* might take us.

The myriad of human social groupings do create a highly pressurized selective environment. Life seems to get more complex all the time. If nothing else changed in the world at all, humankind would continue to increase the complexity of society and social situations. Our competition in that high selectivity environment would keep the selective pressure on. Only the successful can survive to reproduce.

Consider the slow beginnings of human culture and what appears to be its exponentially increasing development in recorded history—a nanosecond in the evolutionary scale of time. Once human, the most salient form of natural selection at work on intelligence may be from within our social and cultural groups rather than from outside forces.

Once humankind had mind and culture it slowly boarded the freight train of focused if not self-directed evolution. Human culture and human thought started to have a feedback effect on evolution. With civilization, roughly equivalent with recorded history, humankind switched to a passenger train.

We are now on a high speed commuter train in that our selective pressure on ourselves is tremendous. As a society we may be misdirecting how we'd like that selective pressure applied. Are we sure that we want the most aggressive corporate executives selected, or the most ruthless sales people, or the most steroidal athlete, or the most drugged out rock star? From that platform of focused selection we now propose to step to the supersonic world of self-selected and self-directed evolution.

One of the premises of the argument that human evolution has ended is similar to one of the anti-welfare arguments (These are not my words). *Individual reproduction is the threshold test in evolution. Is reproduction reserved only for your successful candidates? Or aren't the less successful and the disenfranchised using sex, resulting in children, at the expense of society, as their consolation prize for not succeeding in the world? Aren't they out-reproducing your most intellectually advanced members two, three, or four to one?*

Even if that's true, the pressure and, therefore, the reward for increasing intelligence, or at least social facility, must be at work even in that environment. Social intelligence, which may be the source of much of our intelligence, is called for in any human environment. Further, that social intelligence may be the primary evolutionary pressure in its own environment.

In other words, the presence of social intelligence calls for ever increasing social intelligence in order to cope with the escalating complexity of the social milieu and all competing players in it. This serves to make the evolution of social intelligence a self-feeding upward spiral. (Though evolution is a complex of multi-level selection to the extent that trying to understand evolution from a single source of selection is like trying to understand the process of baking a cake by considering only a single ingredient.)

Our culture may seem static in the short run, but there are actors at work within it that create an environment requiring progressively increasing adroitness. Just my personal opinion, but I think this actually serves to create an environment of hyper-evolution at least with respect to the individual's ability to dexterously handle social and, in fact all, elements of our culture. Just ask your kids; your demonstration of yesterday's cultural acumen is spurned today as being "out of it."

Again, the ability to achieve increased reproductive success is the test of an adaptation. In the arena of social and cultural adroitness, sexual selection is certain to contribute, but it would be difficult to discern or differentiate from other forms of selection, if any are at work.

It was stated earlier that the original source of great ape, then human intelligence may have been the intelligence necessary for primate frugivores to remember which fruits and which trees would be ripe and when. That highly rewarding talent may have underwritten the first blossoming of what would become our intelligence. The mind that could cope with the complex matrix of fruiting flora might do the same for nuanced social situations, or the finesse of language, or the intricacies of culture. Maybe capacity for one allowed capacity for all. Consider the example of the computer; the capacity is there for more than one program. That's what's significant and that's what gives those sets of capacity their potential.

Our dexterous digits are also cited as a point of origin for intelligence. The reason intelligence is of such immense interest is that humanity in its modern, fully actualized form seems to have exploded on the scene in just the last 35,000 to 50,000 years. Human accomplishment has been staggering ever since. Was there a blossoming of intelligence then?

As alluded to before, in the absence of a body of knowledge, especially scientific, natural selection rewarded brains of ever increasing capacity—the only way to make a difference—in any or all of the possible endeavors that humans have faced. It took a long time for our culture and knowledge to catch up to our brain power, but in that void we filled our culture with what we could create from what we thought we had on hand—natural forces, animals, strange occurrences, fortuitous happenings—superstition emerged as a way to explain things and rituals were created to address them—superstitious responses or rituals suggested similar responses for the supernatural.

Religion made a progression from the supernatural into high value social relationships. As it evolved, religion continued to morph into forms delivering more and more value—at least the religions that survived, the ones that didn't disappeared. In newer forms, the body, the group of believers values the individual more and the believer values the body, as well as the other individuals, and him or herself more. The ultimate religion offers services, strengths, aid, solace, inspiration and more to the extent that it forms a virtual psychosocial vehicle insulating, protecting, and transporting the individual toward his or her desired destiny and makes the immediate environment resemble the best of all possible worlds—or at least that's the best of all possible religions.

Does cult behavior support the thesis that religion is in our genes?

So it seems. Certainly the cult leader does tie into the believers' emotions, but is there something else embedded more deeply? It seems the charismatic leaders reach deeper within the believer than the believer knows.

The cult leader may be reaching ecstatically-triggered mechanisms that appear programmed for it (along with likely psychological aspects). The leader doesn't need to know anything about any of these mechanisms to make them work. In fact, they may work better for him if he's committed to his beliefs or delusions rather than knowing how these believers are being manipulated by his actions.

Is this all due to the dominance of religion over the minds of men?

Do psychological mechanisms explain it all or does our hard-wired predisposition to religious/spiritual behavior explain it better? The psychological explanations always seem weak compared to the strength that cult leaders have over their people. Does it appeal to the rewards of our spiritual neurochemistry?

Does psychology explain it all or does our hard-wired predisposition to religious/spiritual behavior also influence cult behavior? Does our spiritual drive make us more susceptible? The psychological explanations always seem weak compared to the strength that cult leaders have over their people.

In an article on *The Psychology of the Cult Experience* in the New York Times published: March 15, 1982, Glenn Collins tells us:

"Dr. Clark is one of the founders of the Boston Personal Development Institute, a nonprofit group that treats former cult members and advises their families. He and his associates there have treated former members of the Unification Church, the International Society for Krishna Consciousness, Scientology, the Way International, the Divine Light Mission, the Children of God, the Church of Bible Understanding and smaller, less-prominent groups.

"Several of the researchers believe that the studies of cult members may revise current theories about the workings of the brain. Dr. Cath and Dr. Clark, working independently, have been intrigued that the experiences described by cult members resemble personality changes regularly associated with disorders of the temporal lobe of the brain.

"The symptoms of temporal lobe epilepsy," said Dr. Clark, "are similar to those seen or reported as resulting from cult conversions: increased irritability, loss of libido or altered sexual interest; ritualism, compulsive attention to detail, mystical states, humorlessness and sobriety, heightened paranoia."

"Dr. Cath said: 'Keeping devotees constantly fatigued, deprived of sensory input and suffering protein deprivation, working extremely long hours in street solicitation or in cult-owned businesses, engaging in monotonous chanting and rhythmical singing, may induce psychophysiological changes in the brain. The rhythmical movement of the body can lead to altered states of consciousness, and changes in the pressure or vibration pattern of the brain may affect the temporal lobe.'"

"Dr. Clark hypothesized that what he calls the 'cult-conversion syndrome' represents an overload of the brain's ability to process information. He said: 'The unending personalized attention given to recruits during the conversion experience works to overload the prospect's information-processing capacity. This has another important function: the induction of trancelike states. Cult proselytizers then exploit the recruit's suggestibility.'"

At first blush, there are some resonant concepts in the article, but perhaps nothing conclusive. Of interest, though, even if some of these psychological mechanisms cited by the researchers aren't solely in the domain of our predisposition to religiosity, they may simply come into play with respect to it. Maybe not even actively actuated by it, but co-opted in the loosest sense.

Consider the following quote, though, from the *American Psychological Association* (APA) and be ready for a slight zeitgeist shift.

Philip G Zimbardo, PhD wrote an article during 1990 for the *APA Monitor* titled: *"What messages are behind today's cults?"* He is professor of psychology at Stanford University and a former APA president. Some excerpts from his article are:

- *"Cult methods of recruiting, indoctrinating and influencing their members are not exotic forms of mind control, but only more intensely applied mundane tactics of social influence practiced daily by all compliance professionals and societal agents of influence."*
- *". . . cult leaders offer simple solutions to the increasingly complex world problems we all face daily. They offer the simple path to happiness, to success, to salvation by following their simple rules, simple group regimentation and simple total lifestyle. Ultimately, each new member contributes to the power of the leader by trading his or her freedom for the illusion of security and reflected glory that group membership holds out."*
- *"Cult mind control is not different in kind from these everyday varieties, but in its greater intensity, persistence, duration, and scope."*

Ronald Enroth wrote in 1994:

"The American Psychological Association, along with nearly two dozen individual scholars and behavioral scientists, filed an amicus [friend of the court] brief in 1987 in behalf of the Unification Church in the California Supreme Court . . . . The APA and its co-amici argued that there was little scientific support for 'brainwashing' theory. Both the National Council of Churches and the Christian Legal Society filed briefs in this same case."

This information seems to counter much of the psychological thought of the earlier day on the cult phenomena as represented by the first article above. Also, it seems that the allure of a cult may be that of a simpler, unambiguous life. That, too, is not so different from what many religions offer.

Once again, our evolution may have cobbled together a loose mishmash of psychological mechanism, functions, or what have you that more or less operates as our predisposition to religio-spirituality.

Or it may consist of a more highly interrelated socio-psychological set of templates. Selection doesn't care how it puts together an organism's functions. It is even more in the dark than a blind watchmaker. It is not a true process; it is only a result.

Solidarity

Consider behaviorally modern humans fifty to a hundred thousand years ago. There must have been evolutionary survival value for early human groups who were strengthened by the solidarity of religious belief. Certainly there would be greater ease in mounting defenses and offenses in groups with cohesive belief systems. An 'All for one and one for all' sense of unity, a kind of an esprit de corps that would be missing if, say, Tarzan believed in Christ, but Jane was a Hindu. They'd have to find some other commonality to bond over—if they could at all—with the divisiveness that those differences in religion *may* bring.

Pity the freethinking rationalist among our ancestors, one who would choose to question the veracity of his group's religion. First, the group might try out some unpleasant labels on him, consider him a candidate for exile, and watch him for other signs that might indicate he is a threat to the stability of the group.

That individual won't be having much fun either. It's not smart to attack one's group—that's how they'll see it—what would be gained, ostracism? At best, it's the path to distrust. The sensible path to the good things in life is to affirm the group religion. Doubt certainly must *not* have had survival value. Who'd pair up with an infidel? But are doubters just the statistical few in any population? Or are they the few honest seekers?

The researchers in pursuit of real science in neurotheology (some who lay claim to the field are accused of psychic pseudoscience) assume that nonbelievers are devoid of the spiritual faculty so they are at a zero on the scale with the truly spiritual having more and more of said faculty. But this scheme has them treating nonbelievers with the standards of the believers—who may not know anymore about these underpinnings of spirituality than the nonbelievers. Maybe the nonbelievers are believers of something else. We could give the researchers this, nonbelievers are not having spiritual experiences within the main stream religion of the culture.

Consider this, are the believers believers because they have had that validating experience that has told them there's a spiritual reality out there? The nonbelievers say that the believers' transcendent experience only shows that there is something *within them* and not something transcendent *"out there."*

As discussed earlier, nonbelievers may lack something that would reward them for spiritual experiences (maybe the religious activities also lack something and fail to bring the potential nonbeliever to a spiritually rewarding experience). If the nonbeliever would be rewarded by a more authentic secular spirituality—something ennobling the human spirit—then such nonbelievers may not lack such a faculty.

Still, there's that optimum religious experience looming out there that only seems to be possible for believers. Do we look at nonbelievers as simply part of a normal distribution of the population, say, two or three standard deviations to the left? As we've seen, such a judgment may aptly describe not only our relationship to faith, but our associated gene compliment as well as our relative number of active dopamine receptors.

If we nonbelievers are that seven percent or ten, twelve, or even sixteen percent of the population, we're not just a fluke or a freak occurrence, we are a legitimate minority. We may just be that segment of the population that keeps the remainder grounded. Without us, a population might have a runaway gene competition to breed ever holier-than-thou believers until they float away into fantasyland in something that might truly pass for a "god delusion." Genomic research should eventually point toward some answers or at least highly refine these questions.

Self-directed human evolution
as a nobler human motive

Humankind has more or less directed its own evolution for fifty to a hundred thousand years, perhaps millennia more. We didn't always know that, but we do, or we should, know it now. It wasn't by committee or planners of any sort. We unknowingly did it when we focused society as a force of evolution on our kind. We did it in exercising sexual selection—and so it was done to us. Our cultures marshal endless tests of our every conceivable ability and over evolutionary time, our skills, features, and characteristics have become nuanced to an incredible degree.

IF we now, with full intent and awakened awareness, purposefully focus the full force of our culture, knowledge, and technology, how great can we become as the product of our own design? We're fantastic beings now and we started out as apes (though they're pretty fantastic, too)! Almost every step on the path that led to us was a form, a mind and body, that we'd not want to trade places with. Yet every step of the way, those are the people whose choices made us what we are today.

We have and we will continue to remake humankind in our own imaginations.

Humankind has become the promise that in its dimmer past it could not have voiced, but only on the path to that assent has mankind seen the greater vision and been able to aspire to it. When enlightened man 'remembered' his evolution, he turned a corner and found his brethren, the other great apes. They helped him to reconnect to his true world, the Earth. (We're surprised at their savagery, but it is we who are driving them to extinction—and we are unwilling to change that course.)

An environment can coax evolution in any direction. If it would have been advantageous for people to become more religious, and that environment held steady for, say, 50,000 or 75,000 years or so, the possibility is great that selection refined a few genes in the direction that would have made the individual more successful in that environment. Nicholas Wade (*The Faith Instinct*) and, for what it's worth, I agree that religious behavior could be selected for, as do E.O Wilson and David Sloane Wilson. While Dawkins, Dennett, Boyer and, it seems, Steven Pinker, Sam Harris, Andy Thomson, and Barbara King disagree. (Apologies to anyone who's revised their position.)

The assertion that religion is not adaptive behavior is based on several arguments. For one, to the extent that religion is group behavior—and as has been redundantly stated several times, there are no genes of a group—there can be no group genes selected.

An adaptation is by definition what has been selected. If there is nothing to select, then no adaptation could be selected. For that argument to be valid for our purposes here requires not only that religion is not of value to its followers, but also that it never has been.

A successful gene, say it carries a proclivity toward religious behavior, will indeed affect the population of which it is a part. If it guides its individual owner to successful reproduction and its "brethren" genes in another individual does the same and this is repeated enough times until this population has greater reproductive success than another population, this may look like group selection, but it doesn't require the group to have genes of its own.

That's not to say groups don't compete. In the modern world, it's difficult to find groups that don't compete. Everywhere one finds a viable group, it more or less takes on a life of its own. In life, everything competes.

Evolution at the group level?

Religious behavior was a valuable adaptation at the group level, or as David Sloan Wilson reminds us, the selection is multileveled. But that doesn't mean selection on the individual level, even sexual selection, wasn't at work (remember: *The holier thou art, the more likely thou art to find a bride—and to be fruitful—and multiply*). Individuals probably fared better who were more social, who conformed to group behavior—something we've been practicing since before we were human, before we were even Homo.

If the most strongly knit groups, clans, tribes were the most likely to survive, and religion is very significant at binding together—what could bind a group more strongly than their beliefs about whom they were, where they came from, and what their destiny would be?

It's not that rather pedestrian litany you might get in response from the man on the corner: "I'm Joe Blow from Cleveland and I'm planning to retire." That's not the strength of binding at depth that takes place in religion. That's not the important identity or destiny we speak of in religion. Others who take only a cursory look at religion conclude there is nothing significant there. The beliefs themselves aren't of primary importance. What's important is that the believers have bound themselves *religiously* together over these beliefs.

The illusive strength of the religious bond and its importance to the individual (and group) can be gauged in this way: Religion "done right" can rival *family* as a value. The third term of allegiance in the triumvirate God & Country & family, is family. You must know how strong the family bond can be. Some families and their ties can supersede the strength of God & Country loyalty, but not all.

Commonality over who the believers' deity was and what their beliefs and group identity were just made them tighter. Challenged from the outside, xenophobia was group defense. Challenged from the inside, ostracism was group preservation—they'd push the offender out into the world to be treated as a stranger. Shunned.

Burning heretics at the stake in the Middle Ages seems like an action that might have purged the gene pool. Will we find that the 50,000+ doubters put to death by the Church were of a like genetic sequence? And that the ultra religious that came to America were of a different, but uniform genetic kind?

Somewhere back in our prehistory, an early human group garnered cherished rituals, sacred knowledge and revealed wisdom, and developed a tradition of handing down their religious thoughts and behavior—along with the genes that made them want it—genes that benefitted from it, by responding to the totality of a life imbued with religion.

At the corner of Religion Street

Consider a crossroads in the path of early humankind. One way led to a casual relationship with the divine—an acknowledgement that their trickster god was quite the curious fellow . . . The early people who went this way thought the deity was an interesting if peculiar spirit as evidenced by the strange events and occurrences he orchestrated in the world and the lives of his people.

Another path led the way for a people who attempted to supplicate their deity and even develop a significant relationship with her. On this path the people became followers, perhaps in some minds even junior partners, of a deity whom they worshiped and to whom they made themselves worthy. They became a people for whom this deity must surely care. Their community was bound together in the most radically deep ways. And it was the highest good for each to do the most they could for the other.

Let's bring these two groups back to the crossroads. As they face off, how will their futures unfold? Is there any doubt that those who know who they are in relation to the deeper reality, who see themselves positively engaged with a transcendent personality, the source of all being, and who have a destiny as a people because of these relationships with their goddess, with their community, and with themselves, is there any doubt that the members of this group have a beneficial adaptation?

The first group are the primitives of the present day who have only "religious thoughts and behavior" in the absence a full-blown religion. The second group has a religion that is optimally effective and evidently near its prime.

To the budding mind of early humankind, life, the world, and the greater reality beyond were mysterious and unfathomable. Cherished wisdom handed down must have been treasured. Such sacred knowledge wasn't expected to conform to the rules of the mundane world—a certain illogic in the mundane world might be revealed wisdom in that domain of illusive symbols and nuanced reality inaccessible to all but the true initiate—so there was an air of otherworldliness connected with the telling of that realm and the deities that came out of it to rule the world and the lives of men.

If, later on, Religious Thoughts and Behavior triggered the squirting of a little serotonin in the brain when they occurred, all the better. And, a little like the drunk who wants more and more to drink, wouldn't anyone like more of the *feel good* neurochemicals—serotonin, dopamine, oxytocin, epinephrine, and the endorphins? And, on the occasion of a rapturously inspired thought or full-blown religious experience, the chemical fireworks in the brain would feel like validation of the thought (a confirmation bias at work) and it might even feel like God was validating that very thought. (It's the neurochemical equivalent of the congregation saying "amen" to each thought the reverend expresses.)

Where those cultures with only religious thoughts and behaviors had to compete with other cultures that similarly only had RTB's, a small incremental edge could mean the advantage. When the carriers of enhanced RTB's, those with a little more enthusiasm for the religion and its community of believers, be it via neurochemicals, a psychological predisposition, or an as yet unknown influence, they have the advantage—until the next better advantaged religious culture comes along. And, if none do? Then RTB's might be all the unchallenged culture has or needs.

Put into place over those, say, 2500 generations of people with religion all forms of evolution, known and unknown, and the game is even more rigged in favor of the house . . . of worship.

It may be that man first (>50K ybp?) learned subconsciously how to release his neurochemicals with chant, dance, and trance. They made men feel especially enlivened—living large on the juice of the gods. (If you think about it, waiting for actual feedback from a deity in the supernatural realm might be a truly interminable test of a believer's patience. Yet, believers so want their religious worldview to be real, they desperately need some form of validation. I suspect that they struggled for it. They craved any crumb of a false positive for it. Each little increment of "receptivity" to the divine would be its own reward.)

They refined those cultural trappings, added rituals to enhance the effects; surely there was some aspect of neuroplasticity that aided the process at least within a lifespan, and slowly over eons, religion's power was ratcheted ever upward. Believers and belief found ways to achieve survival and thrive.

With all the predisposing factors in place today, might "we" all the more easily reach or be led on to the so-called peak experiences? A sanctioned "high," smiled upon by God? These questions lead to the bigger question, *Can the religious person climbing toward a peak simply work themselves up to visions, voice of God, or other singular events?*

Ann Taves in *Religious Experience Reconsidered,* says that many a vision among the cloistered were promoted by the process of a focused visualization with the person concentrating on a sainted personage or even their Savior. It would be interesting to know the nature of those experiences as well as the neurochemistry that might have supported it, and especially what if anything finally triggers the event or whether there is no event threshold.

One view on the effect of visualization—if you obsess over something long enough it creeps into your experiences. Think how that is for yourself. Those distorted images that flash for only a second, perhaps the ones you see out of the corner of your eye, then you turn your head, but they're gone. (If I'm too long at card games, I see them when I shut my eyes to sleep. The same is true of long hunts for morel mushrooms. I could easily imagine doing this with religious icons and the heady emotions they could evoke.)

Previously mentioned were the peyote ceremonies of the Navaho that entail strong drug stimuli to force a religious event (*Fingerprints of God*, Hagerty). Fasting in the desert evidently produced some effects for soul-weary Hebrews. Lesser rituals, too, might edge one ever so slightly toward such events.

Some who have had what they consider a religious experience have said they were facing a serious question, a crisis point with respect to their beliefs, their lives, or their "immortal souls" or salvation. This preliminary phase may have been necessary to set them up for the experience. Perhaps a heightened awareness or sensitivity—a certain expectancy—looking for, or open to, an answer.

Could there be a *sweeping away* of a person's "religious emotions" after a certain threshold is reached? Could there be other purposes why humankind might have evolved the capacity to have the singular, pinnacle experiences—visions, the felt presence, the sense of oneness?

Or are they simply the by-product of a brain stimulated, over-stimulated, or deprived of rest, food, or neurochemicals? I wonder if, some bell curve would apply to the distribution of mystical experiences among the population; say the peak at the middle of the curve represents the typical staid rank and file layman who would never have a religious epiphany. Outliers would be unbelievers on one end and mystics and those who've had peak religious experiences on the other.

It's less certain, but it seems likely that those spiritual leaders who've had experiences could serve as inspiration to others—they are the living icons of faith. They are the miracles and saints of history. Do they allow or even aid that rank and file to reach a higher level of spiritual experience—whether that's measured by PET scan or the type and amount of neurochemical release? Is seeking such an experience on their own barred to some Christians?

The flock at say, the Sermon on the Mount probably thought their souls were responding to the spiritual strength of the speaker and all the while it was their brains releasing, then experiencing the effect of dopamine or serotonin. Christianity may have been the beginning of a new religion, but it was far from the first religion. Humankind had internalized the genes of the spiritual response and, perhaps, the spiritual experience it can spark many millennia before.

Postmodernism and countless other factors have taken a toll on spirituality, especially church-borne spirituality (organized religion). In all but a few denominations—Evangelists, Born-Agains, Pentecostals— spiritual encounters are largely gone in America at least from the Christian American scene.

Before this is misunderstood, let me clarify. I'm not attacking or belittling believers or questioning anyone's faith. What I'm talking about is the likelihood that churchgoers are having spiritual experiences—those above and beyond . . . , elevated to a serene place, looking around the church, thinking, *this is good,* and really feeling it. When I think about black spiritual gospel music, I could believe those folks are feeling it.

Spiritual/religious experiences are so far removed from the typical churchgoer's experience that even the Born-Again Christians' telling of their conversion experiences causes other (non-born again) Christians to raise their eyebrows.

The religiously disillusioned have removed themselves from the subset of the population that can have significant spiritual experiences. Further, it seems highly likely that with them they also pull out of that subset their peers, any number of friends, and acquaintances, and, at least to some extent, they infuse the zeitgeist and collective consciousness with an atmosphere largely inhospitable to the spiritual and to whatever extent banish the spiritual from the public discourse (so, too, do the laity when their eyebrows rise as above).

X. Spiritual Redux

We who suffer a spiritual crisis

Most of us want to achieve a certain level of contentment, fulfillment, and wholeness in our lives. We wish for something spiritually significant to satiate that need inside to quell our angst, our drive for spiritual satisfaction. We do seem to suffer when we deny or suppress our spirituality while those engaged in the practice of the most farfetched beliefs seem to benefit from it. What's working against us in our quest? (For one thing, those of us who are analytical personality types may pick apart any belief to find what's wrong with it. Sorry, full disclosure.)

In spite of the putative growth in evangelical Christians (The most recent Pew surveys show this demographic to be stable, not growing; see the link earlier), there is also a broad skepticism about the existence of a spiritual realm while at the same time the existence of angels and ghosts are given credibility in folklore.

This may be the dilemma of the Postmodern Age: Only ever more energetically observed religions will survive as the light of new knowledge leaves less and less room for supernatural beings to hide. Maybe that will be humankind's perennial dilemma (See *the koan that will haunt us for the next thousand years* in the Spiritual Atheism section ahead).

It has been said that we are seekers of meaning. We will have to seek it elsewhere. It remains to be seen if this spiritual need must be met in order to have a viable and healthy society.

Can a new religion be born in the postmodern world? Can postmodern religions like New Age (if it becomes a formal religion) or Scientology capture a significant percentage of potential believers?

OR is it too dangerous for humanity to be exposed to religion considering our latent religious equipment? Is it a little too easy for us to get religion, for religion to get us, and the depth to which we are taken in by religion?

The best religion has to offer

Have you experienced that interior sense of awe that buoys the spirit at those peak moments in the presence of being and the world? Some have wondered from the earliest, *Am I generating this sense of spirit or is there really something out there?*

For eons humans mistook mind for spirit, especially this expansive, ennobling aspect of it, this temporal spirit enthralled by its own imagination and yearning and no less, the very improbability of being. Who was the first to tap their chest and ask, *Is there really something in here, an essence that's me?*

If we can be lonely in a crowd, perhaps, the most trying loneliness is that of a crowded world, a world that may not care, one that is about something else altogether, or seemingly about nothing at all. This loneliness is being face to face with a society which is alien to us and to which we are equally alien.

Religion at its best urges the individual to turn a loving face to society, to embrace it, love it, love all mankind, for in that love which seems to manifest our spirit outward to the world we see our love reflected back again.

Religion also remakes that indifferent world into one in which we are made ultra-relevant by its solace, its brotherhood, or by providing us with an afterworld that's caring and to which we are relevant and in which all will be made right, whole, just—an afterworld that makes the trials and tribulations of this world more bearable, and makes the world more beautiful, more like the best of all possible worlds—a world fit to be internalized into the fabric of our reality, our worldview.

Our spiritual feeling

Does poetry spark something in your heart? Does music? Does a scenic view do anything for you? Does a life-affirming movie or novel stir you emotionally—or even spiritually—whatever that means to you?

If you feel something in those or other like experiences, those may be distant relatives of the low level spiritual rewards that goads the believer along on her path.

Writing and thought can do that for me. You, like me, may be able to read, write, or think yourself into a better emotional state, even one that feels spiritual. Writing critics like to point out, none too kindly, when they think writers are performing self-therapy on the page.

Nonbelievers may be just as "spiritual" as believers. Since there is no spiritual realm, it all comes from within (though there can be external sources of inspiration). Our spirituality, if we have it, is just as authentic as theirs. In fact, ours may be more authentic since theirs is based on supernatural beings or a supernatural realm or reality behind nature.

The words below gave me something of that spiritual feeling as I wrote them. Use them as a test. They aren't particularly wise or profound, rather, they are meant to stimulate that spiritual *something* within. If those don't do it for you, write some that would. Maybe you'll give us the next generation of religion-free authentic spirituality . . . or something like it.

The metaphorical meanderings of the mind string together events sometimes so momentous or stunning that they change us forever, sometimes too trivial to fully be remembered. Among those meanderings are memories—all too often of mistakes, regrets, opportunities lost that we see forming our lives. The longer we live, the more this flow becomes a swirling vortex within a greater flood.

At such times—and aren't all times such times?—we must find a place of serenity. Find the self beneath all thought. Your life as well as your mind can be a refuge, though not only for the hermit or the ascetic but as a buffer for anyone worn down by the challenges of the world. If you don't have peace and serenity there, you'll have them no where. The more frenetic your search becomes the farther from your goal you'll find yourself. When your inner self is fragile, take the most care. Guard your essence from harm—even from yourself.

Return to this place often to find your strength. Draw it only from a good and gentle source. From that strength breathe, move, work. Choose what you do carefully. Check that for resonance with the self at your center. Do that which feels closest to the achievement of transcendence for you.

That sense of transcendence brings a liberation of the mind which can in turn free the spirit. The mind is the start of every true path to freedom. Your path is there for the finding.

Spiritual evolution . . .
a wholly holy enterprise?

Is it possible? Can we evolve into some sort of ultimate spiritual beings? Some believers certainly hope so. This is something of the domain of the SBNR's, especially New Age. If Christian salvation or reincarnation seem implausible to the believer, maybe there's something else *out there*. Something real.

The pinnacle of spiritual achievement, or so they believed, in our pious past was being the most devout, the truest to their faith, cultivating the purest heart, adhering to the loftiest moral behavior, or verging on a spiritual experience in the achievement, in the pursuit of, the holy enterprise.

Religion, we've said, has had an actual effect on human evolution, bending us in its direction. Can that be stepped up?

Sometimes in the fictional story line of a novel or movie, we do evolve vicariously, through the hero, into a transcendent or spiritual being (admittedly, secondhand, so our transformation may be fleeting) such as in the movies *Powder, Phenomenon* or we seem to communicate with one, *The Abyss, Mission to Mars, 2001: A Space Odyssey*. I'm suggest that we all can feel a certain spiritual tug in these or other experiences that you might not have associated, at first, with a spiritual feeling.

I think some of our fiction is a temporary placebo for our long failed or missing myths. Through some fictional characters we achieve some measure of spiritual fulfillment or at least temporary relief from not achieving it. (Might there be a "self-therapizing" writer at work underneath it all in both fiction and non—as well?)

A thesis, though difficult to test, could be developed around the idea of "our long failed myths." Perhaps we originally evolved to have only the one myth, our origin myth. As the noise and confusion accumulated from the myths of other tribes, they negated, defeated, and otherwise watered down our myth.

Is there another alternative? Is some ultimate generic religion possible?

The question would seem to hinge on the spiritual components of any such neo-religious effort. Does it move us in a spiritual way? It seems that we would have to be honest with ourselves that there isn't a divine or supernatural entity out there to inspire this religion. Once done, does that allow anything that can be called spiritual? We're about to delve deeper into that.

Chasing enlightenment

The spiritually dissatisfied who've moved on to Buddhism, Humanism, New Age, or even more esoteric spiritual paths may not be having full-blown religious epiphanies either. Was it always hard in every culture to seek the supreme sublimity of the ultra-spiritual path? Your friends, relatives, neighbors might take a dim view of your renunciation of the worldly trappings of life, especially if you're leaving a family with children behind.

An analogy suggests itself. Spirituality or its promise seems to beckon in the way that sexual desire does. It keeps a spark alive in your mind—that promise of a sweet spot. A happy answer to the drive, the desire, the need. (Would that our spiritual drive were so easily satiated.)

Believers define it as that within us that responds to a higher power or that which transcends our daily existence. Let's work with it: That within us which we nurture to our higher selves in harmony with our better natures, our hopes and dreams, a greater calling, an ennobling, our "bestwill" toward humankind.

"Saint" Augustine, paraphrasing said, *I am incapable of understanding all that I am*—the idea being that our minds, our souls, are a part of ourselves, but are also a part of the divine—and the divine which is infinite is beyond our capacity to comprehend, thus, there's an aspect of us that participates in the infinite.

An alternate way of considering Augustine's observation of the mind/soul and its self-apprehension is to consider the mind/soul as a "black box" (a mental model that incorporates the unknown internal functions of something not understood) of the type often cited in thought experiments.

Refining that image for use here, a black box is a concept that has known or assumed products—here, the generation of a 'self'—and it may incorporate all sorts of seemingly irreconcilable truths, factors, or assumed realities. For example, in Descartes' dualism the mind is nonmaterial, intangible stuff made of spirit, the same as it is for Augustine.

God as a concept is an ideal example of such a black box. Take the line of reasoning, *Why does the universe exist? Because God created it.* This works for billions of people and yet all we did was to shove the unknown source of all being into a black box and label it God.

With respect to Augustine's belief that our minds share an experience of the divine, a stock criticism of defaulting to the divine starts with the question, Why? Citing the divine or anything supernatural as a causal explanation of something is no explanation at all. It is only the positing of a black box of further mysteries, typically even harder to explain than the primary phenomenon. In short, it really only serves the adherents to a particular religion by affirming their beliefs or dogma.

Augustine (uh GUS tin) might counter thusly: the divine might not be the cause of everything that goes on, but when some events are caused by divine intervention or activity why should we say it was something else?

We shouldn't, but should we suppose the existence of beings and a realm not within the experience of any reliable witnesses for anything we can't explain? Also, such claims can be neither falsified nor independently verified. In short, your explanation is, again, a black box that you say incorporates all the solutions and explanations, and yet, we can't look inside to see any of those inner workings.

Yet another line of reasoning from inside a mind, so to speak, is one in which the mind considers its own nature. As a young human being slowly becomes aware of itself, it finds itself in the world and yet sees no source for the being of its essential, internal self. As it learns from its world, the question of self is 'mystified' and symbolized by the idea of soul. Self, when it is commonly contemplated as a soul, may be reducible to mind plus something of an illusion.

When a person, a mind, contemplates its own being it seems as if this individual being implies some unit of existence, perhaps spiritual, unchanging, and, in a sense, transportable beyond the body. This gives rise to the seemingly logical possibility that the individual as a soul could have had existence at another time, another place. It feels legitimate to ask, "Isn't it simply the luck of the draw? Why was I born as me rather than as Napoleon?"

In reality, that is the illusion. The body and the self are not separable. The mind *and* body are the conscious self, but the self could not have any other form or being. With respect to 'self identity,' it is no more possible that *you* could have been Napoleon than it would be for your dog to have been a frog. It is *your* mind and body, here and now, that generates this presence we call *you*. Why would Napoleon's, or anyone else's, mind and body generate you?

Mythic center

As human life improves, it seems all the more incongruous that the human spirit should dive into the mud, but on occasion it does. Whether the cause is postmodernism, the death of God, socio-economic dis-ease, or some sort of cascade failure of the human spirit, something holds us down now. Humanity has had these types of crises many times.

What Rollo May the psychologist philosopher said about exiles is similar to humankind's situation now. He said they lose their mythic center and that in turn, destroys their psychic life.

Whether people have religious beliefs or not, they all share in the spiritual need. We must all minister to each other's human spirit. If they pretend they have no human spirit, we must nurture that infirmity as well. We should celebrate our new human reality, our greater humanity, should help others to aspire and achieve.

> The new divisiveness and rancor in this country is unhealthy. We used to share a vision as Americans even if we were divided by ideology. Now we play up our differences. We look for points of disagreement with the other camp and we blow them up until they look like the commission of a treasonous act. Not only are we unwilling to listen to different points of view, we pay our polarized pundits to confirm our biased opinions with their biased opinions.

I wonder if the SBNR (spiritual, but not religious, remember?) were offered a new religion made to order, what they'd want their new religion to be about? I'm thinking they'll reject anything that doesn't have that "crème filling." That sweet spot. That little spiritual/ supernatural microchip inside most or all of us that craves—what? Spiritual fulfillment? (For many, if that spiritual worldview doesn't include the supernatural, it's a deal breaker. For nonbelievers, it's a deal breaker the other way around.)

What is the formula for spiritual fulfillment? Is it a certain rhapsody of thought and feeling that affirms and confirms the rightness, the blessedness of all? A swept away satisfaction that knows no bounds? Again, sliding up the scale of spiritual experiences to noticeable events will help to clarify. Some will draw the line beneath the born-again experience (meaning spiritual fulfillment need not reach that level), others will draw the line above it (meaning that it is the minimum for spiritual fulfillment. (Even believers are a little suspicious of apparent out and out spiritual experiences. I think because these experiences seem randomly distributed, perhaps undeserved, and not something that can be had by the "worthy" no matter how hard they might try or wish for it.)

Can the spiritual experience be reduced to a certain structure in the brain, specific neural pathways, a precise discharge of nerve impulses and an ordered, measured release of neurochemicals? Is a particular mood or state of mind essential to set up the event? Is a set of beliefs as well as some particular knowledge prerequisite for the person to have the event?

If you test the believers of our hypothetical religion-of-their-own-design by leaving off the ala carte tray of religion all supernatural beings, big "S" spirituality, a spiritual plane or realm, the soul, afterlife, or reincarnation, how many will sign up for this residual religion, if it can be called a religion? In accord with my theses, not so many will sign on without the psychophysical, neurochemical stimulation. (Does that doom a universal religion?)

I think we will have lost New Agers with that diminished version of religion. Maybe not all Buddhists though. Not until we eliminate enlightenment (Oops, this is the *other* kind of enlightenment. Although the deeper you go into this other kind, the quasi-spiritual kind, its precise definition is elusive. Let's call it Buddha's enlightenment for the moment. Is it a serene wisdom? Who says when we've obtained it? What's the metric of that obtainment?)

I wonder if, for the SBNR, that any religion they'd consider would have to have not only the feel of "authentic spirituality" but some sense of communing with the source of all (many churchgoers have little or nothing of this magnitude beyond the wish). And yet this isn't necessary for many Buddhists or any secular humanists though I think there is some "secular" spirituality for both (See Spiritual Atheism).

It would be extremely interesting to know which elements of religion we need to obtain spiritual satisfaction. I use the Born-again Christians as an example as they are defined by the spiritual experience they've had. There may be more joy, elation, or rapture in another example and so you should consider most other examples as higher on the spiritual meter.

What about the believer whose meter is at zero? What does it take to make them happy enough *not* to leave their church (Assuming that it is more than just habit, which it may not be)? Does a sermon, a communion wafer, and a sip of sacramental juice get them off zero when their spiritual needle sits there pegged at rest?

Reactions must surely vary with the individual. What could be more subjective? Still, there must be something vaguely "spiritual" that comes from the religious trappings. Consider another example, the architecture of the great cathedrals—no greater architecture existed at the time—they must have generated considerable awe and inspiration. And if the cathedrals were not inspiring enough, did taking part in rituals, singing hymns, worshipping among life size iconography and communing with fellow believers bring a touch of the spiritual into a life?

Soul, man

The present conception of the soul is a relatively modern invention and has undergone an evolution of its own. In western culture a number of sources have made contributions to the concept. Some of those have included the New Testament (Most Old Testament authors made no mention of an afterlife or soul), Jesus or his biographers, numerous church leaders, some of the Greeks (Plato's school), Dante's Inferno, Descartes' *Meditations* and other works, such as those of John Milton, and other poets and writers. You can now see through these added embellishments on the myth that Christian fiction is a much older genre than one would think.

Man does not have a soul but is a metaphor for the soul. Would that we could transcend flesh and blood. The self-proclaimed truthsayers hold that we are an indwelling piece of the divine. Rather than an inner-self (some say not that either), are we at least the semblance of a self, the locus of our thought, the focus of our being, that which responds to inspiring talk or thought?

Not an immortal chunk of the eternal. No, but something more rare. It is the illusive self that each of us seeks that we glimpse fleetingly like shadows in a mirror. Unapprehendable if left uncultivated. To know it, we must grow it. We may conjure it as character or psyche, ego, id, or identity. It may not be a "self," but it functions like one.

Is it any wonder that many opt for the familiar traditions? Usually, one signs on for the religious franchise of one's parents. That's not so frightening nor as liberating as truly following the unraveling thread of reality—nor so ostracizing as being outed then shunned, or its modern equivalent, as an unbeliever.

I wonder, too, if by apprehending the world, we feel as if we understand ourselves. If we—or by God and his prophets—understand the world, then our origins, our fate are not such looming mysteries and we are not so exposed to the unpleasant vagaries of chance.

A simple choice?

One may introspect, on the occasion of one of those dark Sundays of the soul . . . that most people seem to support the idea that the belief in a god, a supreme being is a conscious choice. Having gone from yes to no personally, I doubt that it is a simple choice. Maybe both believers and nonbelievers are fooling themselves.

On the face of it, yes, it seems to be choice. But if you tried to prove that thesis by just doing it, do you really think you could make the choice then and there to believe, or not? (The psychology of decision making might give insights into this.)

Still, people cite rational reasons for believing—or not. They have feelings about certain ideas they've taken as fact or rejected. These ideas and associated feelings can change, something shifts. The person sees a disparity, a discrepancy. The larger pattern has internal consistency issues; perhaps the structure has started to crumble.

A person raised in a religion is most likely to follow that religion. The practice, the behavior, the habits, the life creates more than a cultural immersion—the person's reality is or can be based on that religion and its beliefs. If facts in the mundane world interfere with those beliefs, special and sacred knowledge trumps mundane-world knowledge. Certainly individual reason, beliefs, and feelings can sway the person. Given what we now know from brain science, neurochemical influences on the brain may be more relevant than simple choice.

At any rate, with the mainstream religion of the people there's a whole culture, a society, a support system for it, rituals and holidays that are observed and on and on. And there are anthropological forces at work—from the deep time of village life. One shouldn't buck the system. Don't reject the religion of your culture. It can make you a hated outcast.

I think Christianity has adopted and adapted a number of elements that have made it particularly attractive. Repentance, forgiveness, love, immortality, piety, the Golden Rule, justice. I think some of these have worked for various religions because they tie into deeply hard-wired human needs and wants, in short, a more humanistic bill of fare.

Many people who most vigorously espouse religious beliefs have little tolerance for the religion or beliefs of others. Consider the victories of the majority religion (the broader Christian spectrum) at

326

the turn of the twenty-first century in the United States. Those of religious difference, including those of no religion, found the god of the Judeo-Christian traditions to still be foisted on all citizens with little consideration of their right to be free from that religion. Slogans were still on the money, posted in public places, references were in pledges and affirmations. The U.S. Motto was nearly unanimously reaffirmed to be *In God We Trust* (All of these are a mistake unless believers want to fuel New Atheism). The courts have removed piecemeal only the most flagrant offenses, but the resurgent religious fervor may do more than put them back if the Supreme Court becomes more religiously right-shifted.

The Wish to Transcend
An alternate thrust of the Spiritual Drive

Most of the human drives have long been identified: Hunger, thirst, sex, and perhaps the need for shelter. There have long been arguments for and against the inclusion of one thing or another in the category known as human needs or drives.

That's not what this is about. It isn't really important whether the wish to transcend ("spiritual" by another name) is a drive or not. It is, rather, a means by which to understand much of the misunderstood behavior that we all take part in, especially, spiritual behavior. The religious probably think that it's inspired by god. Now we know that it's a little more indirect than that. This particular way of looking at our behavior is useful over a wide swath of human efforts. It can be an especially insightful tool for understanding.

The concept is a simple one. This thread of the spiritual drive, the wish or the will to transcend, is woven through out much of human activity throughout time. The mind of man (and woman) wishes to rise above the everyday world. This wish is an old one. Remember those cave drawings thousands of years old in France and Spain? That art, and a lot of art, is a special activity by which a selected aspect of our world is re-examined or re-presented through a varying array of mediums. This act of art is one way the human mind handles its world spiritually. It's a method for handling the world by which we gain transcendence over our world.

The world, in the sense of all that exists, is an imposing reality. It is literally every thing to us. Through it our needs are met. Within it our triumphs and defeats play out. Its story is largely our story. Our common origin myth connects our story to its place in the larger world's narrative.

329

In mankind's early periods surviving day to day was an ordeal. Life was focused on survival and material needs. Through an integrated whole of man's cultural, social, and physical adaptations, it became easier to meet those needs. And so mankind, through his transcendence from a dearth animal existence enabled himself to survive and become a being with the promise of an ever greater future. Man saw the high road and set out for the peak—To become a being that could envision an open ended future, one that could have the vision to look up and beyond.

In spite of everything, the hurdles and roadblocks remain. The world can still be a figurative jungle. For all that the world is, it is something very difficult to escape from when one wishes to. Isn't it the wish to "rise above" the world that we express when we whimsically beg, "Scotty, Beam me up!"?

What we are really asking for there is kind of cosmic liberation—freedom from the world and its cares. This and such similar wishes are *Plan B,* after we've tried *Plan A*—managing the world—and found that to be too difficult . . . we choose to move on, to leave the world behind.

Other efforts that would fall under 'Plan B' might be escapist literature or movies, recreation, games, hobbies. More serious attempts at transcending the world under the escapism heading would include the use of mind-altering drugs—transcendental *medication*—or even suicide.

World conquest probably falls in this category; a bureaucratic post with a modicum of power might have to substitute for most people.

[Note that the pariah, the school shooter, or the religious renunciate may all have judged the world to be beyond redemption, but they adopt very different paths in reaction to it.]

Mastering the world by transcending it

We all, in our daily activities, interface with the world to some extent, unless we are hermits. (A hermit is one who masters the world by shutting it out).

We recognize the fickle nature of fortune as it ebbs and flows in this existential sea of chance and happenstance. Fates can befall individuals through no fault of their own. Illness and catastrophe appear to strike randomly.

There is no end to the circumstances we might like to rise above—or we wish the world would have risen above, to have been a better place. The best of all possible worlds? How about just a world that's a pretty good place?

Transcendence of the world, for most of us, is not possible physically. It is only mental, maybe spiritual—it takes place in the mind or among minds. The latter from the idea of a community of minds which may come together to affirm their mastery of the world by celebrating the illusive transcendence they would share. Consider a religious gathering of any faith. The group is bound together (the Latin origin of the word *religion*, re-ligre, means to bind together) by common belief. Belief in the supernatural may be older than art as a tool of transcendence.

The mysterious workings of the world were frightening for early man. He paid homage to the Unseen Mover, acknowledged His power, pledged allegiance to Him. Man in his sycophancy was attempting to master his world. His beliefs were a comforting taste of transcendence; if the gods liked him, perhaps they would bestow greater gifts from the unlimited bounty of their transcendent plane: a bountiful harvest, glory in battle, fruitful child-bearing, and the jewel of the faithfull's eye—the ultimate transcendence of the world, life ever-lasting, immortality, and safe passage at life's end.

XI. The path of the Doubtful Sojourner

The Universal Spiritual Experience

It seems for whatever reason that humankind has spiritual needs, greater needs for some, less for others. Religions sprang up, rooted in myth and superstition <u>because</u> they met some of these spiritual needs and the need for community, law, and a comprehensible worldview. Existential philosopher Jean-Paul Sartre, in exasperation with this long inexplicable need, said that society has a God-shaped hole in it. I think he could have extended that God-shaped hole to being in humankind's head and heart as well.

Society has Sartre's "God-shaped hole," by one or the other of two scenarios: 1. Man and society evolved it as an answer to the ultimate questions, that answer being necessary to function and move on. Or 2. They evolved the whole complex—The religious or spiritual need became embedded as the genetic component, perhaps in symbiotic partnership with religion, a cultural meme, the non-genetic component (although, don't be surprised if neither component respects the genetic and cultural boundaries).

Religion does have meme-like qualities, only so much more so that perhaps it is a supermeme. It is more than just a meme of beliefs. It is a vehicle for spiritual needs. It is religion because religion is the spiritual vehicle, the power source, the social force, the energy conduit that holds tenaciously to humans that have been so designed and it reproduces itself as a, if not <u>the,</u> core cultural aspect.

Rituals, tradition, codified beliefs and social and behavioral norms—not to mention ostracism as a punishment for failing to conform—all served to institutionalize religion in society. Religion has often held a position of strength sometimes equal to, sometimes superior to, the governance of the group, tribe, or community. Religion (at least some religions) has done, and still does, a lot for mankind, but this thesis would be a tangent not germane to the present discussion and has been acknowledged multiple times.

Giving credit where it is due, religion has enabled its believers to achieve surprising accomplishments arising supposedly from inspiration attributable to something in the realm of the adherents' spiritual beliefs. Even if the believer is factually wrong in every respect, they some times seem elevated in spirit by their beliefs in the face of hardship or sorrow or simply the challenges of the daily world. (That doesn't mean there's an outside influence at work.)

The challenge for the secular human spirit is to find and enjoy the spiritual effectiveness and fulfillment that the religious experience in the practice of their religion without any of the negative corollaries (Being closed to new or different thinking, having to reject reason and accept beliefs on faith, etc.). Most religionists would scoff at the possibility of unbelievers having a "spiritual" experience, but given all that we know of their "ability" to have such experiences, it isn't quite as far fetched as they may think. Still, what would, what should bring us to a pinnacle spiritual experience? Perhaps we denigrate the utility of such an experience to the class of experiences one would have in an altered state produced by a drug trip.

What would a spiritual experience be confirmative of for a nonbeliever? (Believers seriously ask themselves the same question about the religious experience of their fellow believers.)

We need not New Age religion or New Atheism, but New Age Atheism. Spiritual atheism? Perhaps, as defined, yes. Evolutionary theology? How much more oxymoronic can we get?

Most of us have probably noted that there is both beauty and metaphorical insight to be found in most religions and that on some level these may even seem resonant with something that feels spiritual within us—if you don't push it too far. Rationally, if not spiritually, it seems as if humanity needs to be free to find authentic spirituality—or at least to pursue it. Still, there are few who want to be liberated from their religions or so it seems—they have a high level of tolerance for imperfection and even unknowing in their religious state (*Be still and know that I am God.*)

Research mentioned earlier shows that higher levels of neurochemicals make a person shift in the direction of accepting more spiritual explanations for things (and in this instance this *can* include "woo-woo" type spirituality).

Given what little we do know about religion, it would be the rare believer who understands what has shaped their religiosity—some prototypical spirituality hammered out over tens of thousands of years into the evolving, protean form that underlies what we see manifesting as religion today. We're grappling with an invisible beast in religion—all we see is its avatar—religious man.

Embrace your spirituality

Are these fighting words to the nonbeliever?

The very word spirituality conjures up supernatural beings and a fantastic realm. It can be anathema to us. *"It's an illusion from the believer's world,"* we may have thought. But in our blanket rejection, we could be turning our backs on a satisfying fulfillment of a true, though as we've seen, misunderstood need.

Maybe some or most of us nonbelievers lack some aspect of the need or ability to fulfill that quest for nurturance. We may shy away from anything sounding spiritual, but perhaps we would be better off if we recognized the human need. We should recast that innate need and its fulfillment as the nurturance of the human spirit.

Our human ancestry defaulted to religion, the uber-meme. Its beliefs and rituals had enough "juice" to make our ancestors rally around it. In the long run, those who felt rewarded by religious thoughts and behavior were further rewarded by multilevel selection with more reproductive success . . . and ultimately evolution teased us out to the *Homo religiosus* we are today (There are various users of this term, a Wikipedia article credits it to Alister Hardy, a prof at Oxford, Karen Armstrong, Mirceau Eliade, I also thought it was original to me, as well until I researched the term.).

At every point in human evolution those existing hominids were the most advanced beings that ever walked the planet (barring the effects of a significant die-off from apocalyptic catastrophes). Life was so hard, though, so trying, even so devastating that humanity seldom had occasion to celebrate itself. It needed something that transcended its squalid existence . . . and religion served. It served as a means to placate the powers evidenced by the weather, to ask for help with the hunt, or end famine, or perhaps to spare a sick child. It offered the most control over events, the greatest understanding of life, the greatest condolences for death.

Today as religion's usefulness wears thin, we find ourselves in a scientific postmodern world. We face the question, *Can new religions form where new myths will have to face the scrutiny of science? Will we be able to suspend our disbelief enough to consider new and binding myths? Do we want to? Should we?*

Aren't we too educated, too sophisticated to accept new myths?

Science, evolution, and facts are offered up as the new source of myth material. That's akin to what is being attempted in this book. Will that do it for everybody? Scientism is the negatively connoted word for the worship of science. But the words of Chet Raymo confirm that true knowledge does offer us more.

Are we ready now or must it wait until some day in the future when we can step away from the surrogate that we needed for a time— one with an artificial spiritual objective, a supernatural crutch—and embrace our humanity . . . ourselves?

Spiritual Atheism:
How can a nonbeliever be spiritual?

A secular view of the universe allows for no supernatural beings nor any spiritual realm. It is an unabashedly materialistic view. Few religions can accommodate that stand.

Consider it from this perspective. In this material world, all that exists, all that has happened, all that ever will happen are events that *can* happen in a material universe. Every spiritual-seeming event or occurrence, every accomplishment, every ennoblement of the human spirit, all are possible in a material universe because all have occurred in one.

There are no more supernatural beings in the believers' world than there are in ours . . . . So we are potentially just as spiritual as they are (with our equipment varying from person to person).

Spirituality (or religiosity) as an evolutionary adaptation and now spiritual atheism? What's with all the oxymoronic sounding terms?

Perhaps none seem more oxymoronic than spiritual atheism, but in light of where we now know our spirituality really originated, there seems to be something to it.

Steve Antinoff is his book, *Spiritual Atheism*, cites Richard DeMartino as an early religious atheist and defines his term "natural koan" as "the core question rising out of one's being." Antinoff quotes Kirilov, a Dostoyevsky character in the novel *The Devils* who says, *"God is necessary, and so must exist . . . Yet I know that he doesn't exist, and can't exist."*

Antinoff says, "These lines [. . .] will plague us for the next thousand years. They form the koan that cannot be walked away from." I think, however, that we have a yet more basic koan, the existential koan, *Here I am. I, me, myself. I am, but I cannot be. How can I exist?*

Religion, for man, has connected that unfathomable mystery of ALL Being with the unfathomable mystery of personal being, the self.

The hunter-gatherers of 50K ybp needed answers to go on functioning. They existed, each one a being, but they were in a world that was highly active itself, storms, volcanoes, ice age glaciers, earthquakes, drought, floods, predators. Where did all this power originate? Belief in *something* behind reality organically sprang up. For Kirilov, it had to, but still couldn't. There had to be an unseen mover. He put the world here, he must have put us here.

Coming up with an answer—and let's be clear about this, all that was required was *an* answer, not necessarily *the* answer—that was what was important. Certainly, our answer had to speak to us. We had to *feel* it spiritually. It had to be *of* our myth. It had to have a special meaning that underlay our reality at a level deeper than our worldly reality). Failing to have an answer would have left man sitting on the ground contemplating his toes.

A related effect may help us paint this picture. When missionaries supplanted an African tribe's religion with Christianity—I don't mean the loving evangelists of today—did that mesh well with their worldview, their culture, their daily lives? No! One of the devastating things about such "mass conversion events" is that it almost always causes some degree of cultural or social failure. And that weakness is divisive. It leaves the social fabric in tatters.

Perhaps, a stronger native religion would have warded off such an attack. This may accentuate my point about Pascal Boyer's thesis that primitives have/had RTB's and they aren't religions. If they aren't, they are place holders for religions. And a more "evolved" religion (Yes, religions are Darwinian. There is competition among religions—they are memes, but more—religions are given special status and respect as the powerful adaptations they are.), if allowed to gain a foothold, could overpower the native one.

Instead of two good religions, these African natives then had none. Their own religion was attacked by the white gods and shown to be false. Their new religion was good for some, but not for all. The black man, his culture, and his religion were marginalized in his own society by the white man and his religion; superior technology and some cultural superiority served to underline all of this.

Religions weren't originally designed—didn't evolve—to coexist. Societies and religions, especially in the more distant past, were seldom mature enough to harmoniously accept the presence of other religions. (That made them only slightly less politically correct than religions today.)

With their origin/identity myths conflicted, their social realities seemed artificial, their morality contrived, their very existence seemed out of whack. Again, indecision resulted in inaction, social alliances seemed inadequate to overcome discord at this radical depth. Malaise ruled the scene. Political unrest and dissatisfaction could lead to the disintegration of society or make it vulnerable to attack or revolt.

At an earlier time, perhaps our hunter-gatherer or tribesman didn't reflect on himself as much. Perhaps his world was so fraught with danger and need that the self-absorbed were already "extinct." Maybe his existence wasn't precarious, wasn't in his face, although that's doubtful. The world, though, certainly was in his face, an insurmountable obstacle of oppressive reality, and he was just an object in it, a *me* that only occasionally glimpsed an *I*.

For myself, perhaps for Antinoff, it is only when that *me* becomes an *I* that we are in the realm of spiritual atheism (that may also set up the realm of religion and philosophy). Prior to the *me* becoming an *I*, we were only objects. When *I* and *We* can act, we are subjects, then a narrative can take place. Our narrative can take place.

We understand, now, that there's not a Big Kahuna hurling the storms of the planet at us. We can set him aside in order to consider our own philosophical importance, the implication of our being for us. As we feebly glimpse the other realities of the universe we tentatively examine their meaning for us as well.

The Doubtful Sojourner

As the Doubtful Sojourner makes his or her way through this confusing labyrinth, clues lay sprinkled along the path. Or is that salty red herring strewn along the path?

This meandering path I've been guiding you on has been a spiritual journey for me and I hope for you as well. There have been controversial topics from the title on, that, I hope, have evoked both thought and feelings from you.

We have taken a look at the chosen path of some believers. One can see the ecstatic nature of the born-again experience as the initiate climbs Jesus Peak. Even more interesting is the backslide out of that experience—believers becoming doubters again. So many think they have the truth, so few do. What they have is the burning desire for that which they believe to be true. They are believers on that path, not truth seekers.

Most of us have that sense of being that seems to very much suggest a self and, does it perhaps, hint at a soul?

Figurative speech can help capture the sense of the human spirit, that soul-like thing. There are important things to say about the human spirit that are not necessarily true. Things that have a certain resonance—the metaphorical corollaries of life, let's say. That's one of the better functions of religion. It gives us permission to consider our spirituality. It's a shame that so many religions choose to dictate to us how and what must we believe. Is it at a place in us where memes can attack because we are vulnerable there? And because it is a place where memes can lodge? Is that the special vulnerability that the drive for spirituality exposes us to?

Religion seems to dwell more on the supernatural realm and less on us as individuals. Perhaps in response to our religious urge, historically, we have defaulted to the supernatural because we don't know how to talk about our spirituality. We can project something out there, in the dark, behind the curtain of nature. Some misunderstood reality, the nature of all being, and we on the other end of it. Two polar opposites of reality, transcendence at either end and we the beholder of both.

Religion has come forward with the metaphors, the poetry and the myth that gives us a way to express our spirituality where in its absence we literally don't know what can be said . . . literally.

We, the myth-challenged, have tried throwing that bone to the Fundies before. We've said, "Aren't you talking figuratively or metaphorically about your religious beliefs?" *No*, they have said, *it is literal truth.* Being as charitable as I possibly can, I'll call these "spiritual truths."

Aspirational ideals might be an area of common ground for both believers and the god-free; we all wish the world was a better place. When Sissy's little Poochy gets hit by a car and we cast around for some relief for her grief, we might find ourselves saying, "He's gone to a better place."

Our human spirit reaches, gropes for a handle for this transcendence that poor Poochy seems to have reached. Death is beyond. Poochy is beyond. Poochy is in a better place . . . . Or, at least (as Sissy skeptically inspects the hole in the ground where we've placed Poochy), we reflect that we were once consoled to think so.

Just because I don't believe that there's a human soul or spirit separable from the body, that doesn't mean I don't know there are accomplishments and triumphs of the human spirit. It *does* mean, though, that all accomplishments and triumphs actually *are* of the human spirit.

Who doesn't like to create figurative, even poetic, wordings to express through hyperbole a philosophical thought or to capture the mood or emotion? (Maybe that's a spark from the "divine gene.") In a world without ghosts or supernatural beings, those are 'spiritual' experiences, at least, as spiritual as they get.

In a very limited defense of the religion of the earliest days, I think it may have been something of a denial, consciously or unconsciously, against, if not our apparent animal nature, at least its lingering shadow. Religion rebelled, "There must be something more!" Religion was early humanity's answer to the ultimate questions, *Why do I exist? Where did everything come from?*

Facing the lack of concrete answers (i.e., in a state of ignorance)—religion treated the question with reverent awe—inspiring reverent answers. Soon, there were spirits everywhere (they may have come before, as well, an explanation by way of the hidden [agent] powers that move the world and make it work).

Even now religion envelopes the majority of the Earth's peoples and probably almost always did (it may be as old as humanity). There is some rebelling against that rigid framework. The figurative truths of religion have become dogma, so strongly supported that they are believed to be literal and sacred.

How could a people base their worldview, if not their lives, on something less than immutable truth? A pretty good idea just wouldn't fill the bill. Even if our worldview is based on science, we get invested in it. No one likes to have their worldview rejected.

With the value of religion at stake, it is only natural that selection found a way to reward us for it . . . for it's underpinnings—being reverent about something—something beyond the reach of reason—the supernatural and the mystery of being that it addressed. To that, to those mysterious essences, we became religiously trained within our societal environments and that training sank into our genes (i.e., it had survival value and so, became an adaptation).

Some say without God there is no spirituality. All evidence seems to the contrary. From the individual perspective the core spiritual experience seems to form as emotions peak and an eruption of spiritual feelings happens. We're programmed not only to believe, but to be rewarded psychologically for it. It may be as simple as our forming a spiritual question—contemplating a spiritual possibility—and being internally, psychically, rewarded for it.

That's not only a feel good moment, it also amounts to a powerful reinforcer of the activity. With that activity, when it's communal, religion is what we call what accretes. When the effort is individual, we call it spiritual. And if it is an activity like this writing, it is also spiritual if it feels spiritual. (Potentially verifiable with a look at brain regions and neurochemical activity thus making spirituality operationally describable, if not somewhat quantifiable.)

Secular spirituality:
the intersection of many fields

> To those who say without God there is no spirituality, I say with humanity there is spirituality.

Philosophical anthropology. Human evolution. Humanism. The aspirations of human ascent. Doubt, agnosticism. Spiritual atheism. Maybe some of these fields only share a single sentence or line of thought. Some so illuminate another as to amplify its meaning many fold.

Diverse ideas, areas of study, schools of philosophical thought can form some overlapping intersections that offer to inspire us. Evolutionary psychology, neurotheology, and other synthesized fields offer us much in new insights.

The very existence of the Humanist Chaplaincy at Harvard stirs thoughts of those intersections for me and elevates the imagination with a spiritual feeling, a lightness of being.

What might be surprising, when this thesis is expanded, is that even science fiction shares something in common with some of these areas of thought in an area called philosophical science fiction and there are other related splinter genres as well that explore meaning within these festeringly rich interstices.

En toto, these groupings circumscribe an area of human thought that I term secular (meaning nonreligious) spirituality, perhaps, it's also humanist spirituality. Why spirituality? Again, I think most of us have that sense of being that seems to very much suggest a self and, does hint at a soul.

XII. Heirs of the Enlightenment

The Next Enlightenment

Everyone who reads H.G. Wells' Time Machine probably comes away thinking s/he would be in the Eloy race—the above-ground dwellers, the beautiful people. If we want to be in the enlightened race with a place in the sun, we have to break with being the underground culture. In general, humankind is heading upward.

Admittedly, forms of destruction, even self-destruction may be looming on the horizon. And, as we know, God isn't going to pull our fat out of the fire at the last minute. Still, given the general moral agreement across the civilizations, the Middle Eastern revolutions (somewhat of mixed bag given their religious connection), and the sensitivity to human rights, the respect for humanity has never been greater.

The Descent of Man
and the Ascent of Humanity

The ascent of the human spirit might be more appropriate in the line above. It is, after all, the collective human spirit's climb out of the animal evolution of man that we should be celebrating.

The human mind created tools and language and explained the world with myth and the ritualistic worship of nature and gods. Eventually, . . . and haltingly the human spirit found a glimmer and nurtured a glow that enlightened the world . . . and we understood the world with the light of reason and knowledge.

Religion will evolve or be left behind with the other relics. It is unlikely to regain the prominence it once had unless civilization falls and has to begin again.

Ultimately, the torch will pass to yet unknown bearers who will forge a new world with intellectual might and arm humankind with knowledge that will launch it from this plateau . . . on and on beyond our furthest imaginings.

Brick and mortar institutions

Is it, perhaps, that unbridled spirituality just doesn't leave a trace and religions seem to? Is it that religions build institutions or is it just that religions that happen to build institutions are evident, obvious, and tend to hang around?

Religions take a long time to grow. They are organic. They grow naturally and they can have very deep roots. In many cases, the strength of tradition allows a religion to remain unchanged for many years. No doubt, the rate of change in the society makes a difference in that.

Possibly, man, without something like religion, is man confused. Effective living may require that we have something, maybe anything, in the little "black box" in the corner of our being where religion can often be found. If religion is not hard-wired into us, it has at least proved to be a valuable software program to us and our culture and community.

This doesn't mean that some non-religious belief system can't be substituted to hold that place, it can: Our wishes for ennobling the human spirit, the love of humanity, the multiplicity of meanings we give to life. We can bring those to our spiritual locus, that private place of self within. In this postmodern era, perhaps this secular philosophy will prove to be, if not enough, at least as effective (as competitive, as viable) as the religions of today—or perhaps tomorrow.

In this context, *spiritual*, for us, means whatever shines within us— that essence within us which responds to the greater human spirit and to the ennoblement of both. And so, this is a secular spirit. We can call it "spiritual," in spite of the baggage that goes with that term because it is that same "spot" in most of humanity where human evolution has chosen to "bless" us with a predisposition toward belief, religion, and spirituality [as a sense, a feeling, a human goal].

It is part and parcel of the world's religions that they are survivors. They have evolved along with man, his culture and civilization. The religions are strong; they have the supportive strength of their adherents. They would not easily be dislodged or supplanted as long as they are giving enough of the followers a sense of satisfaction, be it neurochemical or some other satiation of the spiritual need. I strongly suggest than no such goal of eradicating religion be adopted. It is rather, for us to call them to be their best. Let us help them ennoble their human spirit. To that extent, we will have ennobled ours.

If we could pull out the metaphorical "spiritual truths" of the religions, the beneficial ones, the ageless wisdom, we could create or enhance practical philosophies from the poetry of those words.

I predict that over time the current religions will recede in prominence—as we strive to find an essential spiritual identity— and they will become more like the city we hail from. The Christian Humanists will be like the Cincinnati Reds. *Cincinnati* is an adjective but not the be all and end all of the baseball team, not its definitive essence.

"Christian" in this instance means little more than a curious modifier. We'll be Christian humanists (not the ones who believe in supernatural beings), Buddhist humanists, Jain humanists and so forth.

If one is burnt out or spiritually bankrupt, the path to walk is a necessary one of renewal. It is one of reconnecting with your spirituality without forcing a reanalysis of your whole life. If you're one who is turned off by organized religion and its dogma, you may have pooh-poohed the spiritual aspects of life and mind. Yet, the religious don't really have the market cornered on spiritual being. As we've seen, religion isn't a God-given receiving unit for divine communiqués, it is, rather, something that has earned its place as an evolutionary adaptation bolstering self, group, and their mutual bonds.

The aspirations of human ascent

If nothing else proves it, the predictions and promises of the modern religions, the hoped-for salvations, the nirvanas, the heavens—these all tell us rather plainly that we wish for some spiritual validation and that failure is not a good option. It leaves us cold. We learn in our myths that spiritual failure is death or not so directly, it can appear in dreams or myth as a threatening apocalypse looming out there somewhere. That figurative destruction is a symbol for our literal death.

If our literal spirits don't live on, our figurative ones do—in that, our bequest, we leave behind the society we've created. We are most pleased with ourselves when we leave a better legacy. As societies and individuals let's help ourselves create a better us. We don't have to be religious to do that.

Now, we can see that it has always been us, we humans alone, that have made the human spirit soar. Look how far we've come. If we look back to our australopithecine ancestors, we know they could never imagine us, and so, even if we can dimly visualize something ahead, we can rest assured we haven't guessed the best of it.

As secularists, we may have some fuzzy vision of a super-consciousness, maybe a matrix of thought, or a singularity of mind, say, when we are all united by a future iteration of the internet—perhaps then we will be village Earth.

These ideas, even if a bit overblown are a wish for human unity that gives us a metaphoric utopian vision to share. This is not unlike the way that the best people in every religion have brought to the table the best of those religions. Why fight with people of belief over that?

We've seen totalitarian governments so bent on bringing forth utopian societies that they would be willing to kill every man, woman and child if necessary to do it. Let's don't do that again. It's not going to be utopia if you have to force it on people.

"Say, are you preaching religion?" You might ask.

355

Not of the *supreme being* sort. But it is for each of us to seek within ourselves the noblest form of humanity. The best products of religion already had grand aspirations of humanity within them. That's why the best parts of them have had universal appeal while the quirky supernatural content has not. The Golden Rule, which predated Jesus, is a substantial basis for much morality and requires no supernatural being's approval before we adopted it.

If you reflect on all the religions, you'll notice there are a lot of very differing beliefs. According to some there are souls, according to others, not. Some have no deity. Some have several. When you look at what religions have most in common (at least on the high road), it amounts to hope and caring for humankind. In a very real sense what they all have in common are humanistic aspirations.

Given the religious drive, disillusionment with religion, and the doubt about belief, one is left only with humanity. Given where humanity came from and how high we've risen, we must celebrate that as well as where we could go.

The Question of Human Unity

Can we agree to rise above our beliefs and ideologies to embrace the humanity that is everywhere in the world? If we are to be *for* humanity today and tomorrow we must. Let us no longer allow religious belief to divide us. We cannot if we are to accept responsibility for tomorrow's world.

We must acknowledge that it is wrong to judge others by our religion just as it is wrong for others to judge us by their religion. We should reach over the belief divide to our counterparts and offer common cause in our hopes and dreams and good works. Genomic research shows us that we are all truly a part of the one family that is humankind. We should certainly be able to bond over the humanity that unites us.

Citizens of earth: You are charged with the future of the planet and the fate of the human race. Which inhumanities, what oppressions will you allow?

We should be countering religious strife, bigotry, and hatred with reason. We shouldn't directly shame a religion, but by contrast call those people to be their best. If you see that the way as a human spirit-championing humanism, you should be able to see how we can do more.

Conclusion

Among the theses advanced in this book, e.g., the exploration of religion's roots in human evolution, is the idea of how broad religion's base in humanity is. The argument being, if "religion is in our genes," we should find it to be universal in all human cultures. Some researchers in the science of religion, say it is *not* universal, because existing primitive peoples (surviving hunter-gatherer tribes, or their descendants, or gatherer-fisher tribes or subsistence agriculturalists) appear to have, rather than full-blown religions, what anthropologist Pascal Boyer characterizes as Religious Thoughts and Behavior, or RTB's.

I think that the primitives may be exhibiting an example of religion in its incipient phase or perhaps a sideline to the religiosity gene's and the religion meme's multilevel selections, perhaps something akin to an evolutionary dead end. Alternatively, the present day primitives may only have RTB's rather than full blown religions due to the same isolation that held down every other aspect of their culture.

Fully modern man may have taken a slightly different path than the tribes of hunter-gatherers who until modern times lived much as they always did. Modern humans on one path may not be fully explained by those on another path—those who were still hunter-gatherers until recent times are not the direct ancestors of modern humans today. Their isolation in remote areas may have insulated their cultures from the influences of change just as it has continued to do until recently (more and more of today's surviving primitive cultures have taken the seductive slide into modernity).

The Native Americans created a divergence from their indo-european ancestors when they crossed the Bering Straits land bridge to the western hemisphere. They sacrificed cultural advances they would have made in the eastern hemisphere to search for a better life in the west.

Over-simplifying, there may have been those human lineages that retained simple cultures and religions of the past while others were in the lines that led to more complex cultures like our own for whatever reasons. Not that either culture is better or worse, both have their "dark aspects." Survival, however, is amoral.

Post Script

The need for religion

A criticism that has been leveled is that atheists might tear down religion only to find that it's necessary to replace it with another belief system that they would have to create. I tend to agree even though our atheist camps argue that nothing like religion is necessary—it may not be for them. It is for the rest of humanity that the question remains open.

For whatever reason most of humankind seems to need the things that are pulled together in a satisfying religion—creation myth for origin, identity, and ultimate answers, common belief for a sense of community, which also supports a heightened sense of purpose, an iteration of the Golden rule as a moral code for how to act in the world. The more members and the greater their enthusiasm for these and other aspects of their religion, the greater the spiritual rewards (psychologically and neurochemically speaking). As mentioned, the augmented social strength of individual and group, the primary reproductive strategy of religion is often overlooked.

It is by faith, the faithful say, rather than reason that they accept the tenets, doctrine, and dogma of their belief. Take note then that they imply, if not state, that they chose to believe for reasons other than reason. They were born to it; it's there parent's religion; it's the religion of their culture—the primary reasons for everyone's acceptance.

Another reason for someone to join a religion is that they like what they hear. It appeals to them, it's attractive. Christianity has been like that, and successful for it. Although, there were a lot of missionaries bonking heads in a lot of countries that made converts, too. A man once told me he converted to Catholicism because it looked like they had the money and the power.

Not so much these days, but Old Testament preachers successfully scared many into religion with the threat of eternal damnation. In their more recent incarnation of End Times ministries along the lines of the ridiculously successful *Left Behind* series by Jerry Jenkins and Tim LeHaye. (The Left Behind series, the Da Vinci Code, and the all time best seller, the Bible all tie into that spiritual drive, obviously.)

Fortunately, the modern thrust of Christianity—the evangelicals—seem more interested in *spreading the love.* I can see how their enthusiasm will bring the emotional upwelling and neurochemical sense of wellbeing, rewards we all might enjoy. Old Testament sentiments . . . not so much. That, too, is good.

Is it there?

Is there this innate nudge toward religion buried within us, within our three billion lines of "code," the base pairs of DNA? The same genetic predisposition we've been examining and that little jolt of "juice" that it can deliver might also serve to get the average joe off zero, to move off center, to go for the generic religion, especially the one in his face.

I've discussed counter arguments, the way we might *not* have religion in our genes. I hope that the reader will have noted by this point that it is the thesis of this book that there is genetic support for something within us that manifests itself in, or is at least signaled by, the presence of religion.

Sounds like I'm hedging? It's because I don't want the thesis rejected on a technicality such as the claim that because today's primitive peoples have only religious thoughts and behavior, not full blown religion, religion isn't universal, and, therefore, "religion isn't in our genes." Yes, this problem has been dealt with earlier, but it leads to a larger issue.

The genes "for" some specific trait or characteristic are rarely as simple as one pure gene for one, and only one, simple trait. Rather than being intelligently designed, the human genome is a hodgepodge of fragments with one bit turning on this protein or an epigene doing that. In fact, the genome is blind as are all of its active components. "IT'S ALIVE" only because its parents were fit enough to reproduce and did so.

Remember that natural selection is a result and not truly a directed process? Nothing is there to direct evolution (except we have been influencing human evolution as noted, but not consciously directing it), nothing gives it purpose, nor is evolution the purpose of any other entity, process, or thing. Every aspect of evolution and all the amazing science that explains it are simply dealing with the analysis of that result.

In that vein, the genome has been built up in helter-skelter fashion since the first DNA on earth replicated itself. Beyond the basic limits of life and biochemistry as a minimal hurdle, there is no organizing principle, save the ability and actuality of reproducing. And those that don't reproduce have there genes deleted from the gene pool with them.

Yes, there is amazing science that has been done and is being done surrounding evolution. Incredible complexities, subtle nuances, and surprising statistics are continually changing our understanding of evolution. (Consider the simple fact that if one gene enables its bearer to reproduce a few decimal points more offspring than its competition, the competition will eventually disappear.)

With all the amazing complexity of evolution, and probably more that we don't yet know, it is still a result. Sometimes we talk of it as if it is a directed process such as when we say it is "descent with modification." No one specified modification nor did nature choose to. Perhaps the better terminology might be "the variability in the genes that's selected in the ancestors and manifests itself in the descendants," but that doesn't convey the result as succinctly.

I understand the reluctance to even go down the road to religion being an evolutionary adaptation. For one thing, it means believers are a little bit less culpable for believing if it's in their genes. By the same token, the deck was stacked against them. The house wins. It's such a surprise to think that believers didn't have freewill in choosing to believe (there were other "incentives" as well), let alone that religion was a product of natural selection.

Worse for the atheist agenda, though, the fact (well, all right, the theory then, if only for the fact that it does have great explanatory power) that religiosity could be an evolutionary adaptation rather endorses it as having been beneficial at least at some point in human evolution. That's tantamount to saying religion was good . . . and was good for man.

What's good for the goose may be good for the gander, but *good* is at a minimum a relative term. Aggressive warlike behavior no doubt had survival value and would be *good* in the same way religion was, a competitive advantage. These things would both be *good* like the chimpanzees long canine teeth are good . . . . And that's why evolution doesn't win the Peace Prize.

Granted, the public perception would read more into the word *good*. The general pronouncement that religion was good for humankind would be bandied about. Heaven forbid the headline, DAWKINS SAYS RELIGION WAS GOOD FOR MANKIND. The rank and file of Christianity might find it a mixed blessing. Liberal Christians might be buoyed up by the idea. Moderates, too, who accept evolution as a valid theory, might be pleased: *If evolution was God's will, then this is how he gave us religion. It's the Maker's mark.* From that dividing line where Christians no longer accept evolution and on through the Young Earth Creationists to the hate-mongering radical extremists, they will pay little attention to a statement from the science community that says religion was evolutionarily *good* for Homo sapiens.

As the debate wears on, both sides of the divide refine what they mean. Nuance and new insights force both sides to toe the line. The fine line at present seems to be where the *religion as an evolutionary adaptation* camp recognizes that many existing psychological or cognitive systems are put to use in the service of religion.

At the same time, the *no evolutionary adaptations unique to religion* school may concede some territory on their side of the line for the many reasons cited through out this book.

I think there are some aspects of spiritual or religious behavior that the *no adaptation* side fails to explain, or at least fails to explain in a way that makes their explanation seem equal to the effect we see. Some of these are:

The spiritual longing (or need). It's there and not because a deity put it there. Philosophers and psychologists have tried other explanations as have those cited in this book and others which may have been overlooked. Still, nothing short of a genetic adaptation seems to explain the grip religion has on humankind.

Twin studies—there is a high degree of correspondence in the religiousness of twins raised apart. I don't see any explanation for this from the *nonadaptation* camp.

Mystical/religious experiences and perhaps even experiences as common as those who feel the "spirit move within them." Modern humans have the neurological equipment to escalate to and experience a spiritual peak in the absence of any outside input.

Religious cults have an inexplicable power (though they will say it is charismatic leadership, peer pressure to conform, attachment, and so on as there have been well known non-religious cults with a similarly mesmerized membership. Though, I would say they have tied into the power religion has over the human psyche.)

The universality of religion, it seems to me is NOT answered. It is said that religion isn't universal because today's primitives may be living just as hunter-gatherers did, say, 100,000 ybp. Current primitive peoples only have religious thoughts and behavior, not full-blown religions.

Maybe that is what earlier humanity had in place of today's religion. Still, even that seems to be on the scale, on the religious spectrum. We know there had to be a time before religion or RTB's. These two ends of the known spectrum seem consistent with nascent religion being little more than RTB's and perhaps, might have been a little less. Further, these RTB's may be the closest thing to a hunter-gatherer religion. We may see that cultures with this rudimentary form, perhaps this near-religion, did not progress culturally.

If a strong religion is the adaptation it seems to be, those cultures without it may have been left behind in the competition for the niche of modern man. Although, competitive cultures no doubt had other strongly competitive traits and cultural adaptations, perhaps the most advanced language, the most advanced technology/industry, economy/ trade. A strong religion might have been only an arrow in the quiver of culturally competitive characteristics.

So to the question, *Why is religion so universal?* As the evidence shows, on top of Homo sapiens' other skills, religion was a further adaptive advantage that enabled those with it to thrive.

Final Farewell

As we go through life, we grossly underrate the importance of what goes on inside us. Perhaps, it's because the milestones are hard to read. Each of us is the sole judge of what our interior life is like.

We and our world are locked into a continual relationship in which we refine and redefine each in terms of the other. We rebuild the world inside us into a worldview and it is through that mediation that we interact with the world. What we choose to see of the world we recreate within ourselves. Whether it's love, hate, beauty, prejudice, a pinnacle inspiration, or an ignoble depth, when we give it to the world, we bring it upon ourselves as well.

Our self-love can be affected by the world we've chosen to internalize. It is a test of wisdom to internalize the best of all possible worlds. That's the upside of religion. At its best, religion can envision the best of all possible worlds.

Each Man's potential has always been limited by his mind, his intellect. Yet over evolutionary time, we've blossomed. How can we be more than the sum of our parts? Thank human evolution for that. It's the engine of human ascent.

Leave their Myth alone

Now that we have some perspective, I think we should be careful not to take away their myths from the religious. I think that's what they hold onto the most tenaciously. Just about every tribe or society alike has their sacred creation myth. Many of the religious today, especially the middle-aged or older can't swap science for their myth. We can set a better example, one of caring and compassion that is humanitarian. It's the direction we've all been heading.

We'll just have to sustain our humanitarian outreach and support to the religious until they are ready to let their myths go . . . or until humanity comes up with a better one. We've seen examples of the devastation that a loss of myth can wreak on a people.

Once a generic humanistic religion will have accomplished its world wide reach, we will enjoy the oneness of humanity, equanimity in the treatment of all, and even the spread of the best of religion without the dogma, the belief in the supernatural or its quirky, cantankerous deities, the erroneous metaphysics, or the flawed cosmological aspects. An eclectic humanism, indeed, would free humankind to select the best from every religion, every discipline, every philosophy, everything . . . It is where the dialogue of the Earth's future will take place—or not. And if not, the future will be formed without dialogue.

There's been such a dialogue since humankind could form an abstract thought. That dialogue began when a single individual first glimpsed the possibility of the human spirit and humankind's potential existential nature (to the extent that our cultures can define and refine us). That may have been the dialogue that gave birth to civilization. It is the dialogue that will give birth to humanity's future.

We can now dimly glimpse the possibility of a future potential for humankind as much beyond our understanding as we would be beyond that of the first proto-human.

Humanity is our only hope. And as it was said earlier, it's dangerous to deny this. Must we still pledge our allegiances to the gods of an early time in civilization's history? No! Respect the respectable portions of the traditions, but voice the aspirations of humanity. Champion humanity.

*   *   *

Shortly after our sojourn began, I paid homage to Chet Raymo's question from *Skeptics and True Believers*. Raymo asked why aren't modern holy men "transmuting the dross of scientific fact into the spun gold of sacred meaning?"

368

In other words, why isn't someone creating fact-based belief for the worldly spirituality of the indomitable human spirit? I hope that I have accomplished that for you to some extent.

Blog at secularholyman.com

Glossary

Alpha male

An alpha male, sometimes female, is the local nominee for the people's group leader, perhaps a chief or tribal strongman. Within that primate pattern is the allegiance of the group to this title-holder of now legitimate authority.

Alphamalism

Considering the alpha male hierarchy as a source for social, political, and religious, and/or spiritual theories, patterns, or structures.

Axial Age

Several of the major religions began between 1500 and 2500 years ago rededication of one's life to Jesus. One has the feeling of serenity or peace, perhaps, of such magnitude that the source may be Jesus.

Decoupled Cognition

The ability to think about something that isn't present, and, therefore, to decouple one's consciousness from what is in front of oneself at present and think about something at another time or place.

Deduction

Deductive logic is a form of reasoning in which the conclusion is certain because it is a necessary implication of the premises. Fido is a dog. All dogs have four legs. Therefore, Fido has four legs.

Deduction is often contrasted with inductive reasoning. In an inductive argument, a series of examples is examined and the likelihood is estimated of the next case being like the ones before.

The sun has risen every day, so the sun will rise tomorrow (Yeah, I know the Earth really turns toward the east.)

God Gene

The God Gene by Dean Hamer—the VMAT2 gene—might purportedly create a God center in the brain. Richard Dawkins would want to know why a god center would have evolved. I would say it would have strengthened the socio-religious unit/community/ tribe/village. Though there are few who would hypothesize this God center today.

Hyperactive hidden agent detection device

A brain "template" or psychological module that makes us ask, *Who?* At a bump in the night rather than, *What?* It urges us toward a false positive that some agent that we can't see is at work in our world.

Induction

In an inductive argument, a series of examples is examined and the likelihood is estimated of the next case being like the ones before. The sun has risen every day, so the sun will rise tomorrow.

Meme

An item that escapes or otherwise leaves an individual mind and spreads through the culture. Typically, an idea or complex of ideas such as a religion. Where a gene is a biological unit of reproductive information, the meme stands as the cultural unit.

Mulilevel selection

Selection by any or all means. The typical litany is natural selection, sexual selection, group selection and cultural selection and perhaps more?

Neo-atheism

A step beyond new atheism. Offered as a slightly softened position with respect to the religious and other people of goodwill who would choose to have a constructive dialogue with us.

New Atheists

The oft cited Four Horsemen of the Apocalypse are Richard Dawkins, Daniel Dennett, the late Christopher Hitchens, and Sam Harris. The term also means the more assertive atheism, perhaps more rigorously academic and therefore slightly less tolerant of unreasoning belief.

Orthomorphic hierarchy

True to form, correctly formed social or power structure. Ortho— (correct, true)-morph (form, shape). Hierarchy—ranking of individuals or positions in the chart.

Psychic

Or psychical. Not in the sense that one would be said to be "psychic," but rather like psychological factors, of the self or ego.

Religiosity

In its broadest sense, is a comprehensive sociological term used to refer to the numerous aspects of religious activity, dedication, and belief (religious doctrine). Another term that would work equally well, though is less often used, is *religiousness*. In its narrowest sense, religiosity deals more with how religious a person is, and less with how a person is religious (in practicing certain rituals, retelling certain myths, revering certain symbols, or accepting certain doctrines about deities and afterlife). From Wikipedia.

RTB's

Pascal Boyer's RTB's. The argument that says today's primitive cultures have Religious Thoughts and Behavior but don't have true religions.

(Big) "S" Spirituality

Big "S" Spirituality entails a holy host of supernatural beings in a supernatural realm and in a world with all the "signs" of spirits, angels, ghosts, and what have you.

SPECT scans

Single Photon Emitted Computed Tomagraphy—a brain scan that shows activity in centers of the brain with the aid of a radioactive tracer.

Woo-woo

Pseudo-science, ideas that are a little too far out there. From spooky sci-fi sounds such as the *Twilight Zone* musical theme.

Ybp

Years before present.